Library of
Davidson College

VOID

AUSTRIAN SOCIAL DEMOCRACY, 1889-1914

Vincent J. Knapp

University Press of America

Copyright © 1980 by

University Press of America, Inc.™

P.O. Box 19101, Washington, DC 20036

All rights reserved
Printed in the United States of America

ISBN: 0-8191-0907-X
Library of Congress Number: 79-5509

329.9436
K67a

84-8060

CONTENTS

PREFACE		v
I.	THE ADVENT OF SOCIAL DEMOCRACY	1
II.	THE GROWTH IN ORGANIZATION	27
III.	THE POLITICS OF REFORM	57
IV.	THE WIDENING NATIONALITIES QUESTION	81
V.	THE SEARCH FOR A SOCIAL POLICY	105
VI.	THE ACHIEVEMENT OF ELECTORAL REFORM	129
VII.	THE DISINTEGRATION OF AUSTRIAN SOCIAL DEMOCRACY	153
VIII.	THE COMING OF WORLD WAR I	177
CONCLUSION		201
NOTES		205
BIBLIOGRAPHY		273
INDEX		291

PREFACE

Austrian Social Democracy began in the 1860's as a movement on the very periphery of Austrian political life. In part, it was to remain there for nearly thirty years because of its own organizational weakness, and because its main source of voting strength, the Austrian working class, was effectively cut off from the franchise. In the beginning, the ability of the Austrian movement to make its influence felt depended upon its ability to grow organizationally. An organization was developed in the 1860's, but the ties within it were so loose that for many years up to 1889 it was hardly worthy of the name. If an Austrian socialist movement existed, at all, in this period, it did so as a fragmented party, with a definite local emphasis and with the stress seemingly upon what divided it ideologically and nationally.

When one looks for the cause of the isolation of Austrian Social Democracy, the answer does seem to lie in the social structure with economics helped to produce in the western half of Austro-Hungarian empire. To start with, Austria was still an overwhelmingly agricultural society in the last half of the nineteenth century; industry was still a secondary matter. In the 1860's, Austria's political life still reflected its basic social composition for political initiative continued to rest with the aristocracy and the court. The changes that occurred in 1867, which split Austria into two almost completely independent states (Austria-Hungary), had as their sole political result the effect of absorbing the middle class into active politics, but not the peasantry or the proletariat. Once in power, the aristocracy and the middle class effectively kept the working class from the exercise of the ballot into the 1890's. This situation was to hold to 1897 and 1907 when Austrian Social Democracy was finally strong enough to help force a partial and then a total concession on the matter of franchise reform.

It was able to do this only after its numbers had grown, a process that had to wait until industrialization came to the western half of the monarchy in sufficient intensity to produce a true industrial proletariat. That situation had not obtained in 1848 but it did by the 1860's, Austria's Gründerjahre, an era that saw large-scale industry planted in Bohemia, Moravia, Lower Austria and Styria. While the growth of industry at this time was sufficient to stir the development of a Social-Democratic movement and Social-Democratic ideas, it did not produce a large enough class of workers to give a solid foundation to either. Actually, Austria's industrial revolution, between 1867 and 1889, was in an infantile or adolescent stage of development. It would not reach maturity, and neither would the working class, until the decade of the 1890's when production in Austria shot up two or three hundred per cent and so correspondingly did the size of the proletariat.

In a sense, as long as industry was not yet central to Austrian economic development, the working class was bound to be unrepresented. But as soon as their numbers began to swell and they became an identifiable social class in the 1890's, their political interests could no longer be ignored. The real problem was bringing together the multi-lingual Austrian proletariat, a task that was not accomplished until 1889 when the Austrian Social-Democratic Labor Party came into existence. For a number of years, the party, which purported to speak for a labor movement that was still poorly organized, considered itself a determined class foe of both the aristocracy, which it regarded as undergoing a process of embourgeoisement, and the capitalistic middle class which dominated Austria.

Although the party never really did cease its denunciation of the class structure of Austria before 1914, it did gradually move closer to the mainstream of Austrian political developments, demanding and sometimes winning changes in the political structure of the western half of the monarchy. Those changes were

TO JAN, DEREK
COLIN AND KYLE

the result of three factors: first, the type of leadership that the party knew; second, the growing organizational strength of the Social Democrats; and, third, the willingness on the part of the existing order to make concessions at certain crucial points.

Austrian Social Democracy was directed by moderates, such as Victor Adler and Engelbert Pernerstorfer, almost from the beginning. Since both of these men came to social democracy from political liberalism their emphasis was inevitably legal rather than extra-legal. Austrian Social Democracy was likewise made moderate by the very institutions (sometimes called proletarian institutions) which it helped to bring into existence. The party and the trade unions, which the party supported to begin with, were, of course, the two pillars of the movement. But these two organizations spun off other bodies which were either partially or totally under the control of the movement - organizations such as the Krankenkassen, the cooperatives, a womens' auxiliary and a youth group - organizations which had the effect of creating Austrian Social Democracy as a state within a state. But, as it was, none of these organizations could really operate in a vacuum. Increasingly, they came into contact with the larger society of which they were a part and progressively they began to adhere to it. The process was not all one way. Actually, Austrian Social Democracy, even at the moment when Austrian society was acting upon it, was influencing the course of events, creating a greater awareness within the empire of the social problems that were affecting the lower classes.

Austrian Social Democracy was able to move from the very periphery of Austrian political life to the very center: one, because of the organizational pressure that it was able to exert; and, two, because the existing legal structure yielded to some, if not all of those exertions. The Austrian political system, in its various forms, was not nearly as hide-bound in the last twenty-five years of its existence as some historians would have one believe. It yielded at a number of points, permitting the Austrian Social-Democratic party to organize across provincial lines, guaranteeing the right of the trade unions to organize, strike and engage in collective bargaining, lifting the restrictions on the socialist press and finally giving in, in 1907, with the full consent of the emperor, Franz Joseph, to the number one demand of the Austrian Social Democrats, the introduction of universal manhood suffrage. These concessions were in many ways due; they were logical in the more open society that was coming to Austria as indeed they were coming to prevail in much of Western and Central Europe. But the effect of these changes was to absorb Austrian Social Democracy into the existing society to such an extent that it was inexorably bound to the fate of the empire in 1914 and then again in 1918.

The emphasis in the pages that follow is on the major preoccupations of Austrian Social Democracy from 1889-1914, and the ordeal that it endured in order to survive. During the twenty-five years that it can be said to have existed as a movement, it showed itself to be primarily concerned with the pragmatic, almost to the point of excluding the theoretical. The primary focus of the movement was upon its own internal development as it fought to maintain its precarious unity as an international party representing the various national elements in the western half of the Austro-Hungarian empire. Beyond this natural concern, it concentrated upon the nationalities question and the attainment of political and social democracy. These were the matters that occupied its press and these were the topics of intra-party debate. These themes upon analysis do much to illuminate the history of Austrian Social Democracy down until 1914, mirroring, as they do, if not all, then most of the party's development in that era.

Other considerations, such as the role of the Church or the influence of the military never became primarily largely because the movement was beset by other problems. Unlike France, Austria did not have universal manhood suffrage until 1907; unlike Germany, Austria was not a nation-state but a multi-national state; and unlike England, Austria's economy could not support a comprehensive program of social security. The result of all of this was that Austrian Social Democracy often seemed to be the victim of circumstances, for it was forced repeatedly to take on not only the problems of the Austrian working class but the problems of the much larger society of which it was a part. The pressures that it faced did, as Edward Bernstein pointed out, make it opportunistic; it had little choice in a public situation that was dislocated by national dissent, political fragmentation and open poverty.

Because the preoccupations of Austrian Social Democracy were practical, theory weighed upon it only lightly. In its early years after 1889, it was really an ideological orphan in spite of its professed commitment to Marxism. At first, there was a more discernible influence from Lassalle than from Marx but as the decade of the 1890's wore on the ideological hold once exerted by Lassallean thought began to wane and the party, sometime later than is generally supposed, began after 1900 to take on a definite Marxist complexion. The Marxism that it finally accepted was the reformist kind that was gaining popularity in Germany, France and Italy. This is not to say that even when the party was ideologically conscious that it was ideologically committed to revisionism. While it never formally adopted revisionism in theory, it did come close at certain moments in practice, so close actually that it seemed to be reformist and even Fabian in tone most of the time.

The history of Austrian Social Democracy before 1914 is not a spectacular story, maybe because it produced no truly spectacular leaders. Instead it is an ordinary story of a political, economic and social movement that was primarily concerned with bread and butter issues and day-to-day political practices and it was within this somewhat limited realm that its victories and defeats were to come.

Chapter I

THE ADVENT OF SOCIAL DEMOCRACY

The development of Austrian Social Democracy up to the 1860's was inhibited by Austria's backward political and economic institutions; institutions which, in effect, had outlived their usefulness. This fact was proven in 1866 when the Prussians decisively defeated the Austrians at Sadowa and drove them from their traditional place in German-speaking Central Europe. To the surprise of most Europeans, the Hapsburg monarchy emerged from that defeat with a new vitality, adapting itself both politically and constitutionally to the demands of a more modern state. In its search for new formulae, the monarchy, and the bourgeois liberals, who were to follow the lead of the emperor, Franz Joseph, created a more open society that was to see the emergence of a Social-Democratic movement for the first time.[1]

Looking back from the turn of the century many socialists were to insist that it was not 1867, but 1848, which actually marked the beginning of a self-conscious working-class movement in Austria.[2] That view was largely incorrect for Austria lacked a true industrial base in 1848 and had not produced an industrial working class.[3] The workers of 1848 who took part in the revolution were not factory workers, but artisans and craftsmen, whose interests and predilections differed considerably from the group which would come into existence sometime later.[4] What came about in the 1840's was not a proletarian movement but an initial sign that a social consciousness was beginning to develop. It is true that before and during the revolution a number of working-class organizations were formed,[5] but they failed to survive 1848. In sum, then, what developed in the Vormärz period was a socialist spirit which constituted a preview of the future growth of Austrian Social Democracy in the decade of the 60's.

The revolution of 1848 in Austria was primarily a liberal, middle-class movement where political ideas gained a much higher priority than social theories.[6] Still, there is evidence that the ideas that were to become associated with social democracy were gaining some acceptance. A growing social awareness did characterize the poetry of Karl Beck and the plays of Albert Meissner, especially the latter's Ziska.[7] Similar expressions of social concern were present in 1848, taking on a more precise form in such left-wing political journals as the Constitution and the Allgemeine Oesterreichische Zeitung. Some of the demands now being made were so radical that the liberal writer Eduard von Bauernfeld noted the frightening effect they were having on the bourgeoisie.[8]

As for the working class, a close analysis of the situation reveals that they were anything but revolutionary in 1848. All the workers really wanted was economic relief and not even Karl Marx, who arrived in Vienna in the summer of 1848, could draw them on to a more precipitous course. Having exhorted the workers to action, Marx left Vienna in disgust, his calls unheeded. What the workers wanted, it seems, was nothing more than a guarantee for their political rights and a promise of some kind of peaceful economic change.[9]

Austrian Social Democracy did not last into the post-1848 period largely because the reactionary and repressive regimes of Schwarzenberg and Bach created a political climate within which the survival of socialist ideas was made difficult.[10] Even the growth of trade unions was stymied by the anti-strike legislation of the 1850's that remained in force into the following decade.[11] Not even the liberalizing tendencies that were temporarily manifested in the October Diploma of 1860 and the February Patent of 1861 were really enough to revive Austrian Social Democracy. While Austria's political society remained closed, the first real signs of industrialization were beginning to appear. With them came the emergence of a genuine industrial proletariat, making its appearance in Reichenberg (Liberac), Brünn (Brno), Prague and Vienna. These changing conditions were to give rise shortly to the first modern socialist movement in Austria.[12]

During the 60's, liberal and socialist ideas began to circulate again in Vienna, giving life to a revitalized Social-Democratic movement that developed at first mostly under German leadership. Up until 1871, in fact, Austrian Social Democracy was more a product of German developments than of indigenous influences.[13] One of the major factors retarding Austrian Social Democracy, almost from its beginning, was the lack of a program for action. That void was filled in the 1860's primarily by intellectual currents coming out of the German states. But, coincidentally, with the arrival of these new ideas came ideological rivalry that divided the movement into contending factions, with one group supporting the German liberal thinker Herman Schulze-Delitzsch and the other the independent German socialist Ferdinand Lassalle. Before his death in the mid-60's, Lassalle had rejected the liberal concepts of Schulze-Delitzsch, which stressed the idea of workers' self-help, believing that all atomistic attempts at obtaining change within capitalism were bound to fail. His own program called for the achievement of social reform through the agency of the state and by means of political action.[14]

For a short while, Schulze-Delitzsch's call for credit unions and cooperatives to aid the workers in escaping capitalistic exploitation did win some followers. But as the decade wore on, Lassalle's belief in étatisme and the power of universal manhood suffrage converted more and more workers.[15] As the influence of his thought spread, his adherents founded branches of his General Workingmens' Association in Vienna and northeastern Bohemia.[16] Meanwhile, after 1863, the number of trade unions in Austria began to multiply, the vast majority of them without affiliation. To the surprise of the government, heterogeneous organizations sprang up in Asch

(Aš), Reichenberg, Brünn and Vienna. The movement even threw up its own leaders, including Joseph Steyskal in Brünn and Simon Martins in Asch. In some instances, the leaders grew so bold as to demand legal recognition from the provincial government in Bohemia and in Lower Austria.[17] While all of this was going on, socialist ideas were circulated through the pages of Volksstaat and the Arbeiterstimme both of which were published in northern Bohemia, as well as in other socialist sheets elsewhere.[18]

In the main, these new associations took on the character of workers' educational unions. They studied a bewildering array of thinkers, with the result that the ideas of Lassalle, Schulze-Delitzsch, Saint-Simon, Weitling, Darwin and Feuerbach were all embraced in the confusion accompanying this initial outburst of working-class energy.[19] Even the Ministry of the Interior took cognizance of this symptomatic restlessness, noting that Austria's infantile labor movement was taking on an increasingly political character.[20] In several cases, that political action was being guided by the ideas of Lassalle which were finding a wider audience and which were soon to inspire the wave of labor unrest that would take place in Vienna after the promulgation of the Austrian constitution of 1867.

After Austria's defeat in 1866, Europe was astounded by the resiliency which Austria showed in recovering from the debacle. After several false starts, the emperor, Franz Joseph, was able to work out a modus operandi with Hungary in the form of the Ausgleich and to satisfy his subjects in the west with a constitution. The constitution of 1867 was basically a liberal document that guaranteed all Austrians certain fundamental rights, including equal access to the courts and freedom of speech and assembly.[21] The constitution also created a legislative and a judicial system, although the voting procedure for Austria's curial parliament was not decided upon until 1873.

In that year, a new procedure was brought in which openly favored the propertied classes - the aristocracy and the upper middle class - by apportioning seats according to certain socio-economic groupings. The first of these was a curia consisting of 85 great landowners who paid a tax rate of between 50-150 florins per year; the second curia comprised 24 seats, some of which were chosen by all males over 24 who paid a fixed tax, and some of which were elected by the chambers of commerce. The urban chambers of commerce were to send 24 deputies to the third curia; and the fourth was to be elected by a select group of male voters in the rural communes.[22] The complicated geometry that went into the creation of the curial parliament effectively excluded the young Austrian working-class movement and the peasantry from participating in the political life of the empire. The workers welcomed the declaration of rights that formed the preamble to the constitution of 1867. But beyond this, they were disappointed because they had been denied the franchise and because their right to organize had been hedged by a number of qualifications. Their discontent, growing stronger, was to manifest itself in due course in the General Workers' Educational Union now forming in Vienna.

In November, 1867, the German liberals, who composed Austria's first parliamentary ministry under Count Charles Auersperg, displayed a willingness to accommodate the demands of the working class by granting to them the free and unfettered right to organize.[23] Immediately thereafter, a new organization, the General Workers' Educational Union, came into existence in Vienna. This body soon provided the Austrian working class with the dynamic and charismatic leadership that it had been lacking up to this point. From the moment that it was created, the union betrayed its indebtedness to Lassalle in its statutes, regulations which the German-born joiner Herman Hartung helped to write.[24] Over the course of the next three years, Hartung was to be the driving force behind the Viennese Workers' Educational Union, composing both its program and its by-laws. While his position in the union itself remained strong, in time he was overshadowed by another German expatriate, Heinrich Oberwinder, who soon surpassed him as the leading exponent of Lassalle's ideas within Austrian Social Democracy.[25]

In January, 1868, those ideas were reinforced by Johann von Schweitzer, the man who, after Lassalle's death, assumed the leadership of the Lassallean forces in the German socialist movement. Addressing a manifesto to them, Schweitzer tried to win over the German workers in Austria by appealing to their Grossdeutsch feelings.[26] Schweitzer's appeal actually produced little response because, of the multitude of ideas that Lassalle advocated, his emphasis upon narrow German nationalism proved to have the least appeal for the Austrians. Schweitzer was to be disappointed because, from the outset, Austrian Social Democracy showed a willingness to work within an international framework, thus weakening the appeal that German nationalism was to have. Beyond this, national feelings were quite obviously a luxury for an Austrian socialist movement that was concentrating upon the goals of political and social reform. This fact was demonstrated early when both Slovene and Czech representatives were elected to the central committee of the General Workers' Educational Union.[27]

In the summer of 1868, Hartung became the leading instrument in the creation of a new Social-Democratic program, which incorporated most of the major proposals for political and social change that Lassalle had advocated in the first part of the 60's. The program soon attracted wide support, although in one area it did diverge from Lassalle by emphasizing the international character of the Austrian labor movement. As for the program itself, it was an unreconciled mixture of conflicting ideas, some of which were very pragmatic, others not. Specifically, the program called for: the establishment of productive associations by the state; freedom of the press; the right of the workers to assembly, associate, organize and bear arms; the abolition of standing armies; and the right of national self-determination.[28] The basically irenic nature of the socialist movement of the times was poignantly expressed when the Social Democrats insisted that their program be implemented by whatever legal means were open to the state.

Spontaneously, as Social Democracy developed and grew, a political party began to take shape with popular support crystallizing for the movement's principal leaders, Hyppolit Taushinsky, Konrad Grohs, Hartung and Oberwinder. But continual attempts by the party to reach out to the workers were only met by police harassment and arrests.[29] After he was released from jail in 1869, Oberwinder, having first solicited financial assistance in Germany and Switzerland, did manage to found a Social-Democratic newspaper under the title of Volksstimme. Hartung served as the newspaper's editor even though his socialism had undergone a metamorphosis and now included Marxian as well as Lassallean precepts. The motto of Volksstimme became "Proletarians of all countries unite," indicating, one, the conversion of Hartung to the idea of Marxian internationalism, and, two, the steady, if not spectacular, addition of certain Marxian assumptions to the Austrian movement.[30] In spite of this, Volksstimme continued to espouse the tenets of Lassalle even at a time when the impact of Marx was increasingly perceptible and was soon to be underscored by developments in Germany that would, in turn, affect Austrian socialism.

Through the 1860's, the working-class movement in Saxony, directed by Wilhelm Liebknecht and August Bebel, was progressively taking on a Marxian character.[31] The ideas of Lassalle, just gaining the upper hand in Germany over those of Schulze-Delitzsch, were now being brought into competition with those being advocated by Marx and his disciples. The inevitable consequence was that the unity of the German movement was again shattered by the divisive force of ideology.

The open clash between these two ideologies in Germany soon spilled over into Austria where Schweitzer's newspaper, the Social-Demokrat, and the Demokratische Wochenblatt, edited by Liebknecht, were fighting each other over the loyalty of the Austrian working class.[32] Further, the influence of Marx increased noticeably as the ideas contained in the Communist Manifesto and the first volume of Das Kapital began percolating down to the party's cadres.[33] Marxian ideas were given yet another impetus by the personal appearance of Liebknecht in Vienna in 1868,[34] and the rise of a distinctly Marxist element in Austria under the brothers Josef and Andreas Scheu.[35] In the months and years that followed, Andreas Scheu became Marx's principal spokesman in Austria, his own influence reaching to Vienna and northern Bohemia.[36] But, while Marxism was indeed on the rise, it never did succeed in overcoming the faith that the majority still held in Lassallean principles.

Meanwhile, the links binding the German and Austrian movements, already strong, became even tighter in 1869 when Liebknecht and Bebel joined with a splinter group of Lassalleans at the Eisenach party congress.[37] A delegation of Austrian socialists, including Oberwinder and Andreas Scheu, attended the congress. The Austrians did not subscribe to the German program, although their presence at the congress served as yet another means for the transfer of Marxian ideas to Austria.[38] While their German counterparts were moving towards a final accommodation, one that would at last come at Gotha in 1875, the fissures that were dividing Austrian socialism were actually widening. Steadily, the conflict took on an ideological and personal character as Oberwinder daily became more identified with the moderates and Andreas Scheu with the so-called extremists or radicals in the movement.

While all of this was going on, several successive liberal ministries began to take note of the growing tempo of strike activity in Bohemia,[39] and the mushrooming development of socialist unions in Lower Austria.[40] At first, the anxiety was confined to a small group gathered around the minister of the interior, Count Edward Taaffe, but in 1869 it spread to a wider circle, especially as huge working-class demonstrations took place more frequently in Vienna. The growth of labor unrest, evident throughout the decade, reached a climax in December, 1869, when the Social Democrats sponsored their greatest demonstration.[41] On December 13, 1869, nearly 20,000 workers gathered before parliament in Vienna to petition for the unfettered right of association and assembly, for freedom of the press, and for universal manhood suffrage.[42] The demonstration marked the greatest single manifestation of discontent in Austria since the revolution of 1848, and so alarmed the existing Liberal government, which was sympathetic to freedom of assembly but not to what it interpreted to be the imminent threat of social upheaval, that it decided to take action.[43]

Ten days after the demonstration, the socialist leaders were arrested and tried, each being sentenced to long prison terms: Oberwinder to six years; Andreas Scheu, Johann Papst and Johann Most to five.[44] Seven other leaders of the party were imprisoned for periods ranging from two to ten months.[45] Moving quickly, the government also disbanded a number of unions and imposed severe censorship on all Social-Democratic publications.[46] Confronted by massive street demonstrations in 1870, the government relented for a time, momentarily restoring the nominal right of the workers to combine. But relentless police repression throughout the year began to sap the movement's energy.[47] Somehow, during the period, the radicals managed to keep publishing their principal organ, Volkswille, Heinrich Scheu assuming duties as editor after the imprisonment of his brother Andreas.[48]

In February, 1871, the last of several successive liberal governments was turned out of office and replaced by a conservative coalition headed by Count Charles Hohenwart. Regarded by the liberal press as an anti-bourgeois coalition,

Hohenwart's government attempted to galvanize working-class support by extending an amnesty to the Social-Democratic leaders. Almost immediately, the newly-freed socialists fell to fighting among themselves, thus widening beyond repair the rift between the moderates and the radicals in the party. Thereafter, the complete disintegration of the movement was only a matter of time.

The center of the dispute between the moderates and the radicals was the plan of Hohenwart and his minister of commerce, A.E.F. Schäffle, to bind the various nations and classes in Austria to the state by means of language concessions and social reforms.[49] Oberwinder was convinced that the working class was too weak to exert any real political pressure on the government on its own;[50] he therefore proposed that the party join Hohenwart in support of government reform.[51] The radicals were infuriated not only by Oberwinder's apparent surrender to reaction, but also his corresponding attempt to give to Austrian Social Democracy a distinctly German character. Oberwinder's proposals inevitably alienated the radicals for two reasons: one, because the left-wing of the party was deeply committed to the idea of proletarian exclusiveness; and, two, because Andreas Scheu was bent upon establishing a line of communication with the newly-formed Czech Social-Democratic movement of the 1870's, which, like his own faction, favored, at first, an international organization for the proletariat.

Scheu had reason to be optimistic in the early 1870's, especially as the German character of Austrian socialism began to dissolve, giving way to a more international outlook that opened up the prospects for an immediate alliance between the German and Czech working-class movements. The two groups had contacted each other initially in the Viennese Workers' Educational Union, which had enrolled some non-German members and which had published at least one of its proclamations in Czech. As a result of these contacts, both the ideas of Lassalle and Marx had been transmitted to the Czechs, first in the 1860's by way of Vienna and then in the 1870's by way of Reichenberg.[52] Lassallean thought, prominent for a while, failed to maintain a hold in Bohemia,[53] in time fading into the highly eclectic type of socialism that tended to prevail among the Czechs.

For the most part, Czech Social Democracy in the 1870's was not infused by a sense of internationalism but rather by a strongly nationalistic spirit which, at a number of points, threatened to overpower all international sentiment in the movement. Nevertheless, Josef B. Pecka was able to assert himself as the leader of a minority faction which condemned all feelings of nationalism as lower middle-class in origin. Pecka's peculiar brand of internationalism was the logical outgrowth of his own strong cosmopolitanism,[54] while that of his collaborator Ladislav Zapotocky was directly inspired by orthodox Marxism.[55] In the early 1870's, the radicals (the internationalists) in both the German and Czech parties began to move towards one another, a step that was made easier in 1873 when the Czechs accepted a party program that incorporated the plank in Hartung's 1868 Viennese program on international cooperation.[56] As far as the German radicals were concerned, Oberwinder's obstinacy on the nationalities question was the greatest single impediment existing to a united effort, and they attacked him more than once for it in the pages of Gleichheit, their principal organ.[57]

Just as the centripetal forces in Austrian socialism seemed about to win out, the delicate unity of the German movement dissolved. On the surface, the disputes within the party were the result of differences in temperament; but the clashes here only hid much deeper differences over the purposes of the party's organization. Oberwinder was still in a dominant position with that organization when he was challenged from an entirely different direction. That challenge was emerging from a new element, led by Emil Kaler-Reinthal and the brothers Hermann and Wilhelm

Wanke, which was now making its appearance even further to the left than the group headed by Andreas Scheu.

The Kaler-Reinthal faction, drawing its support chiefly from certain radical circles in Vienna, openly favored a more extreme course than the one the party was taking. Most of the members of Kaler-Reinthal's faction were admirers of the extreme methods of the Paris Commune, and Kaler-Reinthal himself announced "that if the current peaceful revolution should fail to be successful then the Viennese workers would not shrink from violence."[58] The startling growth of revolutionary fervor in the ranks of Austrian socialism disturbed Oberwinder, who feared the personal challenge of Kaler-Reinthal as well as his overt call to revolutionary action. As for Kaler-Reinthal himself, he was disposed toward action,[59] a dedicated activist who was seemingly devoid of ideological commitments.[60] An attractive personality, Kaler-Reinthal at first drew considerable attention, but his constant calls to violence left him in time isolated from the main body of the party, which was still disposed to legalistic means.[61] As opposition to him began to mount, he and his followers withdrew from the party. But his faction remained active into 1872 and 1873, attacking the more timid in the movement for their hesitancy. The break with the secessionists, as they were called, had two important consequences: first, it deprived the German movement of its most headstrong leadership and, second, it contributed even more to the centrifugal forces already at work.

The tendency of Austrian socialism to splinter was temporarily arrested in 1874 when the international wings of the German and Czech socialist movements met at Neudörfl to hold a unity conference. The conference convened in Hungary in order to escape the police and eventually accepted the credentials of some 74 delegates, of whom 10 were Slavs. All told, the delegates claimed to speak for more than 25,000 workers, most of them in Vienna and Prague.[62]

At the conference the delegates agreed upon a common program and a plan for a party organization.⁶³ The new program accepted at Neudörfl was indebted to both Lassalle and Marx, with most of the proposals listed coming from the writings of Lassalle. This connection became obvious when the conference came out for universal manhood suffrage, social and legal reforms and state assistance to productive associations.⁶⁴ A number of supposed Marxists, including Andreas Scheu and some of the Czechs, acceded to the program even though it was only partially informed by the ideas of Marx. The conference went ahead and laid down plans for a central committee, a control commission and local party organizations, a plan that never did amount to anything.

The hopes engendered by the conference at Neudörfl were never realized, for the movement, begun in 1867, was actually about to collapse. Within the space of two years, Oberwinder, Andreas Scheu and Kaler-Reinthal all emigrated,⁶⁵ robbing the movement of its most talented leaders. These defections coupled with continuing police pressure spelled a virtual end to active party involvement in the politics of the empire. Meanwhile, the trade-union movement was itself about to go under, the result of the economic crash of the mid-1870's.⁶⁶ In the inhospitable atmosphere of the 1870's, what was left of the German and Czech movements went their own separate ways. In German Austria, the remnants of the party were being drawn toward anarchism and, in Bohemia, Pecha found it increasingly impossible to overcome the attraction that Czech nationalism was having for the vast majority of Czech party members.

Nothing demonstrates the dilemma of Czech Social Democracy in the 1870's more than the editorials contained in <u>Budoucnost</u>, the paper that Pecha and Zapotocky had set up in 1874. From the paper's editorial stand, it was clear that Pecha and Zapotocky still strongly favored agreement with the Germans, but not even their resolve was enough to undermine the anti-German feelings held by most Czechs.⁶⁷ Efforts were made by Ferdinand Schwarz and Josef Ulbrich, on the German side, and Wilhelm Körber, Adolf Burian and Zapotocky, among the Czechs, to bring about an accord in the years that followed, but they failed to produce any results.[68] Meaningful contacts between the two national groups became less and less frequent, the last one taking place in 1876 when a small faction among the Czechs decided to adhere to the newly-created Gotha program, the official program of the then unified Social Democrats in the German <u>Reich</u>.

In the late 1870's, a few bare ideological connections still existed between the Germans and the Czechs but they were not strong enough to prevent the formation of an independent Czech political party at St. Margareten in 1878. This new party, like all the rest, was ultimately to dissolve, but, before it did, it rejected any and all ties with the scattered groups of Social Democrats still left in Vienna, Reichenberg and elsewhere.[69] The cause of internationalism, already obviously on the decline among the Czechs, was curtailed even further in 1882 when both Pecha and Zapotocky were arrested and sentenced to jail. Shortly after their departure, a Czech anarchist, Josef Hybeš, gained control of the movement and turned it away from the principles of social democracy.[70]

Elsewhere, German Social Democracy in Austria was moving along an even more precarious course, its radical wing falling under the sway of Johann Most and Josef Peukert, both prominent anarchists. Most had been active in Viennese trade-union circles ever since the late 1860's, first as a moderate and then as an anarchist. Driven from Austria, Most emigrated to England where he commenced publication of a new anarchist sheet, <u>Die Freiheit</u>, a newspaper that was smuggled into both Germany and Austria.[71] In Vienna, Most's views were represented by Peukert, a native-born Austrian, who succeeded Andreas Scheu as the leader of the party's left-wing. Peukert was instrumental in converting the left-wing of the party, which prior to this time had been committed to a type of philosophical radicalism, to the ideas of anarchism. As the party grew more extreme under these influences, Most kept calling for the creation of a more highly disciplined and conspiratorial party, predicting that such a "new party would grow, while the old one would shrivel away."[72] Peukert was soon echoing Most in his own newspaper, Die Zukunft. A bitter and resolute man, Peukert believed that the workers had absolutely nothing to look forward to within capitalism. Speaking before an assembly in June, 1882, Peukert declared "every effort at reform within the existing order of society only makes inevitable a continuation of the material and spiritual servitude of the working class."[73]

The moderates in the German party were now completely on the defensive, the legalistic note that they sounded in their principal organ, Die Wahrheit,[74] going unnoticed by the younger Social Democrats. Spellbound by the anarchist Bakunin and by Russian populism, Austrian anarchism was now able to enlist a number of enthusiasts, many of whom later were to form the second line of command in the Austrian Social-Democratic Labor Party after 1889. Included here were Hybeš, Julius Popp, Anton Hueber and Jakob Reumann.[75]

The introduction of anarchism had a devastating effect upon Austrian Social Democracy, almost decimating as it did the internal cohesion of the movement. The extent of the difficulty found expression in an article that was published in August, 1880, in Georg von Vollmar's émigre newspaper, the Sozialdemokrat. The article reported that "the Austrian party is disorganized, its approach to most...questions is dictated only by...impulses which in turn are affected by... incoherent controversy. One cannot speak any longer of a unified party,...provincial organizations barely exist, if they exist at all.... It is undeniable that the Austrian movement is in decline and its ability to give direction and to engage in agitation has vanished."[76] The paralyzing effect that anarchist influences were having on the movement continued right on through the 1880's, what with the moderates powerless to deal with the anarchists and the latter's admiration for the Russian revolutionary tradition remaining unbounded.[77]

Partially stimulated by the inflammatory tone of Die Zukunft, a wave of anarchist unrest struck Vienna in 1882. The first outbreak occurred during July, when two anarchists robbed a shoe factory for "revolutionary funds" and killed the owner.[78] A few months later, labor demonstrations, incited by anarchists, led to clashes between workers and police. In 1883, the violence grew worse, with cases of arson and several policemen shot. The whole development reached its peak in 1884 when "radical socialists" brutally murdered the proprietor of a money-changing house and his two sons.[79]

The government of Count Taaffe, which had been in power since 1879, was now called upon to act. At first, Taaffe hesitated; one, because he was not sure whether the police were strong enough to handle the violence, and, two, because he had personal reservations about suspending the workers' right to assemble.[80] But finally in early 1884, he stepped in. Police inquiries led to the arrest and subsequent execution of two of the anarchists,[81] and, shortly thereafter, martial law was declared for Vienna and Lower Austria. Still another blow fell on January 30, 1884, when some 100 Social Democrats, roughly lumped by the police into the same category as the anarchists, were excluded from the area under martial law.[82] Acting through an 1869 law, Taaffe then suspended freedom of assembly, provided for the expulsion of provocateurs and eliminated trial by jury in the district courts of Vienna and Korneuburg.[83] The government deliberately kept its enabling legislation in force for seven years,[84] all the while jeopardizing the revival of Austrian Social Democracy.

The exceptional laws passed in 1884 suggest a parallel with the anti-socialist legislation of the Bismarkian era in Germany as do, of course, the social reforms that were about to be introduced in both places. The reforms enacted in Austria were not originally designed as an answer to anarchism. Actually, Taaffe's government had been committed to them ever since 1879, and for years now a social reform committee of the Austrian lower house had been at work trying to prepare a satisfactory bill.[85] Partially as a response to the situation facing Austria, the Austrian parliament between 1883 and 1885 passed several acts that made Austria one of the most advanced countries in all of Europe in the field of labor legislation.[86] The bills accepted regulated working conditions in the mines, limited the workday for women and children, provided for factory inspection and reduced the overall workday in Austria to eleven hours.[87] The social legislation of the 1880's was the work of Catholic and aristocratic forces whose conservatism did not prevent them from expressing sympathy for the workers and miners.[88] As it was, the social legislation of the time turned out to be an adequate beginning, but the socialists of the 90's insisted that it had to be extended in order to be truly effective.

The events of the 1880's marked a low point for Austrian Social Democracy. Membership in the German movement dropped off considerably, although here and there men, such as Josef Hannich in Brünn, did continue their educational efforts among the workers.[89] It was during this sparse period that one of the co-founders of the Austrian Social-Democratic party in 1889, Karl Kautsky, first began to make his name known.[90] Actually, the revival of Austrian Social Democracy was to be the work of two men, Kautsky and Victor Adler. Kautsky brought to the Austrian movement one of the most sophisticated minds that European Marxism was to see before the first World War. His ultimate mastery of the nuances of Marxism far outdistanced that of any of his contemporaries, with the single exception, perhaps, of Rosa Luxemburg. By contrast, Adler was not a philosopher, but a pragmatist, whom his close friend Engelbert Pernerstorfer once described as a "genial tactician."[91]

Kautsky's conversion to socialism came during his student days in the 1870's.[92] While a student at the University of Vienna, Kautsky was drawn toward the left-wing of the German Social-Democratic movement,[93] where the ideas of Marx were being aired as nowhere else. Later on, under the intellectual influence of Johann Schwarzinger, the editor of a socialist newspaper in Wiener Neustadt, Kautsky went on to read the works of Marx.[94] In the process, Kautsky was to become one of the few men for whom Marxism was a definite philosophical commitment. At the beginning of the 1880's, Kautsky drifted away from Vienna, moving on to Zurich and London before he finally settled in Germany, there to become editor of the Marxist theoretical journal <u>Die Neue Zeit</u>. In the years that followed, Kautsky returned to Austria to attempt to unify the party but his efforts failed until he joined with Adler. Together, in 1888, they masterminded the Hainfeld party congress which at last brought to an end the doctrinal differences that had been dividing the movement for more than a decade.[95]

While Kautsky's name was better known at the time, it soon became clear that Victor Adler was the real architect of party unity at Hainfeld. Adler had been born in 1852 in Prague to wealthy Jewish parents, who, shortly after his birth, moved to Vienna. During his student days in the late 1860's and early 1870's, Adler won a reputation as a diligent reader who liked to engage in intellectual arguments. While Adler was sympathetic to the workers' movements then going on, his interest stopped short of participation,[96] as he simply remained within his own close circle of friends and acquaintances.[97] When Adler finally did turn to a consideration of some of the great social issues which were then being debated, Adler's thinking was evidently influenced by Pernerstorfer, who had visited a number of meetings sponsored by the Viennese Workers' Educational Union and followed up these initial contacts by reading in Lassalle.[98]

Adler's views concerning socialism seem to

have derived from his reading of Lassalle, Proudhon, Rousseau, von Stein and others,[99] but not from Marx and Engels, whose works were relatively unknown at this time. For a short while, Adler even became involved in the controversy raging between the followers of Lassalle and Schulze-Delitzsch, displaying in the process a rather thorough acquaintance with the ideas of Lassalle.[100] Adler's youthful exposure to Lassalle, especially Lassalle's philosophical emphasis upon the concept of the social-service state, left an indelible impression upon him, one that he would carry in time right into the Social-Democratic movement.[101]

During the 1870's, Adler deserted philosophy in order to study toward a medical degree.[102] When he did become politically active again around 1880, he emerged as a German liberal and nationalist obsessed, for the moment, by the rising Slavic threat in the empire to German culture and the German language. Motivated by this concern, Adler joined the nationalistic German Progressive Party and with Georg von Schönerer and Pernerstorfer helped to found the German-National Union in Vienna.[103] The union included radical elements which felt that Taaffe, who openly favored concessions to the Slavs, was trying to destroy the favorable position that German culture had had up to the 1880's. Mounting German frustration on this score found expression in 1882 in the so-called Linz Program, composed by Heinrich Friedjung, Adler and Schönerer, which called for the restoration of Austria as a German state under the implied protection of Bismarckian Germany.[104]

After the publication of the Linz Program, Adler separated himself from the German national movement and from von Schönerer, whose professed anti-Semitism, while more political than racial, proved to be unacceptable to him.[105] By the middle of the 1880's, Adler had identified himself with socialism and the cause of the Austrian working-class. The transition for him was much smoother than might be supposed since both the nationalism, of his early days, and the socialism, which he was now accepting, shared a common belief in universal suffrage and nationalization.[106] Equally, his change of mind was not unexpected, considering his personal acquaintance with socialist ideas. Moreover, Adler's youthful interest in socialism had been revived in 1878 when he married the sister of Heinrich and Adolf Braun, both former Lassalleans,[107] and then again in the early 1880's, the result this time of his friendship with the ex-Communard Leo Frankel.[108]

By 1886, he was publicly a socialist, but the change in his case was more a product of sentiment than anything else. A trained physician, Adler had been taken aback by the poverty that he had witnessed in the city of Vienna.[109] Slowly, as a result of this experience, Adler formed the conclusion that only Social Democracy could raise the level of the unfortunate in society above subsistence. The solutions which he came up with for the problem of poverty were drawn, in the main, from his reading of Lassalle, concluding that the workers must first win political power and then bring about economic change. The fact that he favored indirect rather than direct action was clearly summed up in his famous statement, "not bread, but political rights." Speaking before a rally in 1886, Adler, paraphrasing Lassalle, put it more precisely when he said, "with political rights, the working class will be able to obtain not only bread but power. It is a majority of the population, and the prerequisite for it is merely that it knows what it wants."[110]

In December, 1886, Adler used funds inherited from his father to establish a new daily newspaper, <u>Gleichheit</u>.[111] Kautsky viewed the reports that Adler intended to found a new socialist newspaper in Vienna with a good deal of alarm, being suspicious of the editorial stance that the paper would take. Unable to prevent its establishment, Kautsky wrote to Friedrich Engels that at least Adler would now have to decide whether he was "<u>for</u> us or <u>against</u> us."[112] Actually, Adler <u>did</u> not indicate an ideological preference; rather it was clear that he was trying, through the pages of Gleichheit, to bring a greater degree of unity to the movement of Austrian Social Democracy.[113] To this end, Adler's editorials kept advocating the need for both the moderates and the radicals to set aside whatever differences they had.[114]

Although sympathetic to the moderates, Adler's own position was not by any means set in these years.[115] His socialism tended to be highly individualistic. While he read Das Kapital, he never accepted Marx as dogma.[116] An undogmatic man, he viewed most problems from a practical rather than a preconceived point of view. By his own admission, he was simply not given to speculation, for as he explained, "In an unconscious way, my mind works on economy, taking up and holding that which I can use practically; everything else runs through my mind as if it was going through a sieve."[117] As for Marxism, he saw it as an integral part of a much larger movement,[118] as a contribution to that revolution in the way men think that Lassalle said must come if socialism was to be victorious.[119]

If Adler accepted Marx at any point, it was because Marx helped him to think in sociological terms.[120] As far as socialism was concerned, Adler once described it as the right of all men to good health.[121] If Adler was ideologically paired with any man, it was with Oberwinder and the contention of the early Social-Democratic leader that the workers must gain their political rights before their economic wants could be satisfied. But unlike Oberwinder, Adler did not believe that the working class should ally with the bourgeoisie to achieve these ends, but rather remain on its own. In sum, Marxism provided Adler with an overall view of history; but Adler tended to see that development tactically the way that Lassalle and Oberwinder had once described it.

From 1886 on, Adler pushed himself forward in the movement, alienating a number of party leaders including the moderate Josef Bardof.

Along the way, Bardof complained bitterly to Kautsky that Adler was adding to the divisions in the party, an accusation that only compounded Kautsky's own suspicions.122 Those suspicions persisted into 1887, with Kautsky telling Engels that Adler was overly ambitious and was trying to advance the party, and presumably himself, no matter what the price.123 But when Kautsky returned to Vienna in the fall of 1888, his distrust declined, giving way at first to admiration and then to affection as the two men began to work together more intimately. Kautsky was impressed as Adler maneuvered adroitly, winning the confidence of radicals like Popp and Hybeš and bringing to an end the schism that had once seemed so permanent.124 In time, Kautsky looked upon Adler as an ideal spokesman for the party, possessed of many of the same qualities as the German leader, Bebel.125

After 1885, the problem of uniting the two halves of Austrian Social Democracy was facilitated by the declining appeal of both Peukert and anarchism in general. After this, Peukert's position was taken over by Johann Rissmann, who remained, until the early 1890's, Adler's most resolute opponent.126 Through those years, Rissmann kept attacking Adler in the pages of his newspaper, Die Arbeit;127 but gradually his power also declined as his former followers began to go over to Adler.

The first clue that a rapproachement among the various factions in Austrian Social Democracy was in the offing came in April, 1887, in Vienna at a meeting of the socialist union, Wahrheit. There, moderates and radicals joined to support a resolution that would lead to more far-reaching agreements later on. The resolution adopted began with a statement condemning the capitalist system and blaming the presence of poverty in Austria on class hatred and the absence of political rights.128 Adler viewed the Wahrheit resolution as the opening he had been waiting for, ultimately seeing it as the beginning of that process that would bring party unity at Hainfeld in 1889.129

Meanwhile, the division between moderates and radicals that had characterized the German party had found expression among the Czechs as well in the late 1880's.[130] Only here, the Czechs had managed to terminate their differences in 1887 and to form a unified Czech Social-Democratic party.[131] The Czechs created their party in December, 1887, at Brünn. There, some 53 delegates from all over the monarchy had met and agreed not only upon a party structure but also that a unified Social-Democratic movement was imperative for the working-class of Austria.[132] As the congress showed, the Czechs were now willing to soften their previous opposition to a joint effort between the Germans and themselves, a fact that soon proved itself in Bohemia where the Czechs and the Germans began to negotiate for a common editorial stand in the press.[133] Adler's brother-in-law, Adolf Braun, was now convinced that unification was only a matter of time, a view that Kautsky received only with skepticism.[134] Into 1888, Adler continued to work on the Czechs, drawing radical leaders, such as Hybeš, and moderates, like Körber, closer to him.[135] By the end of the year, the spirit engendered by the Wahrheit resolution of 1887 and the Brünn congress of the same year was inspiring the various factions in the two movements to come together, something that they would do in December, 1888, at Hainfeld.

When the actual congress, called by Kautsky and Adler, convened on December 30, 1888, at Hainfeld, outside of Vienna, it was attended by 110 delegates, most of them Germans and Czechs, along with a few Poles, Slovenes and Italians.[136] As it was, the Polish, Slovene and Italian parties did not amount to much, all three of them being more than a decade away from organizational maturity. In essence then, the party that was formed in 1889 was nothing more really than a loose alliance of Germans and Czechs.[137]

The main task of the congress, which had already agreed upon the need for unity,[138] was to overpower the suspicions that had divided moderates and radicals, on the one hand, and

Germans and Czechs, on the other. To accomplish this, the congress drew up a declaration of principles. The principles contained within this statement were essentially a compromise aimed at creating a doctrinal position that all could agree upon.[139] The almost insurmountable chasm separating moderates and radicals was quickly closed by a carefully-worded statement in the declaration on tactics, the two sides agreeing that "the party would make use of every expedient...that corresponds with the people's sense of justice."[140] The ambiguous wording contained here satisfied the moderates because it precluded a definite anarchist stand, and it proved acceptable to the radicals, who felt it restrained them only slightly. As it turned out, the wording in the declaration lost its importance, after a while, what with the almost immediate decline of Austrian anarchism after 1889.[141] Meanwhile, Czech fears were set aside before the congress by Adler's repudiation of his earlier ties with German nationalism,[142] and by the declaration's condemnation of "all privileges based upon nationality."[143] By finding the middle ground between nationalism and internationalism, which is what the Hainfeld program did, a unity was finally brought about between the Germans and Czechs that had been long eluding them.[144]

During the congress, the veteran Austrian socialist leader Josef Hannich declared Austrian Social Democracy to be a Marxist movement.[145] It may have been in form,[146] but, unlike the German Erfurt program of 1891, the Hainfeld declaration was not the product of pure Marxist thinking.[147] Actually, the ideas of Marx and Lassalle blended in that program to such a degree as to produce a highly synthetic approach. The introduction to the Hainfeld declaration was clearly Marxian in tone, speaking as it did of economic determinism, class conflict and an international proletariat.[148] Yet, the ideas of Lassalle, now more subtle, remained in the document in the form of proposals for universal suffrage and social reform through the agency of the state. At Hainfeld, Austrian Social Democracy undoubtedly moved closer than it had ever been to Marxism, but there was still a strong residue of Lassallean ideas left in the party and the fact that they were there was evidently due to Adler, who prepared the declaration,[149] and who defended those parts before the congress that emphasized political and social reform.[150]

In the main, ideological concerns did not long occupy the delegates at Hainfeld; they focused upon the question of suffrage and the need for further social reforms. Politically, the party demanded an immediate extension of the franchise to the working-class and peasantry;[151] while, economically, it called for the right of the workers to bargain collectively, the eight-hour day, the abolition of night work, the extension of factory inspection, welfare legislation and the designation of Sunday as a universal day of rest.[152] Opposition to the new party program was non-existent except for the irascible Rissmann, who criticized both Adler's moderation and the commitment of the congress to reform. Actually, his protests got nowhere, especially as Burian and Hybeš, among the Czechs, and Popp and Hannich, among the Germans, kept giving Adler their full support.[153]

After Hainfeld, Adler emerged as the real leader of the party, what with Rissmann quitting the movement and Kautsky returning to Germany.[154] Now, the party could begin to develop a mass following, a goal that it set for itself in its party newspaper, the Arbeiter-Zeitung,[155] and at the foundation congress of the Second International in Paris in 1889.[156] As of that year, Austrian Social Democracy had at last come up with a stable group of leaders that included Adler, Hybeš, Popp, Hannich and others.[157] Not all of them were moderates; in fact, a large number of them still considered themselves revolutionaries. In time, they would become more moderate under the influence of Adler and as a result of their exposure to the labor movement which was about to develop along parallel lines with the party. What the unions wanted was piece-meal reform and their desire was to exercise a moderating influence upon the political party which was not quite reformist and not quite revolutionary in 1889.

Chapter II

THE GROWTH IN ORGANIZATION

Austrian Social Democracy grew to maturity during a period of profound social change in the 1890's. During that decade, the social patterns that had characterized Austria for generations began to break down under the influence of Austria's intensifying industrial revolution.[1] As the process continued, the aristocracy, the peasantry and the artisans had to give way to the industrial middle-class and the industrial working-class. This latter class, growing in numbers, was ultimately to provide the recently united Austrian Social-Democratic Labor Party with the popular support that it had been lacking up to this time. Estimates as to the size of the industrial working-class in 1900 vary; but the figure usually given is between two and a half and three million.[2]

The major effort of Austrian Social Democracy during this period was to establish itself as a mass movement with a firm organizational base in the old Austrian state. As it was, however, the political situation in Austria after Hainfeld was one that tended to inhibit rather than to aid that growth. This was especially true of the major industrial areas where close police surveillance and restrictive governmental legislation severely limited most organizational and political activity among the workers.[3] Reaction still featured that period and no one satirized that reaction better than Adler did in 1889 before the founding congress of the Second International. Caustically, he described Austrian liberty there as a facade, German in form and Russian in practice. More dramatically, he insisted that Austria was a despotic state and that the government was deliberately inhibiting the political and economic development of the working class.[4]

Both the labor movement and the party during

these years were so disoriented that the trade unions and the party had to function without any sort of centralized direction or control.5 Up until the Viennese Parteitag of 1892, the Austrian party had no executive whatsoever; and the same was true of the Czech party, which maintained its independent identity up to 1893. During this period of organizational anarchy, what direction there was came almost exclusively from the editors of the various party newspapers.6 Contributing even further to the disorder in the party was the fact that it proved impossible at the time to unify the local German and Czech party organizations, which, after Hainfeld, continued to stand aloof from one another. Singular successes like the one scored by Hybeš in Brünn, where harmony between Germans and Czechs was actually achieved, proved difficult to duplicate.7 The reluctance of the German and Czech parties to fuse their locals seriously damaged the party's strength at a time when unity seemed a greater imperative than ever. This inherent weakness was exaggerated as time went on and as industrialization proved an inducement to migration. Between 1880 and 1900, some 500,000 Czechs, attracted by the prospects of employment, migrated to predominantly German-speaking areas in the empire. A full half of that total headed for the lignite fields and industrial districts of northern Bohemia, with the remainder gravitating to the commercial and industrial areas of Moravia, Silesia and Lower Austria. This intermingling of population had an inestimable impact upon the cities especially, as areas like Budweis (České Budějovice) lost their predominantly German character and as Vienna and Wiener Neustadt acquired larger and larger Czech minorities.8 Inevitably, as this process of national migration continued, it tended to exacerbate national feelings, adding further to the stresses already disturbing the German-Czech coalition of 1889.

In spite of these obstacles, attempts were made after 1889 to build up the party in the industrial centers of Vienna and Lower Austria and the mining and industrial districts of northern Bohemia. In Vienna, this development was encouraged by Ludwig Bretschneider's Workers Education Union, which was completely committed to the ideas of socialism, as was the Austrian Student Union at the University of Vienna, an organization that at first adhered to the ideas of liberalism but then went over to Marxism.[9] In northern Bohemia, socialist education unions sprang up among both the miners and the workers with most of the activity emanating from Reichenberg, the principal industrial city in the area.[10] During these early years, party membership began to increase, climbing from 15,498 in 1888 to 47,160 in 1891; simultaneously, the number of local party organizations also expanded, increasing from 104 to 209. Two and a half years after Hainfeld, watching these stirrings, a delighted Adler wrote to Engels, "We are advancing from a sect or a horde of ruffians to a political party."[11]

From an organizational point of view, Austrian socialism was still in its infancy in the early 1890's; despite, that, it was able, nonetheless, to make its influence felt, especially within the ranks of the Second Internnational. Within the International, the Austrians were among those who were determined to turn the May Day celebration into a realistic expression of working-class solidarity.[12] In both 1890 and 1891 they were able to carry their resolve into practice, staging in Austria several successful demonstrations that were backed by a number of work stoppages.[13] Adler was especially enthusiastic for the idea, seeing May Day as an opportunity for the party to reach out to those members of the working class who were still not committed to the movement. Emphasizing the psychological impact of May Day to the Second International in 1893, Adler remarked, "We Austrians are not dreamers...when we recognize the May Day celebration as a superior form of agitation, a recognition that does not stem from illusion, but from reality. Reason is certainly an important consideration, but the feeling of international solidarity that May Day is capable of producing in those workers whom we

have been unable to reach with our arguments...
is equally a reality for us."[14]

What May Day demonstrations there were in this period tended to be centered in Lower Austria and northern Bohemia and to be confined to German workers. The rising degree of German involvement in these demonstrations reached its height in 1893 when some 150,000 workers marched around the Ringstrasse in Vienna in support of the idea of the eight-hour day.[15] Meanwhile, although still without a solid organizational base, the party felt strong enough in January, 1891, to enter the elections for the Austrian lower house (Abgeordnetenhaus). Without real hope, because the working class was without the ballot, the Social Democrats, nonetheless, nominated candidates for the most part in the working-class districts of Vienna and northern Bohemia, in order to popularize their name and their principles.[16]

The steady expansion of the party in the early 1890's made it obvious that it could no longer continue without systematic direction. Although this feeling was widespread, it was not until 1891 that the party finally began to evolve the type of organizational structure that would in the end transform it into a truly viable political force.[17] Up until 1891, local party organizations had operated largely on their own, often without any communication with one another. The most serious challenge facing the 193 delegates, who met in Vienna in 1891 for the second congress of the Austrian Social-Democratic Labor Party to deal with this problem, was to bring together these scattered locals and to try to make party unity more of a fact than it had ever been before. The moment seemed opportune, since the congress was in a highly receptive mood, a feeling that was sustained by both the growing strength of the movement and the recent removal of the exceptional laws that had been militating against the development of the party's organization ever since 1884.[18]

In his opening address to the Congress,

Adler, in line with recent developments, called for the creation of provincial party organizations and for a party treasury to support political agitation and to extend financial aid to the trade-union movement.[19] The actual blueprint for party organization, one that had been drawn up by the leaders of the party before the congress, was presented by Rudolf Pokorny. Pokorny reminded the delegates of the colossal gains that the party had made since Hainfeld and of the necessity of setting aside the disorganized and self-defeating practices of the past that were preventing the party from achieving a higher degree of organizational maturity. He was especially critical of the older and more informal practice whereby locals had looked to the editors of the leading party newspapers for guidance and direction.[20] To end this haphazard practice, Pokorny proposed a series of resolutions to the delegates which defined the nature of party membership and which called for the strengthening of the party's apparatus at the intermediate or provincial level.

Largely as a result of the freer political atmosphere in the empire, the congress eschewed the need for secrecy and agreed, in accordance with Pokorny's first proposal, to extend party membership to anyone who accepted the principles of the Hainfeld declaration.[21] According to Pokorny's second resolution, which was also adopted, it was now the duty of party members to set up new party organizations which would, wherever possible, extend to entire provinces. These new associations were hereafter to be primarily responsible for the conduct of all political, economic and educational agitation at the provincial or Land level.[22] The focal point of all party activity, as specified by the resolution, was to be the party congress, which was to be called into session by the editors of the nine party newspapers, and whose agenda was to be prepared by the editors of Adler's newspaper, the Arbeiter-Zeitung,[23] chosen presumably because it was centrally published in Vienna. The aim of these resolutions was clearly a pragmatic one: to coordinate party activity by superimposing upon the existing structure of locals, intermediate and central party organizations.

As it turned out, these reforms were not enough to end the organizational diversity still existing in the party as of 1891. The party was at the time without a central executive organ that could decide policy and its financial position was so shaky that it could barely support its own elementary effort. But while organizational problems seemed paramount, the party's real weaknesses were, in actual fact, more psychological than structural what with the claims of the Czech party leader Hybeš that the Czech party was, in spite of Hainfeld, different and deserving of as large a degree of autonomy as possible.[24] Hybeš' continual reference to Czech particularism gave ample evidence in the early 1890's that the Czechs were still not completely reconciled to a totally unified party within which they might lose their own separate identity. Philosophically, they adhered to the same program and, tactically, they pursued the same goals; but all the while they insisted on maintaining a distinctive posture and spoke in terms of an alliance instead of a unified party.[25]

The truth of the matter was that up to 1892, the Austrian Social-Democratic party lacked a truly unified organizational structure. But all of that changed as a result of decisions made at the party's third general congress held in 1892 in Vienna. At the congress, a new party organization, pyramidal in structure, was brought into existence by the creation of a clear line of command stretching from the central to the intermediate to the local level. The new and more rigid system, fashioned in 1892, was decided upon, but only after a good deal of debate and some bitter opposition.[26] The principal defender of the change was Adler, who warned the delegates that party activities would soon turn to chaos unless the growing number of party locals was absorbed into some kind of hierarchical party structure.[27] A solution was imperative,

Jakob Reumann told the delegates, because the number of locals had proliferated to 311, a sum that was fast becoming unwieldy.[28] This new arrangement, Pokorny said, speaking as Adler and Reumann had for the party leadership, would bring changes in personnel because henceforth party activity would be directed not by the editors of the various party newspapers but by Vertrauensmänner (unpaid party functionaries).[29] The Vertrauensmann system was not new to the party, but before this time the administrative duties of these officials had never been spelled out. Now they were going to be, for the Vertrauensmänner were to be formally elected by local party organizations and, once elected, they were to set up district party organizations and nominate in turn, from their own numbers, representatives to provincial party organizations.

The principal task of these provincial bodies was to carry on political agitation within each province without regard to national (or by implication, linguistic) boundaries. To cap this system, every two years a general congress of the party (Parteitag) was to take place with the delegates to it elected by the various party locals. In between congresses, the party's business was to be conducted by a nine-man central executive committee, which was to be elected by the delegates attending each party congress. For the sake of continuity, it was originally provided that one-third of the members of the party's central executive committee be chosen from among the editors of the party newspapers. Finally, in order to maintain a check upon party activity, a five-man control commission was established.[30] Of the two commissions, the latter was to go into eclipse while the central executive committee was destined to emerge as the most powerful body in the whole party apparatus.

During the course of the debate accompanying these changes, the question inevitably arose as to whether the party was to be organized in the future along centralist or federalist lines. Responding to the question, Pokorny refused to admit to either label. What the party was looking for, he said, was the most practical means possible of organizing the proletariat in Austria, and this new proposal fit that requirement.[31] The creation of a new central executive committee in 1892 meant a tightening of the party's organization and an imposition of a greater degree of uniformity. Even before this, in 1891, a number of dissidents, alarmed at first by the party's participation in the Reichsrat elections and now by its growing emphasis upon bureaucracy, split off from the movement to form their own Independent Socialist Party. The Independent Socialists broke with the party because of their unshakable conviction that any involvement whatsoever with the existing order was tantamount to a surrender to it and to the system of capitalism. The Independent Socialists, in fact, were so angered by what they considered to be the party's, and especially Adler's, overly cautious policies that several of them, including D.S. Friedländer, Cajetan Valenci and Josef Lax, joined with Adler's old enemy Rissmann to create a new socialist newspaper that was vehemently hostile to the moderate course that the party was following.[32]

The defections from the extreme left-wing of the movement tended to play up the widespread uneasiness inside of the party over the direction that the party was taking in the early 1890's. The real question dividing moderates and the radicals still left in the party was whether the expanding organizational strength of the party was going to be used to serve the cause of social reform or social revolution.[33] Replying to anarchist taunts in 1892, Adler denied that the Austrian proletariat was ready for revolution, dismissing the whole idea with the quip that "Whoever is the poorest is the least revolutionary."[34] In defense of the policies that he had been following, Adler pointed out that the Hainfeld declaration had clearly charged the party with responsibility for organizing the proletariat politically and for imbuing it with an awareness of its own historical mission, something that the party was doing. Once the task was accomplished, he argued, the results would be inevitable, for in time the separate and distinct interests of the workers would dissolve into a single collective outlook which would then express itself in the form of social change beneficial to the working class. This being the case, Adler continued, it logically followed that any attempt by the party to organize the workers politically or, for that matter, to secure social reform for them was ipso facto revolutionary effort.[35] It is clear here that Adler was following a line of reasoning previously expressed by Lassalle to the effect that social change could only come about after the achievement of social awareness by the workers. What is even more obvious is that he blurred the distinction between reform and revolution in such a way as to bestow upon his own policy of gradualism a seemingly incontrovertible philosophical cover.

In contrast to the German Social-Democratic Party, which was not legally permitted to organize across state lines until 1899,[36] Austrian socialism had brought into existence by the middle of the 1890's a highly streamlined and centralized organizational structure. But, as it was, the very strength of that organization proved to be its undoing. For as the power of the party under German leadership steadily expanded and as the influence of the central executive committee threatened to reach down to the local level,[37] the tradition of Czech autonomy, left unchallenged, for the most part, in the years after Hainfeld, now seemed to be in danger for the first time. Only a determined effort by the Czechs actually prevented the process of absorption from taking place. In 1894, it was clear that the Czechs were opposed to assimilation and that the general party had failed in its attempt to integrate the Czech party apparatus in Bohemia and Moravia. Resigned to Czech opposition, the central executive committee, in its report to the fourth Austrian Social-Democratic Parteitag held in Vienna in 1894, admitted publicly that while the Czechs had indeed acted with the general party, which had now been formally expanded to include a

Polish element,[38] they did in fact constitute a separate and distinct political element.[39]

The true extent of the division between the general party and the Czechs was revealed in the reports read to the congress on the status of the party in Bohemia and Moravia. With the single exception of the district party organization in Aussig (Ústí nad Labem), the Czechs had steadfastly refused to mesh their organizations with those of the Germans.[40] In Bohemia, the various Czech locals had remained completely outside of the jurisdiction of the Land organization; while in Moravia, Czech and German organizations had grown up side-by-side without any links whatsoever.[41] The party executive sensitive to these developments, moved quickly in 1894 to prevent what was now a case of Czech particularism from developing into a full-fledged separatist movement. Speaking to the congress, in the name of the executive, Reumann asked the delegates to recognize the existing state of affairs in the party by formally dissolving the Länder organizations and substituting for them a system of Kreis organizations.[42] According to the definition Reumann gave, a Kreis organization was an administrative unit that might encompass an entire province or only a part of one.[43] By adopting this proposal, the party was able to mollify the Czechs and, at the same time, to maintain its own unity by setting up an administrative system that permitted the Czechs the greatest amount of freedom possible this side of actual autonomy.[44]

The organizational changes introduced in 1894 turned out to be ephemeral primarily because they failed to overcome the growing sense of national identification that was coming to overtake the non-German members of the party. By 1896, the Czechs were pressing new demands, only this time they were to take on even greater urgency because they were being backed by the South Slavs, who, like the Czechs, were demanding a general reappraisal of the traditional role that the Germans had played in the leadership of the party. At the fifth Parteitag of the

Austrian Social-Democratic Labor Party, held in Prague in 1896, nationalistic feelings, which previously had been held in check, now began to find expression. Adding further to the tensions was the fact that the Czech particularism now had a new champion in the person of Anton Němec, a man who was destined time and again to assert the right of the Czechs to stand organizationally apart from the remainder of Austrian Social Democracy. Not too unexpectedly, Němec put forward the arguments of the non-Germans at the congress. He announced himself in favor of a close working alliance with the Germans, something that the Czechs had been doing ever since 1889, but he was just as equally disturbed, he argued, by the prospect that the party might continue to be guided by German leadership as it had been down to 1896. His loyalty to his party's program and principles, he insisted, was unequivocal; but, for the sake of party unity, he declared, the party's general executive would have to be reorganized so as to include, on a more representative basis, non-German as well as German elements.[45]

It was clear from the way in which Němec's speech was received that events had caught up with the Germans. For almost a decade, the socialist movement in Austria had been expanding to include Poles, South Slavs and Italians, all of whom, like the Czechs were now clamoring for an expansion of the party's central executive committee so as to make it more truly reflective of the party's actual composition. The success that the Poles had had since 1894 tended to underscore this particular development. Under the leadership of Ignaz Daszyński, the Poles had very rapidly built up important bases of support in both Cracow (Krakow) and Lemberg (Lvov).[46]

Paralleling these developments, another Social-Democratic organization had sprung to life among the South Slavs with party activity here centering upon the city of Laibach (Ljubljana). However, in striking contrast to the situation in Austrian Poland, the South Slavs were actually slow to win converts. The problem, as Ferdinand

Zavertnik told the party congress in 1896, was that it was much easier to conceive of a party organization in Croatia than to bring one into existence.[47] At almost the same moment, a group of Italian socialists, under the leadership of Valentino Pittoni, began to create a solid Social-Democratic organization in both Trieste and the South Tyrol.[48] Obviously overwhelmed by the force of Czech, Polish, South Slav and Italian feeling in the party, the party executive, with its old German majority, could do little more in 1896 than to bow to the demands that Němec was about to put to it. The resolution that he presented and which was ultimately passed automatically bound the party to provide the Czechs and the Poles with a larger representation on the central executive committee and to accord the South Slavs and Italians, with their smaller organizations, more appropriate representation than they had enjoyed up to this time.[49] The acceptance of Němec's resolution brought to an end the party's short-lived experiment with a highly centralized political structure. That trial was about to give way to a plan inspired by federalism, one that would be worked out the following year.

In 1897, after years of searching, the Austrian Social-Democratic Labor Party finally came up with a plan that would allow the various national groups within it to work together in relative harmony over the course of the next decade. And it was Adler who saw clearly now that change was virtually inevitable. In a speech that was alternately forceful and direct, Adler told the 159 delegates who met in Vienna in 1897 at the party's so-called Wimberger congress, that a realignment of forces was now imperative if the party was ever to overcome the threat of separatism that was now confronting it. Without a single major reservation, Adler endorsed fully the decision that had been taken a year earlier at Prague to broaden the party's policy-making central executive committee, calling that decision logical and natural when one took into account the progress that the Czechs and the Poles had been making.[50]

As it turned out, the congress went far beyond its original intention by granting to the non-Germans in the movement virtual organizational independence, a move that had the effect of dividing Austrian Social Democracy along national lines.51 As a result of demands put forward by the Czechs, Poles, South Slavs and Italians, the Wimberger party congress created a radically new organizational structure for Austrian Social Democracy, one that turned the history of the party around almost completely. What the congress did was create an entirely new central executive committee (Gesammtvertretung), to be composed of representatives of the German, Czech, Polish, South Slav and Italian parties, each of which was to enjoy de facto autonomy within the larger party.52 The central executive committee was to have jurisdiction over the various national parties, each of which was to control its own politics by holding its own independent congress. To maintain a degree of coordination, joint congresses of the party as a whole were to take place every two years.

Adler hesitated at the congress to describe this new set-up as federal; but one of Němec's closest allies in the Czech movement, Franz Soukup, did not share his reservations. Soukup told the delegates that centralism had been an historic necessity before 1897 because the movement had been in an infantile state of development, but now he argued, all of that had passed. The future of the movement demanded, he continued, a more federal system, one that would correspond more closely to the multi-lingual character of the Austrian proletariat.53 Němec, of course, was delighted by the party's decision to decentralize. Optimistically, he predicted that while the new arrangement would not bring into existence a common party, it would have the effect of creating a united one.54 Speaking after Němec, in an obvious attempt to play down the strong nationalistic stand taken by the Czechs at the congress, one of their leaders, August Radimsky, seeking to settle the uneasiness that some delegates were feeling, insisted that the party's decision was entirely in accordance with the Communist Manifesto.55

 Whether it was or not, the decision taken in 1897 turned out to be momentous for the party. It recognized implicitly the depth of national feelings coursing their way through the various parties and sought to accommodate those feelings for the sake of the unity of the working-class movement in Austria. The Arbeiter-Zeitung, commenting editorially, hailed the decision as the only feasible one for a problem unknown in most of the other socialist parties of Europe.56 Adler accepted what was, on the surface at least, a blow to German prestige and power with grace;57 and non-Germans, like Ignaz Daszyński, never questioned for even a moment the appropriateness of the change.58 But doubt plagued Pernerstorfer, who at long last had joined the party in 1896,59 as well as other German leaders who felt that the division of the party into a number of completely independent Social-Democratic organizations had somehow weakened the entire movement. From his point of view, the party had compromised much too readily with the force of nationalism. But years later, philosophizing on the accommodation worked out in 1897, Pernerstorfer granted that no power on earth could have prevented it from happening at the time.60

 Meanwhile, events outside of the party were about to compel yet another change in the party's organizational structure, the last significant one before 1914. Through the decade of the 1890's, popular pressure in favor of an extension of the franchise to the lower classes had grown considerably. Several conservative ministries had toyed with the idea of opening the franchise, but nothing was actually done until Count Casimir Badeni became prime minister in 1895. When, after some delay, Badeni finally brought in a bill with reform in mind, it became all too clear to the Social Democrats that it did not contemplate a complete overhaul of the system at all. Its sole proposal was to add to the existing curial system a fifth curia, of 72 seats, whose members were to be elected, it is true, by universal manhood suffrage. The remaining members of the lower house of parliament, some 353 individuals, were to be chosen as they had been in the past by a weighted system of voting directly favorable to the upper classes.[61] At first, the Social Democrats condemned the bill because it failed to grant the vote to the working-class in any sort of meaningful way; but, as time went on, they grudgingly came to accept it as at least an opening wedge.[62]

Once the bill became law, the Social Democrats prepared to participate in the Reichsrat elections of 1897, the first to be conducted under the bill, in an active way. All together, the party ran candidates in 70 of 72 districts for the fifth curia, winning a total of 14 seats and capturing 223,679 out of 607,131 ballots cast, or thirty-eight percent of the votes in that curia.[63] The party was so encouraged by its showing in 1897 that it decided to carry through still another administrative change, one that would tie it as never before to Austria's existing political structure. In this area, the German party initiated things by establishing a series of Wahlkreisorganisationen which were deliberately created so as to coincide with the electoral districts created for the Reichsrat elections in 1897.[64] The reason given for this move was the very pragmatic one that the party's future involvement in elections could best be facilitated if the party's organizational structure at the local level coincided with the existing system of electoral districts.

As the decade wore on, Austrian Social Democracy could rightly claim that it had become a significant political force in Austrian politics. Largely as a result of sustained organizational effort, both the Germans and the Czechs had created rather tightly disciplined political parties, each with an active membership of more than 50,000.[65] The growing power of the movement in the German and Czech-speaking portions of the empire was reflected to a large extent in the movement's two great daily newspapers, the Arbeiter-Zeitung and Pravo lidu. Each had its bias, the Arbeiter-Zeitung tending to give the

German side and Pravo lidu acting on behalf of
the Czechs;[66] but that bias did not reduce the
high intellectual level that each paper achieved,[67]
a fact that sometimes prevented the average
worker from understanding what was being said.[68]

At just about the same time that the party
was passing through its formative age, the
Austrian trade unions, after almost a decade of
inactivity, finally won back their initiative.[69]
The turning point came in 1890, when the total
number of locals established exceeded those
founded during the entire preceding decade. This
period of growth, which saw almost 100 locals
created in 1890 and the same number in 1891 and
1892, closely paralleled the unprecedented
development of the factory system then taking
place in Austria.[70] Before this period of
industrial expansion, the greatest the empire had
ever known, the organization of the Austrian trade
unions had been characterized by a rampant
parochialism. In the past, local unions had been
small and had guarded their autonomy against any
and all attempts to create a centrally-directed
trade-union movement. As a result, provincial
organizations (Landesvereine), which might have
imposed a bit of discipline upon the movement,
were virtually unknown in the 1880's. The
organizational backwardness of the Austrian trade-
union movement was finally brought to an end in
1891 and 1892 by a series of high-level meetings
(Fachtage) that were set up, at the time, by some
of Austria's leading trade unionists. At these
meetings, deliberate attempts were made to join
together locals that previously had refused to
contact one another. In these sessions, there
began to develop a growing consensus in favor of
more coordinated trade-union efforts and an
increasing desire for more industry-wide unions.[71]
An example of this pattern was set in 1891 by the
congress of construction workers. There, agreement was quickly reached in favor of a centralized union, with the delegates telling their
leaders that a shorter workday and a minimum wage
should be the two major aims of their new union.
At the same congress, the union created a reserve
fund to support its own unemployed and founded

its own newspaper, the Österreichische Bauarbeiter Zeitung.[72] At this and other congresses, resolutions were passed which summarized succinctly the aspirations of the newly invigorated Austrian labor movement. As might be expected, priority went to economic issues but the various congresses also declared for universal manhood suffrage and stressed, in their resolutions, their connection with the Austrian Social-Democratic party.[73]

As trade-union membership advanced to more than 46,000 in the early 1890's and the number of locals to 500, pressure mounted from within the movement for even more coordinated activity.[74] However, the institution around which the unions were actually going to unify came into existence purely as a result of chance. In 1892, a number of Viennese unions met in order to consider an invitation to an international congress in England. The invitation was declined, but the delegates did decide to create a standing committee to act on matters of common concern to all the various trade unions in Vienna. In a matter of months, this committee grew into the Provisional Commission of the Austrian Trade Unions, the organization that would soon become the force behind the creation of a unified trade-union movement in Austria. Immediately after its foundation, the commission began to encourage the development of a pyramidal organization that would follow lines of growth that were already starting to emerge. At the base of this evolving system were the numerous Ortsgruppen or local organizations whose activities were now being directed by provincial bodies that were just beginning to form the middle rung in this emerging organizational ladder. As time went on, these provincial bodies found themselves more and more subject to the jurisdiction of industry-wide labor executives, who by 1892 had formed 10 different industry-wide unions.[75] Resting on top of this pyramidal structure, de facto at first if not de jure, was the provisional trade-union commission, its members drawn, for the most part, from the leaders of the various industrial unions. From the beginning, the commission naturally favored

a system of vertical integration since it was the
only type of labor organization that would prove
susceptible to centralized control. Any other
system, the commission reasoned, would only keep
alive the sense of autonomy already found in the
Austrian trade-union movement.

In June, 1893, E.F. Kleedorfer, the acting
secretary of the provisional trade-union commission, published in the first issue of the official
newspaper of the Austrian trade-union movement,
Die Gewerkschaft, an urgent call for a trade-
union congress. When the congress convened a few
months later, a total of 270 delegates attended,
representing some 69 Viennese unions and 125
unions from the provinces.[76] The congress was
featured by an address by Karl Legien, the leader
of the German labor movement,[77] but its real
highlight was a speech given by the veteran
Austrian labor leader, Karl Höger. Höger was, at
the time, not only a member of the central
executive committee of the Austrian party but
also the most respected man in the entire trade-
union movement. In his address, Höger, still
mindful of the divisions of the 1880's, called
upon the workers to end their differences and to
unite in a single cause that could give its
backing to the emerging Social-Democratic movement in Austria.[78] Höger's call for unity set
the tone for a congress that was already pervaded
by a sense of amicability, a feeling that was
progressively reinforced as one after another of
the resolutions put to it by the provisional
commission passed almost unanimously.[79]

Taken together, these resolutions, which
were presented to the congress by Johann Smitka
of the clothing workers' union, had two very
important consequences. First, they gave sanction
to the highly centralized structure that the
trade-union movement was evolving; and second,
they permitted the trade-union commission to
shed its tentative nature and to take on the
character of a permanent governing body. The
delegates also gave their approval for the
creation of a secretariat, with the secretariat
forming an integral part of the commission and

the trade-union secretary enjoying the same voting rights as any other member of the commission.[80] In time, this office was to emerge as the single most important position in the whole labor hierarchy, with the trade-union secretary recognized in the years thereafter as the true leader of the movement. As of 1893, the trade unions had achieved their primary goals: they had brought unity out of diversity, even if that unity was, to a large extent, German to begin with; and they had reduced to insignificance, at least for the moment, the imminent threat of federalism and localism.[81]

In 1893, just as that unity was being attained, a controversy that had been building in the party spilled over to affect the trade unions. The actual conflict within the party centered upon the tactics that the movement was going to employ in pursuit of its primary political goal: the achievement of universal manhood suffrage. The left-wing of the party in the mid-1890's, led by Anton Hueber, Franz Schuhmeier and Wilhelm Ellenbogen, while less extreme than the Independent Socialists of a few years before, was, nonetheless, in favor of using a general strike in order to achieve the aims of the movement.[82] As far as Adler was concerned, the idea was preposterous since it would have committed the still fragile resources of the party and the trade unions to a conflict that could only have meant disaster for the cause of Austrian Social Democracy.

Adler had long been in favor of pooling the resources of the party and the trade unions, but not for precipitous causes. Besides, Adler had serious reservations about the political sophistication of the Austrian working class. Speaking before the Viennese trade-union congress of 1893, Adler expressed the hope that close and intimate ties would develop between the party and the emerging trade-union movement. However, in the same speech, Adler revealed his lack of faith in the working class when he told the delegates that he was personally looking forward to the time when the trade-union movement would actually develop a political consciousness, one that would eventually equal the workers' obvious awareness of bread-and-butter issues.[83] In his own mind, Adler was convinced that the workers lacked political awareness. And in an attempt to overcome this discrepancy, he pushed in 1893 for a measure that would make it incumbent upon every party member to join a trade union, presumably thereby to infuse trade unions members with a greater degree of political awareness.[84]

In spite of Adler's misgivings about the political capacity of the working class, support for a general strike mounted within the party, especially after the prime minister Taaffe publicly decided to destroy the power of the middle-class German Liberals in parliament by overwhelming them with a flood of lower class voters. Taaffe's projected reform, which was evidently urged upon him by his minister of finance, Dr. Emil Steinbach,[85] turned out to be little more than a modification of the existing curial system. Although, the extension of the franchise as he proposed it would have injured the vested interests of the Catholic Conservatives, German Liberals and Polish gentry in parliament, Taaffe had hoped to undermine the voting strength of the German Liberals by eliminating the old tax requirement for voting which had previously held down the number of voters in the urban and rural curiae.[86] If his plan had been adopted, it would have added some 2,230,000 more voters, primarily from the peasantry and working class, to the some 1,770,000 individuals who already enjoyed the vote.[87] At first, the attitude of the party toward Taaffe's reform was ambiguous. But Adler quickly convinced the party that it represented a further democratization of Austrian political life and should be accepted in spite of its piece-meal nature.[88]

While a substantial number of party members were in agreement with Adler, the left-wing of the party was convinced that it would never become a law unless it was forced upon an obviously reluctant parliament by means of a general strike. The general strike had only recently been tried in Belgium, where the socialists had exacted electoral concessions from the hesitant government. The success of the Belgian socialists naturally encouraged those in the Austrian party that were now in favor of more direct action.[89] Hueber's faction had from the first hoped to draw the Austrian trade unions into a general strike but, as it turned out, they were soon to be disappointed by the opposition that was raised to it by Höger.[90] Höger condemned the idea as useless and irresponsible and by so doing contributed to the moral pressure that Adler had already been building inside of the party against a general strike.

In spite of threats to do so, the party failed to unleash a general strike in either 1893 or 1894. What the party feared the most now was a loss of prestige in the eyes of the working class. In an attempt to counterbalance that effect, the leaders of the party engaged in a fitful and prolonged debate over the nature of the general strike at their 1894 party congress. The debate on this point ultimately narrowed down to the question of whether, henceforth, the general strike would be invoked solely for political ends or whether the goal of the eight-hour day would also be joined to it. The dissidents once again backed Hueber, who was outspokenly in favor of using the general strike whenever and wherever it might bring about dramatic results.[91] Adler, however, as it turned out, was really not to be challenged on the issue. His own resolution, far more moderate than that desired by the left-wing, carried the congress but not until after an unbelievably heated debate which revealed that sentiment in favor of a general strike was actually running very deep. Adler's resolution was, generally speaking, a cautious one, providing, as it did, that henceforth the general strike would be used exclusively for political ends and only then as a last resort.[92] A sequel to the events of 1894 came a year later when Hueber was named to the post of trade-union secretary. As his power grew in that office, Hueber, one of Adler's staunchest opponents in 1894, became known as one of his strongest backers.[93]

During Hueber's early years in office, trade-union membership grew only slightly. What gains were made in membership came at a time when the economy, after years of growth, was finally slowing. In spite of this obvious drawback, trade-union membership did inch up, reaching 100,000 in 1896.[94] The internal peace that the trade-union movement experienced during these several years was abruptly shattered during the later part of 1896 by Czech demands for a greater degree of autonomy and independence, demands that seemed to run parallel to developments within the party. The Czechs were quick to direct their criticism against the trade-union commission, which, they claimed, was unrepresentative since it included only one Czech, Karl Kořinek, among its members.[95] The Arbeiter-Zeitung, speaking for the Germans, denied that the existing composition of the commission justified, in any way, the desire of the Czechs for a greater degree of independence or autonomy.[96] The Czechs, however, were simply not to be dissuaded. In December, 1896, still dissatisfied, they carried their demands to the second Austrian Trade-Union Congress.

At the congress, the Czechs insisted upon the immediate creation of a separate Czech trade-union commission, one that would share power with the already existing commission based in Vienna.[97] The Czech aim here was clear, for it would have forced a reorganization of the Austrian trade unions along federal lines and would have spelled an end to the principle of trade-union centralism. The commission, realizing the proportions of the challenge, fought back with a series of resolutions that had the effect of reaffirming the movement's faith in centralized trade-union activity.[98] Hueber, speaking for a majority in the congress and on the commission, at first tried to appeal to the dissidents. He pointed to the immense benefits which the existing system had to offer, one in which the more well-to-do unions (presumably the German ones) were able to aid those (presumably the Czech unions) which were less well-off. Further, he argued, if the grievances of the Czechs reduced themselves to a matter of language, the commission would be more than happy to work out an accommodation for the use of both languages in labor business. But, he went on, if the Czechs were actually going to push for a separate commission, that was too much because such a proposal would place national feelings before the needs of the working class. Besides, Hueber continued, the Czech demands were really misplaced, since the Czechs were already represented by <u>Vertrauensmänner</u> who sat in Prague and Brünn and who acted as intermediaries between the commission and the Czech working class.[99]

The first Czech spokesman to reply to Hueber at the congress was Josef Hybeš, the veteran Czech party leader, who had worked with Adler in 1889 to bring about the original alliance of Germans and Czechs upon which Austrian Social Democracy had first been founded. Hybeš, siding with the Czech dissidents, denounced for them the trade-union structure in Bohemia, arguing that the interests of the Czechs were being lost to the hegemony that the Germans were developing there. He insisted that the desires of the Czechs for organizational and financial independence were really quite legitimate and if recognized would have the result of strengthening the ties between the Germans and Czechs in the Bohemian working-class movement.[100] After Adler had countered Hybeš's remarks by coming to the defense of Hueber,[101] Němec retaliated with a ringing attack upon the centralized system of control that the Germans were devising for the Austrian trade unions. Conscious that what he had to say could conceivably be misunderstood, Němec denied vehemently that the desire to decentralize was in any way inspired by nationalism; rather, he said, it was motivated by a desire to give provincial bodies a greater voice in determining trade-union policy than they had known in recent years.[102] As far as Němec was concerned, the existing system was unjust precisely because it did concentrate too much organizational and financial power in the hands of the Austrian Trade-Union Commission.[103]

The Czechs, already angry, were aroused even more a short while after this when the congress dismissed several of their more moderate proposals, some of which were really only mildly reformist in character. Convinced that the congress was dead set against them, the more radical elements, led by Josef Roušar, walked out of the congress.[104] A month later, in January, 1897, Roušar called together a congress of dissident trade-union officials and with their support set up an independent Czech trade-union commission based upon Prague.[105] The Prague commission, after attracting some 13,000 workers to its standards in an initial rush of enthusiasm, found it impossible to go beyond that point. The bulk of the organized Czech unionists in Bohemia, Moravia and Silesia, workers whom the dissidents believed they would win over, failed to respond to their nationalistic calls.[106] For the most part, the Czech working class did not go over to the Prague commission because it was financially weak and could not compete economically with the amount of support that the Viennese commission was able to extend to the Czech unions.[107] The split created in 1897 was never really ended but it was covered over three years later when the two commissions agreed, at the third Congress of the Austrian Trade Unions, to recognize each other formally and to work hereafter in close conjunction.[108]

The agreement between the two commissions helped to contain the threat of Czech separatism for the time being, but it did not necessarily improve the economic prospects of the Austrian labor movement at the turn of the century. If anything, the movement was about to suffer a series of reversals. The first setback came as a result of the general strike of the miners, a strike that left the union's organization, long one of the strongest, shattered and its resources devastated. Still another blow to the movement was the economic downturn that took place at the turn of the century, a depression that severely limited all trade-union activity.[109] During this period of retrenchment, the organization of the trade unions was actually strengthened by a number of organizational changes that were accomplished in 1900. These reforms led to the formation of new intermediary trade-union bodies (Ortsverbände), which were created in order to coordinate, to a much higher degree, the activities of locals which still showed a propensity for independent action. At the same moment, provincial commissions and provincial secretariats were founded to open up a more direct line of communication between the trade-union commission in Vienna and the unions closer to the bottom of the organizational pyramid.[110]

Largely as a result of the inhospitable economic climate of the period, trade-union membership advanced only slowly, reaching some 132,000 in 1902 and 189,000 in 1904. However, immediately after this, trade-union membership, coincidental with rising wages and greater prosperity, shot upwards, jumping to 323,000 in 1905, and then climbing the following year to 448,000. Eventually, membership in the Austrian unions reached a figure of one-half million, staying at that level until the outbreak of the first World War.[111] While the trade-union commission was gaining consistently in most of the principal industrial areas of Austria, it did find itself in competition from two other groups besides the Czech trade-union commission. The first of these challenges came from the Catholic trade-union movement, which, while it did not even have a program until 1901, was, nonetheless, vigorous enough to enroll some 46,553 workers by 1910.[112] The second serious source of competition for the commission was the right-wing, anti-Czech, German-nationalist trade-union movement with its centers in northwest Bohemia and Moravia and the cities of Vienna and Graz. By 1909, the German "national-socialist" unions associated with this movement had drawn to themselves more than 37,000 workers.[113]

Within Austrian Social Democracy itself, Adler was one of the leading exponents of still another dynamic social institution, the system of consumer cooperatives, a number of which were already in existence. Adler based his arguments upon Belgian examples, where the socialists had already created and were successfully administering a system of cooperative stores.[114] Adler's idea to move in on the already existing system in Austria was met at first by strong resistance from Franz Schuhmeier and a majority within the party. Differing views about the cooperatives crystallized at the 1897 congress of the party where a resolution, backed by Adler, was presented to the delegates urging them to join in the cooperative movement. Schuhmeier attacked the resolution, calling the whole scheme adventurous and warning the delegates that the cooperatives were bound to go under financially.[115] He was so vehement, in fact, that he even denied that the cooperatives would help the workers' standard of living.[116] Schuhmeier's argument won out in 1897 and Adler's resolution was defeated, somewhat narrowly, 40-34.[117]

Two years later, at the next congress of the party, the decision taken in 1897 was reversed, largely through Adler's urgings.[118] In his speech, Adler once again drew attention to the Belgian precedent. Adler assured the congress that the system had retained its basic proletarian character and that a binding link had been forged between the party and the cooperatives.[119] Glowingly, Adler envisioned the time when the cooperatives would encompass hundreds of thousands of members and would, as a matter of course, help to serve the vital needs of the Austrian working class. To make certain that this would be the case, Adler called upon the members of the party to join the cooperatives already in existence and transform them into thorough-going social-democratic institutions.[120] Hereafter, the party-sponsored cooperatives, especially in Lower Austria, made important strides, paying dividends and accumulating capital for future investment and growth.[121]

By the end of the 1890's, it was becoming clear that most of the party's energy was being caught up in a process of social involvement. The movement itself was continuously expanding its popular bases of support in the old Austrian state, becoming more intimately involved with the larger society that it now touched at a number of points. In addition to what it had already done, the party, with somewhat less success, was able to build two other auxiliary agencies that widened its base of support even further: a women's subsidiary and a youth movement. At the same time, it reached out in an attempt to bring still another public institution, the system of Krankenkassen, under its control.

The origins of a movement in favor of womens' rights within the party actually dated back to 1891 and the foundation of the Arbeiterinnen-Zeitung. During the decade of the 1890's, the movement, which concentrated on the creation of educational associations, was unable to develop any real momentum; this, in spite of the vigorous efforts of the movement's most dynamic personality, Adelheid Popp.[122] After the turn of the century, the movement continued to produce outstanding leaders such as Theresa Schlesinger and Emmy Freundlich but no really substantial following.[123] As late as 1909, the feminist cause had attracted only some 6,000 followers to the party's organization.[124]

The history of the socialist youth movement in Austria can also be traced back to the early 1890's, even though the movement through that decade survived with little or no guidance or support from the party.[125] It was not until 1907 that the party's long-standing neglect of its own youth movement was finally ended. In that year, due largely to the efforts of the trade-union secretary, Anton Hueber,[126] the party at last began to funnel significant monies to the Austrian Social-Democratic Youth Organization. Before this, membership in the youth movement had fluctuated just below 5,000, but with the party's revitalized patronage the figure jumped to some 12,000 by the year 1912.[127] Increasingly, in the years before the first World War, the party began to attach more importance to its youth work, seeing in its burgeoning organizations, as the party's educational expert Robert Danneberg put it, a means of introducing the young to "the intellectual world of socialism."[128]

The party did move with more alacrity in its attempt to penetrate the Krankenkassen in the 1890's. The Krankenkassen were specifically semi-autonomous health insurance organizations that had been created, by government legislation, to help workers, artisans and professionals defray the high costs of medical expenses. The program originated in 1837 when an imperial decree made it mandatory for employers to provide some kind of medical care for sick employees.[129] In 1868, the government moved to give the welfare provisions of this law even greater scope by passing a General Workers' Sickness and Accident plan for all employees.[130] In the 1880's, the program was expanded once more, providing for the first time full compensation for the victims of accidents and increasing the benefits that were normally paid to the sick.[131] Finally, in 1888, the various categories within the program were made more exact so as to streamline the payment of health insurance benefits.[132]

Local Krankenkassen were funded in a variety of ways, a condition that pointed up the uneven character of the entire program, which, in spite of government efforts, nevertheless, remained haphazard. For example, in the General Workers' Krankenkassen created in Vienna as an amalgam of industrial and professional groups, the subscribers contributed most of the costs.[133] While, in the separate Accident Insurance Program for Workers, which was finally established to cover some one million industrial workers, heavy contributions were forthcoming from the employers.[134] Far worse was the fact that most of the cash payments distributed by the Krankenkassen were inadequate to meet expenses, so that the program fell far short of a comprehensive system of social-security benefits.[135]

The number of Krankenkassen seems to have been countless, and the organizational methods that were used complex.[136] General supervision for the system was the responsibility of the imperial government, while local administration was in the hands of popularly elected officials.[137] Local Krankenkassen were subject to the jurisdiction of district organizations which were in their own turn elected by popular vote. These elections often produced a good deal of campaigning especially on the part of the Social Democrats who tried, with limited success, to penetrate and take over the system in the 1890's.[138] Besides the positive benefits that the Krankenkassen provided, benefits which the party wanted to associate itself with, the Krankenkassen also occasioned a trained bureaucracy. Indeed, both Franz Schuhmeier and Leo Verkauf, the party's expert on social legislation, made their way into the party hierarchy after first becoming known in the Krankenkassen.[139]

The Krankenkassen represented then still one more means by which the party was beginning to make an impact in the 1890's.[140] By a series of legal maneuvers, the party had by 1900 pretty well attached itself to Austrian society. It now had tens of thousands of loyal party members and it had already demonstrated its growing power at the polls. The movement's labor organizations, with increasing mass support, could now affect the economy either by striking or by means of collective bargaining, preferring the latter. The party had penetrated the institution of parliament, the system of cooperative and the Krankenkassen. Organizational effort was giving to the movement a reformist air, one that grew naturally from the course it had taken in the 1890's. This is not to say, however, that the party or the movement had been absorbed by Austrian society in 1900, for it had not. The working class was still disenfranchised and its standard of living was still low, and as long as that was so, the movement would still be at odds with Austrian society. But the process of day-to-day involvement with Austrian society had begun and it was the direct outgrowth of a decade of organizational effort.

Chapter III

THE POLITICS OF REFORM

In 1889, Austrian Social Democracy declared itself committed to the ideas of Karl Marx.[1] That declaration was not a true indicator of the party's ideological loyalties for the principles and programs decided upon at Hainfeld were really quite eclectic, combining in an uneven manner both the ideas of Marx and those of Lassalle. In spite, then, of the party's self-proclaimed adherence to Marxism, its policies were in actuality far from Marxist in the 1890's. The hold that Marxism exercised over the movement at this time was by and large incomplete largely because it was not adequately nourished by any powerful intellectual influence, as it was to be after 1900 by minds of the caliber of Otto Bauer and Max Adler. The still somewhat hazy connection between Austrian Social Democracy and the original teachings of Marx during this era was the outgrowth of two basic considerations: one, the inconsistencies inherent in Marxism itself; and two, the power and personality of Adler who brought to Austrian socialism certain preconceived ideas that he had acquired prior to his exposure to Marxism.

The first of these problems revolved around the difficulties inherent in applying certain Marxist categories to the practical problems confronting the party in the 1890's. In a number of instances, Austrian Social Democracy was to know the frustration that other socialist parties were to experience, a feeling that derived from the obvious fact that Marxism was devoid of the type of immediate guidelines that would have helped it to grow organizationally.[2] Faced with this realization, Adler could do little more than fall back upon the approach that his earlier exposure to political liberalism and the ideas of Lassalle now suggested to him. As a result of these early experiences, Adler continued to see promise in the ideas of Lassalle, ideas which he continued to champion, along with those of Marx, within his own party. He was, at times, highly critical of Lassalle's shortcomings, but it was clear that Adler considered Lassalle's emphasis on the attainment of universal manhood suffrage the only proper course that Austrian socialism should take. Adler was concerned not only about the results that a democratization of the vote could bring, but also the process involved. For it was his firm conviction that any attempt to achieve the right to vote would have the added didactic benefit of bringing the proletariat to an ever greater level of political consciousness.[3]

This is not to say, of course, that Adler dismissed Marx; actually, Adler not only read Marx but agonized over the dilemma that he found himself in.[4] Still, when it came to strategy, he opted for electoral reform. In part, he was encouraged in his resolve by the successes of the party in Germany at the polls, successes that he hoped to repeat in Austria.[5] As far as Marxism and Austrian Social Democracy were now concerned, there was an ideological coming together in 1889, but the connection was far from firm. Actually, the process by which the ideas of Marx were to permeate the party was an extended one that would take years to unfold.[6] In the interim, whenever the ideas of Marx failed the movement, the ideas of Lassalle turned out to be useful. The second factor complicating the ideological picture in Austria was Adler's rather unorthodox reading of Marx. At several points, Adler admitted that he possessed neither "the ability nor the inclination for theory."[7] Yet, on numerous occasions, Adler had been called upon either to interpret Marx directly or to interpret those sections of the original Hainfeld declaration that had been inspired by Marxism. The inevitable result of all of this was that Adler tended to use Marxism as a tool, either to criticize his political opponents or to support his own preconceptions. Far from seeing Marxism as a dogma, Adler viewed it as a free-wheeling force that could be utilized for the sake of his pragmatic ends. An example of this took place in

1894 at the congress of the Austrian party where
the issue of the general strike had provoked
intense debate. Characteristically, Adler used
Marx to support his opposition to a general strike
and to buttress his policy of gradualism by
declaring, "What I have learned from Marx is that
the highest rule of all party tactics and, above
all, the highest rule in revolutionary tactics
is to look to what is possible."[8]

Adler's instincts were, of course, to remain
within the legal framework of Austrian society.
The question of whether his party would follow
the same course had been left open at the time of
Hainfeld. Both options were conceivable from the
point of view of the ambiguous stand that the
party had taken on tactics in its original
declaration.[9] During its early years of existence, the party had been pulled both in the
direction of reform and revolution. The more
extreme pull had been exerted by the anarchists
and the radicals still in the party, who shared
a common apolitical attitude which led them to
disavow all political activity in favor of more
direct action. Many of the leading figures
around Adler to begin with had come out of this
tradition, including Hybeš, Höger, Pokorny, Popp
and Hueber. Their opposition to political action
was reinforced, to Adler's disappointment, by
the government of Count Taaffe which had harassed
the party during the 1880's and circumvented its
activities with exceptional laws.[10] In such a
climate, neither the party nor the trade unions
felt that they might expect much from a parliament dominated by the aristocracy and the upper
middle class.[11]

However, by the early 1890's circumstances
had begun to change. For one thing, the government and the police began to make a clear distinction between anarchists and Social Democrats, a
move that greatly facilitated the hold of the
moderates on the party. The police systematically
destroyed the anarchist organizations in Austria
and with them whatever revolutionary elan the
party still possessed.[12] The destruction of the
anarchists, coupled with the withdrawal of the

Independent Socialists,[13] eliminated the movement's most uncomprising elements. But they were not, as it turned out, the only forces compelling the party in the direction of moderation. Of equal importance was the drive and energy of Adler, who somehow convinced the various elements in the Austrian party of the need for legal reform.

As Adler progressively involved the party in what were more normal political processes, he justified his actions both by redefining the concept of revolution in terms of reform and by drawing the party away from apocalyptical visions and toward a solution of more practical problems.[14] Goaded by these events, Austrian Social Democracy steadily gravitated toward a qualified acceptance of the existing system. Adler was aided in his efforts to give to Austrian socialism a greater degree of respectability from two directions. First of all, there was the approval which Engels gave to Adler's policy of gradualism.[15] And second, there was the constant pressure exerted by the trade unions for the kind of welfare reform that would have raised the workers' standard of living and reduced the degree of economic insecurity which they knew. The demands of the trade unions for social security were from the viewpoint of the Austrian labor movement the real reason why it had attached itself to the party, and those demands were of a type that could only be satisfied through Austria's existing political and economic structure.[16]

By 1892, the outlook of Austrian Social Democracy had taken on a definitive character. Shorn of its radical elements and increasingly responsive to the demands of the trade unions, the party manifested its new sense of responsibility by acquiescing in Adler's symbolic dissolution of the difference between reform and revolution. Called upon, at the party congress of 1892, to draw a distinction between the two, Adler declared, "As far as I am concerned they are words, only words, and it is really a matter of indifference to me whether you call our party a 'reformist party' or a 'revolutionary party'."[17] More openly gradualist than at any previous time, Adler went on from here to provide his own definition of revolution, one which came close to that given by Lassalle. "I can identify," he said, "the introduction...of a shorter workday as revolutionary because it really does revolutionize the masses, it revolutionizes them and makes it possible for people who had no awareness at all of their position, people, who had vegetated, to come up with a greater awareness and new goals and the strength to pursue those goals; when this happens I call it revolutionary."[18]

At the time of Hainfeld, the type of piecemeal reform of which Adler spoke seemed to be a distant prospect, largely because the Austrian parliament had been dominated by older political parties like the Polish Club, the Old Czechs, the Clerical Conservatives and the German Liberals, parties which represented the interests of the church, the aristocracy and the middle class.[19] Given the class nature of the Austrian parliament, the party, during its early years, denied that representative government was of any value, seeing it essentially as a form of class warfare.[20] After this, however, during the decade of the 1890's, the party's opinion underwent a major change as Austrian Social Democracy became much more favorably disposed toward parliament.[21] In part, the metamorphosis was a product of Adler's persistent belief that the Austrian parliament might eventually become democratized.

The Hainfeld program had proclaimed a myriad of principles. Of the many, Adler chose to disregard those that involved direct action and to concentrate instead upon the indirect goal of universal manhood suffrage.[22] Adler expected political democracy to lead both to social reform and inexorably to a future socialist state. What is more, he was able to convince a majority within his own party and within the trade unions of the efficacy of his plan.[23] In committing his party to political reform, Adler explicitly recognized that the Austrian state, with its multi-national character, would necessarily continue to exist.[24] Adler was conscious that his goal was not strictly speaking a Marxist one. "We know," he said at one point, "that universal suffrage is not really socialistic, but we also know that we must have it if we are going to survive politically."[25]

The Austrian Social-Democratic party was not the only political party to support the idea of opening up the suffrage. It was joined by the Young Czechs, the Ruthenians and the South Slavs, all of whom favored franchise reform in the hope that it would expand their own representation.[26] In March, 1893, the Young Czechs kicked off a new campaign for franchise reform. In the middle of the growing conflict that it occasioned between liberals and conservatives on the question of franchise reform, Adler wrote his most famous political pamphlet, <u>Das allgemeine, gleiche und direkte Wahlrecht und das Wahlunrecht in Oesterreich</u>, a work that was to become the party's standard interpretation. In his pamphlet, Adler argued that the social and economic problems facing the empire were each, in turn, definitely susceptible to a political solution. He made his point clear by declaring that:

> Political conditions in Austria have always been unconscionable; they have now reached a stage where they are impossible. The working class is forced... to exist under an unbearable economic strain, having been sacrificed to the exploitation of both landed property and capital. Their awareness of the conditions around them is now growing by the day, and their desire for change is becoming stronger by the day.... [Exploitation in Austria] is being perpetuated at this very moment by legislation that benefits the upper classes alone....This grim state persists primarily because two thirds of the population of Austria is totally without representation in parliament.... They are bitter because they are being denied what, in a modern constitutional

state, is normally considered to be inalienable: the right of every citizen to participate legislatively and administratively in the political life of a country by the election of representatives.

Economic repression is a common feature of all countries that are in the grip of capitalism; political repression is its necessary concomitant....The only alternative, the only weapon that the people have against it is political power. In Austria alone, of all the modern states, is this right denied to the have-nots, to those without property.[27]

Beyond this, Adler was convinced that feelings of nationalism and the conflicts that they engendered were a mask being used by upper classes to disguise the more important social and economic problems in the empire.[28] In his view, the lower classes were largely immune from feelings of national identification and would remain so. On this point, he said: "If our parliament was a product of the will of the masses, just as it is today but an expression of the misdirected desires of a few, then it would become clear that below the national antagonisms that prevail today, totally different pressures have now emerged. It would become obvious that class conflicts would come to replace national conflicts."[29] The only way out of national controversy, in Adler's opinion, was the introduction of universal manhood suffrage.[30] Such a move, he reasoned, would logically remove the focus from national to economic questions. Adler's thinking was a product of his deep and unyielding commitment to political democracy and to the benefits that it would bring. He was convinced that the right to vote would reduce national hatreds, usher in an era of mass rule and raise the standard of living of the overwhelming majority of the population; and he passed this bias on to his party which likewise came to see the ballot as a kind of cure-all for the ills of society.

In October, 1893, the party's somewhat abstract discussion over the value of parliament and the ballot took on a much more serious character. In that month, Taaffe laid before the curial parliament a plan that would have democratized completely the system of voting, if not the system of representation, in Austria. According to the plan devised by the minister of finance, Steinbach, the right to vote was to be extended to both the urban and rural workers in Austria, enfranchising in the process two-thirds of the adult male population. Although the plan envisioned a change in voting procedure, it did not disturb the system of representation which gave to the aristocracy and the chambers of commerce some 115 deputies to represent their special economic and social status.[31] The introduction of Taaffe's proposed reform drew a good deal of support from Austrian Social Democracy. The party had been building up to this point ever since Hainfeld.[32] Not only had Adler been preparing the party for this eventuality,[33] but the whole Second International had been moving in this direction.[34] The only group resisting the trend were the anarchists who were decisively defeated by Bebel in August 1893 at the London Congress of the Second International on this very same issue.[35]

In the summer of 1893, the drive for franchise reform increased in intensity. In parliament, the government was overwhelmed by the demands of the Young Czechs, the Ruthenians, the Christian Socialists, the German Nationals and assorted political democrats for a wider suffrage. While outside, street demonstrations were taking place, the largest of which saw 40-50,000 demonstrators gather in front of the Rathaus in Vienna to insist upon the introduction of universal manhood suffrage.[36] Once Taaffe introduced the bill, Engels, who had been following Austrian developments intently, sensed that the prime minister had set into motion forces that he would not be able to control.[37] Meanwhile, Adler, after some hesitation, began to swing in the direction of supporting the bill. He carried with him a majority within his own party, but failed to hold down those who wanted to impose upon Austria a general strike to force the bill upon a parliament which was, generally speaking, unwilling to receive it.[38]

Adler was frankly fearful of using the general strike, believing that any direct confrontation with the power of government might bring down the still fragile edifice of Austrian Social Democracy.[39] But not even Adler's stubborn opposition was enough to prevent the idea from spreading through the party's rank-and-file, especially at a time when a number of party leaders, including Jakob Reumann and Wilhelm Ellenbogen, alluded to it in their public speeches.[40] Those who were in favor of the general strike pointed to the Belgian example where the socialists had paralyzed the country for a short period. Adler fired back by telling the opposition that there was a vital difference between Belgium and Austria; one was a highly industrialized state and the other was not. The differing circumstances, he insisted, called for differing tactics. But as it was, few listened to what he had to say.[41]

During the summer and fall of 1893, the campaign for electoral reform gained in momentum. But after this, disillusionment soon set in as it became apparent that the bill would soon be defeated by its conservative opposition.[42] As the intensity of the campaign lessened, Adler was able to reassert his moral leadership over the exponents of a more extreme course.[43] Austrian Social Democracy, as a result, emerged from the conflict with its evolving organization still intact and still untested. In 1893 and the years thereafter, Adler's critics played up his failure to swing the power of the party and the trade unions to the side of Taaffe's bill. But, years later, Otto Bauer, reviewing the events of 1893, concluded that the party would have been compromised if it had supported a general strike and that Adler had actually saved the party, still in an infantile state of development, from dissolution.[44]

Once the controversy surrounding Taaffe's reform bill subsided, resentment spread through the party over what was regarded as Adler's overly cautious approach. That feeling gripped the party even more intently in 1894 when Taaffe's successor Prince Alfred Windischgrätz, who had taken office with the intention of submitting to parliament an acceptable reform bill, brought in a proposal that was nothing more than a pale reflection of Taaffe's bill. Windischgrätz's bill fell far short of the goals that Taaffe had set. All it did was add onto the existing curial system a fifth curia that would have contained some 43 deputies. Those 43 representatives were to be elected by certain interest groups, with the right to vote to be determined by one's economic or educational status in the society.[45] As far as the advocates of a democratic suffrage were concerned, Windischgrätz's proposal was nothing but a slight addition to the existing system, one that made Taaffe's bill all the more significant in retrospect.[46]

Prior to 1893, the Social-Democratic movement in Austria had been able to retain a surprisingly high degree of cohesion. In part, that unity was a product of the threats posed to it on the left by the anarchists and on the right by governmental surveillance. In 1894, that unity threatened to dissolve largely as a result of the humiliation that the party had experienced in the campaign for electoral reform.[47] The discontent over Adler's policies broke out into the open at the 1894 congress of the party where both Hueber and Kleedorfer assailed Adler for his hesitancy.[48] As far as Kautsky was concerned the whole affair had lost its urgency and had now become an abstract consideration.[49] What Kautsky evidently failed to realize was that the residue of revolutionary sentiment still left in the party from the 1880's was finding its final expression in support for the general strike. It was this force which was behind Hueber's contention that the general strike, or direct action, should be used whenever the major goals of Austrian Social Democracy were within sight.

The one and only victory that the opposition scored in 1894 was in placing the general strike on the agenda for the party congress in the first place. The move forced Ellenbogen, speaking for the party's central executive committee, to defend its failure to call a general strike a year earlier. Ellenbogen fought back with the contention that the cause of electoral reform could best be served, not by bloody confrontations, but by the continued efforts of the party to organize the workers and to overcome their sense of political indifference.[50] Ellenbogen and Adler were supported at the congress by Bebel, who backed the party's policy of gradualism and who assured the delegates that franchise reform in Austria was just a matter of time.[51] In spite of the support that Adler had gathered, he was unable to beat back the opposition's desire for a showdown vote on the matter of the general strike.

For a time, the two sides tried to outmaneuver each other with a series of parliamentary devices.[52] After an extended debate, Adler's forces were finally able to bring to a vote Adler's own resolution which committed the party to the use of the general strike but only as a last conceivable resort. The vote in favor of the compromise was 66 to 42 with 30 abstentions,[53] indicating a considerable difference of opinion. Adler took advantage of his narrow success to push through the congress another resolution which reaffirmed the party's commitment to indirect political action, thus repudiating those who wanted to go into the streets.[54] Adler reflected upon the events of 1893 and 1894 in an article which he wrote for Die Neue Zeit a short while after this. In it, he argued that the price the party would have had to pay for a general strike was too high and so he opposed it. The decision, he said, was the right one even if it meant the alienation of a certain portion of the working class.

In the summer of 1894, the Social Democrats staged new demonstrations in favor of electoral reform. During these rallies, party spokesmen again threatened a general strike, but their cries did not have much of a ring to them. Windischgrätz, meanwhile, repudiated these tactics of the Social Democrats by declaring that he would not be swayed by "arguments from the street."⁵⁵ In spite of these disclaimers, Windischgrätz brought in a new reform bill in June of 1895. The bill was so unambitious that it satisfied neither the conservative opponents of reform nor the advocates of a democratic franchise. What Windischgrätz proposed to do this time was enfranchise two special interest groups, the members of the Krankenkassen and all of those who paid a minimum tax rate. The bill would have permitted these two groups to elect some 57 deputies to a fifth curia to be tacked onto the already existing curial system.⁵⁶ The Social Democrats reacted strongly to the bill, declaring as they had on a number of occasions before, that they would not accept half-measures.⁵⁷ Meanwhile, Windischgrätz's halting attempt to bring about electoral reform came to an abrupt end in the same year when his Conservative-Liberal coalition fell to the combined strength of the Slavs over the famous Cilli affair.

Windischgrätz had tied the fate of his coalition government to the question of electoral reform but his fall from power was hastened not by politics but the nationalities question, a question that threatened now to intrude more and more upon Austrian political life. During his short-lived ministry, Windischgrätz had backed a rather controversial school bill that would have permitted the construction of a Slovene gymnasium in the Styrian city of Cilli. Almost as soon as the bill had been proposed it became locked in a dispute between Germans and Slovenes. The Germans viewed the school as a challenge to their hegemony in the area, while the Slavs saw it as a clear opportunity to break away from German control and domination. When the Slavic majority on the budget committee of the lower house of parliament, the Abgeordnetenhaus, voted the necessary appropriations, the German Liberals, their sense of national identification outraged, withdrew from Windischgrätz's coalition.⁵⁸ The socialists were delighted with Windischgrätz's ensuing resignation. They had always considered his government as little more than a coalition of Taaffe's enemies, the very people who had undermined the process of electoral reform in 1893.[59]

Windischgrätz's government, which had produced little, if any, change,[60] was succeeded by an interim coalition headed by Prince Erich Kielmansegg, who, in turn, surrendered office almost immediately to Count Casimir Badeni in the latter half of 1895.[61] As soon as he took office, Badeni was confronted by two gigantic problems: first, to placate the growing demands of the Czechs in the empire for linguistic parity; and the second, to satisfy the demand of public opinion for some kind of electoral reform.[62] Of the two, Badeni decided to settle the political question first. Before he had a chance to table his reform, rumors circulated to the effect that it would add an additional curia to the system. The Social Democrats responded to these reports with a major shift in policy, indicating that they might accept a half-hearted bill, if it was not too ridiculous.[63] The party's rather sudden turn-around in 1895 was most unexpected, especially since Badeni himself had denounced the Social Democrats and their tactics on more than one occasion.[64]

Badeni submitted his new proposal to the house on February 15, 1896. While the bill was not as abbreviated in its scope as those of Windischgrätz, it was, nonetheless, a disappointment to the Social Democrats. What Badeni proposed to do was to add to the existing curial system a fifth curia comprising some 72 seats. These new deputies would be elected by a democratic franchise to consist of all adult males over the age of 24 who had a fixed residence-- all told some 5,000,000 voters. The old curiae with their 353 deputies would continue to be selected, as they had been since 1873, by the 1,750,000 voters who composed the old electorate and who were now to be permitted to cross over to vote in the fifth curia as well.[65] The bill won parliamentary support and became law on June 14, 1896.[66] In that interval, the Social Democrats held still another party congress at which the question of accepting Badeni's proposed reform became the central issue. Some within the party felt that it should hold out for a more comprehensive measure.[67]

At the congress, the Mid-Moravian <u>Kreis</u> organization immediately stirred memories of the party's agonizing debate two years before on the question of the general strike. The party's organization in central Moravia contained a number of dissident and radical Czechs, who laid before the congress a proposal to repudiate Badeni's reform and to hinder its introduction by whatever means the party might decide upon.[68] The proposal failed to win any significant backing at all,[69] in the main because the mood of the congress was much tamer than that of 1894. If anything, the party had lost much of its impatience by 1896. As it turned out, the proposal of the Mid-Moravian <u>Kreis</u> organization did win some expressions of sympathy, especially from such prominent Czech party leaders as Josef Steiner and Karl Vaněk. But in the end both men agreed that the party had no practical alternative but to accept the reform.[70]

Adler admitted to the congress that the bill violated the interests of the working class and that it was full of irregularities. Yet, he said, the bill was, in spite of its shortcomings, a step forward and should be accepted because it would add some three million or more voters to the voting lists, most of them factory workers.[71] Austrian socialism had now spread its organization over the whole western half of the monarchy and it was eager to test its strength against the Liberals, Young Czechs and Christian Socialists, those political parties which might also draw working-class support, even if it was on the somewhat confined grounds of the fifth curia. This was the real reason why Adler denounced the proposal of the Mid-Moravian <u>Kreis</u> organization as impractical and why he exhorted the delegates at the party congress to vote in favor of a resolution supporting Badeni's reform, something that they did nearly unanimously.[72]

The old curial parliament that Austria had known since 1873 concluded its final session in the early part of 1897.[73] Immediately after this, the party turned to the electoral campaign at hand to stand candidates in 70 of the 72 election districts, the only exceptions being rural ridings in Galicia and Dalmatia.[74] The results of the March elections tended to reflect the party's own view of its growing electoral strength. In Vienna, the Social Democrats failed to take a single seat but they did score a major success by winning 88,350 of the 217,000 votes cast, a figure that compared favorably with the Christian Socialist total of 117,000.[75] On the other hand, the Social Democrats were disappointed by the Christian Socialist victory,[76] and by the personal triumph of Karl Lueger, the party's dynamic mayor and one of Austrian socialism's principal foes.[77]

The real breakthrough for the party actually took place in the industrial areas of Bohemia, rather than in the artisan center of Vienna, where it captured some seven seats, five of them German and two Czech. The party's voting appeal there turned out to be international as it scored strongly among the German factory workers of northern and western Bohemia and pulled down a heavy vote among the Czech miners further to the east. Included among the winners were a number of men who headed the Bohemian wing of the German party. The most outstanding names among them were Josef Hannich, who won out in Reichenberg, Wilhelm Kiesewetter, who took the seat in Trautenau (Trutnov) and Eduard Zeller, who was elected from Saaz (Žatec). In addition to the seats won in Bohemia, the party also elected three candidates in Moravia, one in Silesia, two in Galicia and one in Graz. Also elected to the lower house of parliament, besides the above, were the German spokesman Leo Verkauf in Eger (Cheb); the Czech party leaders Josef Steiner in the Prague suburb of Smichov and Josef Hybeš in Brünn; and Ignaz Daszyński, the leader of the Polish wing of the party, in Cracow.[78] The total number of Social Democrats elected, 14, paled in comparison, however, with the totals established by other political parties. For, in the elections, the Young Czechs emerged with 60 seats, the Polish Club 59, and the German Liberals 47.[79]

The entrance of the Social Democrats into parliament worked a profound effect upon the party. More deeply committed to political democracy than ever before, the Social Democrats soon emerged as staunch defenders of the rights of parliament, a position that contrasted with their previously stated opposition to the institution.[80] What the Social Democrats wanted now, of course, was to transform Austria's curial parliament into an institution that was more democratically based.

The changing attitude of Austrian Social Democracy toward parliament expressed itself at the sixth congress of the party, held a few months after the elections. There, Daszyński, the elected leader of the Social-Democratic faction in parliament, announced that the party intended to make use of its new position to advertise its beliefs. But, he pointed out, the party did not intend to carry its opposition to the point where it would do harm to the institution of parliament. The Social-Democratic faction, he declared, would never delay or obstruct the workings of parliament as, for example, the Young Czechs had done only recently.[81]

The party congress of 1897 represented a personal victory for Victor Adler, whose faith in the efficacy of political reform had been borne out by results.[82] The party had not penetrated the first four curiae but it had taken a number of seats and rolled up a large vote in the fifth curia.[83] Moreover, the party might have been more influential than it was in the years after this if it was not for the fact that the old curial parliament literally ceased to function in the period after 1897.[84]

Beginning in 1897, the activity of parliament was brought to a standstill, as first the Germans and then the Czechs disrupted normal procedure.[85] The vehicle of these obstructions was Article 42 of the house's standing rules of procedure (Geschäftsordnung), which provided that upon the initiative of only twenty deputies, a motion of urgency (Dringlichkeitsantrag) had to be considered by the entire house, the motion taking precedence over all other business. The result of all of this was that a handful of deputies was all that was required to paralyze parliament. The pace of obstructions increased so over the years that during one two-month session in 1902, the lower house was forced to consider some eighty-six different motions of urgency.[86]

The only way out of the dilemma created by these deliberate obstructions for the various ministries of the time was a regressive one. They could issue legislation under Article 14 of the constitution but in so doing they were forced to do so without parliamentary approval. Article 14 of the constitution guaranteed to the emperor the right to decree legislation while parliament was not in session. Those decrees were subject to parliamentary approval or rejection at a later date, but few were ever thrown out because the lower house could not collect the necessary majorities to overcome them.[87] The reason why the government hesitated to use these extraordinary powers was because they represented a return to absolutism; but on some occasions, it was left without an alternative.[88]

Between 1897 and 1901, Austrian Social Democracy sought to defend parliament against those political parties which used Article 42 to upset the normal routine of the lower house and against those ministries that used Article 14 to push through legislation that was not desired by parliament.[89] Throughout these years, Adler consistently opposed the use of obstruction by the party faction,[90] feeling that restraint in this matter was an indication of the party's political maturity.[91] Moreover, in November,

1899, the party resorted to a new technique in an attempt, once and for all, to return the legislative powers of government to the Austrian parliament. In that month, Leo Verkauf introduced a resolution calling for the immediate abolition of Article 14. Because the issue involved a constitutional matter, the resolution required, but did not receive, a two-thirds majority.[92] The bill did manage, however, to win a majority, indicating the degree of discontent in the house over the misuse of Article 14 by the government of the day.[93]

Meanwhile, disorderly sessions threatened to become the rule of parliamentary activity,[94] so much so, in fact, that the frenzy even overcame, at one point, the normally staid Social Democrats. In November, 1897, the floor of parliament became the scene of a number of fist fights. On November 25, Badeni moved through the German Clerical leader, Count Falkenhayn, to put an end to the disruptions.[95] Falkenhayn proposed to suspend any deputy who failed to come to order after two warnings.[96] The Social Democrats wanted an end to the disorders but they feared that the move might eventually be directed against opponents of Badeni's program. They feared, in particular, that Badeni might try to force through parliament the more unpopular financial provisions of the Austro-Hungarian *Ausgleich*, using the resolution being put forward by Falkenhayn. The Social Democrats reacted by claiming that the proposed change in the rules of parliament was unconstitutional. The *Arbeiter-Zeitung* asked rhetorically, "What will be done about this unconstitutional maneuver?"[97] The party's reply came on November 26, after the presiding officer, David von Abrahamowicz, moved to adopt Falkenhayn's resolution.[98] The Social Democrats, in order to prevent its adoption, stormed the president's chair and had to be evicted by the police.[99] The *Arbeiter-Zeitung* justified the actions as a necessary defense of the integrity of parliament.[100]

By 1900, it was becoming increasingly apparent that the old curial parliament was no longer viable. The leader of the Social-Democratic faction in the house, Daszyński, expressed the party's growing disenchantment with the political pace to the 1901 general congress of the party when he declared: "When I think about the future I am overcome by an almost insurmountable sense of skepticism, a feeling that everything we have worked for might never come to be.... We do not have a real parliament; the chaotic parliament that we have now is not a parliament and can never become one."[101]

By 1901, the party's partial optimism about parliament had turned completely sour. For the most part, that reaction grew out of the party's experience during the imperial elections of 1901. In those elections, the party took 799,461 votes out of a total of 5,753,462 cast in the five curiae. That total, 14 percent of the popular vote, placed the Social Democrats far ahead of the Young Czechs who attracted 578,662 votes, the Czech Nationalists with 525,558 and the German Clericals with 350,700. Yet in the distribution of seats in the curiae, where the number of mandates did not actually reflect strength at the polls, the Young Czechs and the German People's party emerged with 53 and 51 deputies each, while the Social Democrats dropped from 15 to 10 seats.[102] The party had done well in the fifth curia but its showing was not great enough to overcome the appeal that Czech and German nationalists had for most voters in the democratic curia.[103] The party's only consolation in 1901 was that it picked up two seats in Vienna and sliced further into the Christian Socialist lead.[104] But these victories failed to compensate for the loss of seats that the party suffered in Bohemia at the hands of both Czech and German nationalists.[105]

In the lower house of the Austrian parliament, the Social Democrats refused to enter into any political alliances in line with the decision of the 1896 London Congress of the Second International, which maintained that the various socialist parties in Europe could only succeed if they maintained their own separate political identity.[106] In terms of technique, the party did not oppose every measure that the central government proposed; rather its response was usually dictated by the nature of the legislation being considered. Between 1897 and 1900, the party did find itself, however, often in opposition. In part, its opposition was the result of two decisions taken by Badeni. The first resulted in the dissolution of the railway workers' union. The government, which owned the railways, took the step because the union attempted to establish firmer links with the Austrian Trade-Union Commission.[107] This, along with Badeni's intemperate use of Article 14 in order to force through parliament a series of supplementary budgets, alienated the socialists who remained bitter in their opposition to Badeni until the time of his final fall.[108]

The immediate cause of the fall of Badeni's government was the unrelenting pressure that the Germans and the Czechs were applying toward each other in parliament. That conflict, which reduced parliamentary activity to discord likewise affected his successor Baron Paul Gautsch, who succeeded in piecing together a government which lasted only a few months into 1898.[109] The Social Democrats opposed Gautsch because his government, like that of Badeni, included a number of reactionaries, who represented the interests of the nobility and the church rather than the lower classes.[110] The party was no more enamored of Gautsch's successor, Count Leo Thun,[111] who used Article 14 on so many occasions that Pernerstorfer charged that he was out to kill the constitution.[112]

After the caretaker governments of Count Manfred Clary and Count Heinrich von Wittek failed to survive for more than a few months apiece, the emperor for the first time named a commoner, Ernst von Körber, to be prime minister.[113] The Social Democrats interpreted the appointment as an indication that political power in Austria had passed from the aristocracy to the bourgeoisie, a fact they argued that reflected the underlying economic changes taking place in the country.[114] Many expected Körber to continue the efforts of Thun during his final months in office to liberalize Austria's somewhat closed political society. Thun had introduced a new press law, lifting some of the restrictions on publication.[115]

Körber did seek further liberalization and for a while gained the respect of the Social Democrats as he progressively lifted the restrictions on freedom of speech, assembly and press.[116] For a time, Körber was also able to intervene between the Germans and the Czechs and to check the use of obstruction in the lower house of the Austrian parliament, but his victory turned out to be temporary and parliament once again slipped back into inactivity. Faced with obstruction Körber responded to the collapse of parliament by using Article 14, the only way he could make his government function.[117] The Social Democrats never resorted to obstructionist tactics during these years, although they were tempted in 1901 and again in 1903 when the government moved to win legislative approval for a series of military and recruitment bills.[118] Körber made his last move in the curial parliament in 1904 when he proposed a new social-security package. The Social Democrats greeted the announcement with optimism but Körber's legislation remained stalled in committee and failed to emerge before Körber's ministry collapsed.[119]

The failure of the curial parliament to produce even piece-meal reform had the effect of dividing the Austrian Social-Democratic party. By and large, the party's policy was a hesitant one that anticipated social and political reforms from the curial parliament, reforms that never were achieved. The hesitancy that the party felt revealed itself on one occasion in a conversation between Robert Danneberg,[120] head of the party's youth organization, and a young socialist thirsting for revolution. "The working class," Danneberg said, "must mature intellectually to its revolutionary task, and it is our job to fight for the conditions for this spiritual process. Do you believe," he went on, "that the boys who have to work twelve and sixteen hours a day can develop the mental and physical conditions for the Socialist Revolution?"[121]

The leading party theoretician of the 1890's, Wilhelm Ellenbogen, likewise gave expression to the party's belief that the workers could only develop slowly to their historical mission in his pamphlet of 1899, <u>Was will die Sozialdemokratie</u>? Moreover, Ellenbogen's writings on this subject reflected the way in which the ideas of Marx and Lassalle tended to mingle at this time without any seeming contradiction. Ellenbogen assumed with Marx that a basic transformation of society could not take place unless there was a fundamental change in a society's economic base. But after this, Ellenbogen proved almost totally dependent upon Lassalle. Revolutions, Ellenbogen pointed out, need not be bloody. It was ludicrous to think of them only in terms of pitchforks, something that Lassalle had once noted. Europe had been torn by revolution in 1789, 1848 and 1870-71 but that did not make violent revolution inevitable, Ellenbogen declared. Many revolutions, he went on, like the advent of the plow or Christianity, have taken place without being noticed in their own times.[122]

If the party favored any course by 1900 it was surely the less spectacular one outlined by Ellenbogen. Adler still placed his faith in parliament even though there were renewed cries for direct action from within his party. The dissidents came from either the newly emerging school of Austro-Marxism the force that was ultimately to draw the Austrian party closer to Marx,[123] or old-line radical elements who were now stirred to greater activity. Between 1900 and 1904, a number of these people began to demand a return to extra-parliamentary means in order to achieve the goals of the movement. Frustrated by the failure of the curial parliament to act, both Karl Renner, [124] and Anton Hueber,[125] began to look for a different approach.

Adler tried to keep the dissidents in line.

Speaking to a German party congress in 1902, he denied that the party should return to the streets, as it had done in the 1890's. In those years, he declared, direct action was the only option open to the party; now it was not so. Adler granted that the era was one of stagnation; that was all the more reason not to call the working class to "arms,"[126] since it would be for nothing. As it turned out, neither Adler's call for restraint nor Pernerstorfer's counsel in the same direction,[127] was enough to limit the criticism within the party of Austria's inactive curial system.[128] The party still believed that electoral reform was a way out of the dilemma that confronted it. But, as pressing as political questions were in the period before and after 1900, they were constantly being pushed into the background by the ever intensifying nationalities question.[129] As national antagonisms increased the party began to realize that the political question could not be settled aside from the great nationalities question which now threatened to overwhelm it. Because it was an international party, Austrian Social Democracy had to deal with both not only to save the empire but, also, to save itself.

Chapter IV

THE WIDENING NATIONALITIES PROBLEM

In a work that he published somewhat after 1897, Otto Bauer noted that the development of the Austrian state after that date had been characterized by one fact, the progressive nationalization of all public life.[1] This neverending process, which had reduced almost all public questions to national prejudices, had two conspicuous results. First, it increased the centrifugal forces that had been pulling at the state.[2] And second, it made it clear that the German and Slavic national movements were running so close to one another that they were contributing to each other's growth and intensifying the antagonisms that the two had for one another.[3] This rising antipathy was accelerated by the creation of a democratic franchise in 1897; for the new law not only gave greater expression to national feelings, it also demonstrated the extent to which the masses had come under the influence of nationalism.[4]

By the year 1897, nationalism had become a pervasive force in Austrian life, touching every region, every class and every party.[5] Yet, the hold that it had on Austrian Social Democracy down until 1900 was unique in that feelings of nationalism within the party were balanced and checked by the party's long-standing commitment to the idea of proletarian internationalism. That tradition, which went back to the 1860's, represented a strain that was sometimes weakened and sometimes strengthened but never broken in the history of the movement. The tendency of Austrian socialism to go back to this theme was poignantly demonstrated in 1887 at Brünn. There, the Czech Social Democrats formed a new party and proclaimed their willingness to join in the creation of an all-Austrian Social-Democratic party.[6] A year later, this same spirit emerged at Hainfeld and inspired the newly formed Austrian Social-Democratic Labor Party to renounce both national prejudices and national privileges.⁷

Two years after Hainfeld, the strength of the Czech party's commitment to internationalism was tested at the 1891 congress of the party. There, the deliberations of the congress were disrupted by the arguments put forward by a dissident group of Czech national socialists under the leadership of Jan Vǎvra.⁸ To start with, Vǎvra aroused the congress by insisting that the Czechs had identified themselves in 1889 with an entirely false conception of internationalism. Attacking the party's stand on nationalism, Vǎvra argued that Social Democracy could be conceived of as being international only in an economic sense and that in every other respect it was a nationalistic phenomenon.⁹ From here, he went on to condemn the party both for its anationalism and for its failure to recognize the principle of national self-determination.¹⁰ Pushing the congress to the limit, Vǎvra tried to reverse the stand that the party had taken at Hainfeld by introducing a resolution that would have changed the wording in the original declaration and reorganized the party along national lines.¹¹

Vǎvra's resolution was, at least administratively, close to the actual situation that existed in the party. But the resolution only incensed the party's leaders who responded with their own resolution accusing the Czech dissidents of being unduly influenced by nationalism.¹² Whatever moral position Vǎvra had, he lost it when the Czech party leader, Hybeš, got up and denounced him for accepting the Hainfeld doctrine while, at the same time, gravitating in the direction of bourgeois nationalism.¹³ Vǎvra denied Hybeš' accusation, but his arguments were lost to the passions that he had helped to stir.¹⁴ Unable to check the paroxysm that had mounted against him, Vǎvra, and his band, quit the congress.¹⁵ He failed to turn the party around because in 1891 the party was as united on the question of internationalism as it ever was going to be.

The same could not be said a half a decade later, for by then national feelings had deepened both within the empire and within the party. By 1897, feelings of national identification had overtaken the party; so much so, in fact, that at one point Adler admitted that the word "internationalism" had, by this time, lost a portion of its meaning.[16] What was evident in 1897 was the fact that the party could no longer continue to accept a purely doctrinal approach to internationalism and that it had to find some kind of middle ground between the internationalism of the past and the nationalism of the 1890's. The whole problem appeared to be a dilemma, but the dilemma proved soluble because there still existed within the party a reservoir of sentiment in favor of the idea of working-class solidarity. Finding itself in the an extraordinary situation, the party looked around for precedents, but it could not find them either in Lassalle's rather supercharged nationalism or in Marx's somewhat abstract internationalism.[17] Because this was true, Adler told the party in 1897 that it would just have to experiment if it hoped to find a balance between its own desire for unity and the growing feeling of national identification arising in some of its members.[18]

In spite of the early commitment of Adler and Pernerstorfer to German nationalism and the nationalism that underscored the remarks of Němec in 1896 and 1897,[19] the party came up with a new plan for organization in 1897 that helped it to suspend the kind of animosities that everywhere else in Austria had led or were leading to disorder and disenchantment. The party's reorganization along national lines was a victory for the principle of administrative decentralization.[20] But once the change was achieved, the results were somewhat unexpected in that they stimulated again the party's desires for joint effort.[21] This feeling did not prevent the division of the party into six distinct national groups,[22] but it did strengthen the commitment of the Slavic and German elements alike to the principles that united the Social-Democratic movement. That commitment was echoed often in the public speeches of moderates like Daszyński and Hybeš, middle-of-the-roaders like Němec and Soukup and even, for that matter, in the remarks of dissidents like Roušar.[23] What the party lost in 1897 to the ideas of federalism and national identification then, it regained in places like parliament where Social Democrats, Germans, Czechs and Poles alike, worked side-by-side in a way that reflected their belief in a common set of ideals.[24]

The decision that the party took in 1897 did go a long way to accommodate the new nationalism,[25] but that decision was a practical one that succeeded in reestablishing the unity of the movement. The flexibility that the party showed was not, however, matched by the trade unions. For just a year before this, in 1896, the Austrian Trade Union Commission rejected similar demands by dissident Czechs for autonomy. The results there was a rift,[26] one which likewise threatened the party, but never did materialize.

Over the course of years, the Czech trade union commission drifted back into the orbit of the Austrian Trade Union Commission, with the two bodies formally reestablishing ties in the year 1900.[27] After this, the Czech unions grew, but not in any spectacular way, reaching 21,022 in 1902 and then 34,147 in 1906.[28] Through the period after 1900, the two commissions continued to work in close harmony, coming up with agreements on strike policies and wage demands. The cooperation that they extended to one another helped to reduce some of the friction that was arising as rural Czech workers continued to migrate into major German industrial areas. While the flow diminished somewhat, the Czech population in Vienna still went above one hundred thousand and Germans and Czechs continued to mingle patch-work style in Bohemia, Moravia and Silesia.[29] Although challenged at times, the ties between the German and Czech parties and the German and Czech unions, as Karl Vaněk pointed out in 1902, remained, nonetheless, strong.[30]

Just as the Social Democrats had quieted national animosities within their own ranks, the Austrian prime minister, Badeni, stirred them within the empire as never before.[31] On the eve of Austria's decennial negotations with the Hungarians, Badeni tried to win the extra parliamentary support that he needed for those accords by satisfying the long-standing demands of the Czechs for linguistic parity in the Austrian civil service in Bohemia and Moravia. The emperor, fearful of the consequences, refused to support Badeni on this sensitive issue. In spite of this, Badeni went ahead and issued his famous language ordinances in April, 1897.[32] The ordinances aimed at the creation of a bilingual civil service in Bohemia and Moravia by making it incumbent on all civil servants in the two areas to command a knowledge of German and Czech by June 1901,[33] a demand which from the beginning seemed to be excessive to the Germans.[34]

The Social Democrats were obviously taken by surprise when the ordinances were issued. They neither understood the significance of the ordinances nor the results that they would have.[35] They had calculated the depth of national feelings within their own party, but failed to gauge it for the empire as a whole.[36] For, as it turned out, the opposition to Badeni's plan was much greater than either the Social Democrats, or, for that matter, Badeni expected.[37] As soon as the ordinances were published, street demonstrations began in Bohemia and in other areas, with the Germans insisting that the ordinances would bar them from public service in the two crownlands. The ferocious character of these street demonstrations was matched inside of parliament by the activities of Pan-Germans, the German People's Party and the German Progressive Party, all three of which disrupted parliament with obstructions demanding that the ordinances be lifted. Unable to keep parliament in session, Badeni prorogued it on June 2, his own political future in doubt.[38]

The Social Democrats backed the language ordinances in their public statements,[39] accepting wholly the principle which lay behind Badeni's proposal, the right of the Czechs to linguistic parity.[40] The German Social Democrats, however, did express some misgivings about their practicality. Their suggestion was that the changes envisioned by the ordinances might better have been accomplished in some other way.[41] Beyond this, the party said very little about the reforms. What was evident was that the party had given up on the ordinances, an impression that was confirmed in June when the party's parliamentary faction declared that the language problem in Austria would never be settled finally until the people had a voice in shaping it through universal suffrage.[42] Later on in June, Badeni finally stepped down,[43] his last parliament all but paralyzed.[44]

Kautsky attempted to draw a lesson from Badeni's failure by telling the party that the time had come for all nationalities to expect and to receive equal treatment.[45] It was assumed that the Czech Social Democrats would pick up this theme in 1897 and develop it, but instead they remained curiously silent. Their silence was eventually broken but only by accident in 1901 at the general congress of the party when the subject of Badeni's language reforms came up in the party's deliberations purely by chance.

The event that led the Czechs to break their silence was a report by the party's general executive that, to some degree, downgraded Badeni and his attempt at linguistic reform. When the report was read, Vǎnek attacked those parts of the report that suggested that the party had not been satisfied with the content of the ordinances.[46] Following Vǎnek, Soukup made a clear distinction for the party between means and ends. He told the congress that he had been opposed to the manner in which Badeni had tried to introduce the reforms, but that the ordinances were both fair and just and historically and constitutionally valid.[47] Soukup had praise not only for Badeni but also for his successor, Gautsch, who had tried to divide Bohemia into German, Czech and mixed language areas for the purpose of reform but who had also failed.[48] The two Czech spokesmen were backed by Němec,[49] who gave to the congress all the evidence that it needed to prove that the Czech Social Democrats had been bitterly disappointed by the failure of Badeni's and Gautsch's reforms, ordinances that had later been rescinded by succeeding governments.[50]

In sum, Austrian Social Democracy was anything but anational in its outlook and in its approach in the 1890's. The party's consistent view was summarized by Kautsky who declared at one point that "proletarian internationalism does not mean the dissolving of nations, but the freedom and equality of nations."[51] The very same idea was emphasized by Pernerstorfer who, on another occasion, noted that internationalism had as its basic presupposition nationalism.[52] Adler understood also the depth of national feelings in the party when he repeated Daszyński's formula: "I am a Pole, and I am a Social Democrat."[53] Even in that order, the internationalists in the party hoped that the first consideration would at least be balanced by the second.

After solving the nationalities question within the party, the Social Democrats turned to a study of its impact upon the whole empire. The party was convinced that unless some remedy was found, national strife would cripple the empire and end all hope for social and political reform.[54] As national hatreds around it intensified, the party moved toward a more definite policy, one that finally emerged at its 1899 general congress held at Brünn. The policy that was first presented to the congress was largely formulated by Germans, which accounts for its biases, some of which were removed and some of which were not at Brünn.[55]

The party's attitude toward the nationalities question in June, 1898 was still vague when Friedrich Austerlitz tried to make it more definite in an article that he wrote for the Arbeiter-Zeitung. In his article, Austerlitz immediately touched on one of the basic presuppositions of the whole Social-Democratic approach.

As Austerlitz saw it, what the various nationalities in Austria wanted was a recognition of their respective languages. It followed from this that the nationalities question was, in the main, a matter of culture, a point that Austerlitz made here and which the whole Social-Democratic party stressed at Brünn. Austerlitz reminded his audience that the party had been a long-time supporter of the idea of linguistic parity in Austria, but he also cautioned that the question went deeper than a meré recognition of the right of all languages to be used freely and equally. Up until now, he declared, language had been used to keep down the subject nationalities; now it would have to be used for their development.[56]

Once Austerlitz began to move into the question, he discovered what the party was later to learn, that the nationalities question was really not susceptible to a ready solution. Austerlitz realized this when he noted that language parity could be recognized in theory but that it would be impossible to achieve it in practice. What he meant by this was that every nation had, by nature, a right to be dealt with in its own language, but that right could not be universalized in a state that was not one and the same as a nation. Practicality dictated, he contended, that in a multi-national state, all languages could not be used equally.[57] In his own cautious way, Austerlitz implied that a language of communication would have to be employed if the Austrian state was ever to function and that language would presumably be German.

At best, Austerlitz's article represented little more than a halting attempt by one of the party's leading intellectuals to work out a more acceptable position on the nationalities question. Yet, even at an elementary level, that position was hemmed in by Austerlitz's implied insistence that nationalism was devoid of both a political and an economic character. That bias, which limited the party's interpretation of nationalism, was carried over into the intra-party debate on the nationalities question that was conducted a year later in the Arbeiter-

Zeitung, just prior to the opening of the Brünn party congress. Taken together, the articles that appeared there written by Adler, Austerlitz, Pernerstorfer and Daszyński, amounted to a policy. But that policy, which was mainly German, was eventually to be modified, primarily by the Czechs,[58] but also by the Poles.[59]

Adler began the party's search for a broader and more comprehensive approach to the nationalities question with an article that traced the problem historically. 1899, he recalled, was not the first time that the party had been occupied by the nationalities question. It had faced it in 1891, 1896 and 1897, but in each instance the problem had centered upon the party; now it had taken on an entirely new dimension and would have to be analyzed as it affected the various classes and the various nationalities within the empire. The working class, he noted, had had to pay for national feelings, especially since they had impeded political reform and were making social reform unlikely. As far as the party was concerned, Adler admitted that it had been touched by nationalism but that those feelings had not, in any way, impaired the movement's effectiveness.[60] Pernerstorfer reinforced Adler by pointing out that the type of nationalism that had found a place in the party was really very different from the kind of nationalism that existed outside of it.[61] The reason why this was so, Adler added, drawing from Marx, was that the class interests of the proletariat had proven to be stronger than the supposed bonds uniting the various classes in each one of the nationalities.[62]

According to Austerlitz, the only way that the empire could be saved ultimately would be to restructure it along the lines suggested by the organization of the Austrian Social-Democratic Labor Party. The plan had worked within the party and should be taken as a model for what the future Austrian state would be like. The party was a logical model, he added, because it alone allowed for the type of autonomy that the various nationalities had demanded.[63]

Adler added to the party's expanding dialogue by insisting that the greatest existing impediments to the further development of the subject nationalities in Austria were the Kronländer, the historic provinces, each of which had come to embrace a number of nationalities. They would have to be done away with and replaced, he insisted, by entirely new divisions that accorded more closely with national boundaries. Only within these new types of units, Adler concluded, could the cultural and linguistic rights of the people be adequately safeguarded.[64] Under this new type of system, the party thought, national hatreds could at last be ended.[65]

Just before the Brünn party congress, Daszyński added one more point to the party's discussion of the nationalities question. Writing in the Arbeiter-Zeitung, he told the party that the general executive had decided to come out in favor of the division of Austria into self-administered national territories. The extent of these territories would be determined by the criteria of ethnic similarity, language and national affinity. The concept, Daszyński declared, was revolutionary and would prove so once it was adopted.[66]

Daszyński had now carried the party's discussion as far as it was to go in 1899. On the surface of it, the party had taken what amounted to a federalistic position on the matter of linguistic and cultural nationalism. But, in a sense, it had gone further for it was about to break with the older territorial conception of nationality and was coming closer to the idea that Renner and Bauer were later to develop, the concept of personality.

The nationalities program that grew out of the party's deliberations in Brünn was predicated upon two assumptions: one, that the Austrian state would continue to exist in its then present form; and two, that real social progress for the Austrian working class would be impossible unless a solution was found for national animosities.[67] The resolution that the general executive presented to the Brünn congress started with a proposal to eliminate Austria's historic provinces and to replace them with new autonomous national areas.[68] This process was to be aided by five major changes in the administrative and linguistic structure of the Austrian state. According to the resolution, they were to be: one, the transformtion of Austria into a democratic federation of nations; two, the creation of autonomous national territories, adjusted as closely as possible to existing linguistic boundaries; three, the formation of national associations made up of the various autonomous national areas of each nationality, with each association controlling its own linguistic and cultural development; four, the protection of the rights of national minorities; and five, in the absence of any other alternative, the acceptance of German as a common language for the empire.[69]

The resolution split the congress twice, dividing first the internationalists and the "nationalists," and then the Germans and the Slavs. As soon as the congress convened, it became apparent that a significant portion of the party was convinced that the party had already paid far too much attention to the nationalities question. Antonio Gerin, the Italian delegate from Trieste, recalled when the party was less involved with the issue of nationalism and then went on to describe nationalism as a bourgeois but not a proletarian concern.[70] He was followed by the Polish representative, Aron Liebermann, who turned to the congress to say: "National questions absorb too much of our effort."[71] Even Pernerstorfer was disturbed by this trend and indicated, in his speech to the congress, a longing for an older type of internationalism.[72] While it was obvious that a minority in the party opposed any further concessions to the principle of nationalism, it was just as clear that a majority wanted a program that would acknowledge the idea of cultural nationalism. The resolution of the general executive on the matter of cultural autonomy was presented to the congress by Josef Seliger. Rebuking the internationalists, Seliger contended that the question of national identity

and the perpetuation of the Austrian state were
concerns that affected the working class and that
what the party wanted, above all else, was to
find a solution that would finally rationalize
the behavior of the various national groups
towards one another.[73] The problem, he argued,
could be solved but only if each nationality
was free to develop itself culturally.[74]

As far as Němec and his Slav supporters were
concerned the cultural freedom that the party
conceded would be limited if the congress accepted the notion that a common language would be
mandatory for any reconstituted Austrian state.
That kind of proposal, Němec told the congress,
would only increase, all the more, the centrifugal forces at work in the empire. To prevent
that from happening, Němec insisted that the
language question be set aside and that a new
committee, representing the various nationalities
in the party, be established to redraft the proposals originally made by the general executive.
The congress agreed,[75] in spite of a speech
delivered by Pernerstorfer where he speculated
openly why the Czechs always seemed to be a step
or two ahead of everyone else on matters concerning nationalism.[76]

Meeting in secret, the temporary committee
established by the congress worked out a compromise that included a number of concessions to the
Czechs. The new resolution departed from the
original twice, differing on both points 2 and 5.
The second point in the party's emerging program
was made more explicit when it was rewritten to
read: "In place of the historical provinces
(Kronländer), nationally delimited, self-govern-
ing area will be created where legislation and
administration will be the prerogative of national
chambers (Nationalkammern), elected by universal,
equal and direct suffrage."[77] Bowing to the
Czechs, the committee decided to drop from the
resolution the section calling for the use of
German and to substitute for it, under point 5,
the more nebulous statement that: "We do not
recognize any national privilege and therefore
reject the demand for an official language

(Staatssprache). A parliament of the empire will decide if a language of communication will be necessary."[78] Whatever divisions the original resolution had caused, they had been resolved by the end of the debate and the Brünn program was unanimously accepted by the cheering delegates.

The party's attempt at a federal solution to the nationalities question recalled the past and other projects for the revitalization of Austria. Historically, the Brünn program was a direct descendent of the Kremsier constitution of March, 1849. That ill-fated document, inspired by the humanitarian nationalism of the great Czech patriot Francis Palacky and the ideals of the revolution of 1848, had likewise envisioned a redivision of the empire along the lines of ethnic federalism, with each nation able to deal singularly with its own cultural interests.[79] The only difference between the two documents may be found in the fact that the Kremsier constitution provided for the continuation of the various historic provinces, administrative units which time and migration had made obsolete by 1899. The Brünn program also shared certain similarities with the proposals that Adolf Fischhof had put forward in the middle of the nineteenth century, shorn, of course, of their assumption of German moral superiority. What Fischhof aimed at was a situation within which the rights of each nationality would be guaranteed legally and administratively.[80] Lost for a while, the idea that the rights of each nationality would have to be safeguarded institutionally surfaced again in the party's Brünn program of 1899.

In a sense, history had already passed the Brünn program by, even at the instance when it was being composed. Nationalism in the empire, as in Europe as a whole, had taken on a political character, a fact which most pragmatists accepted but one which Austrian Social Democracy consistently refused to recognize.[81] But, whatever shortcomings the Brünn program possessed, including its failure at a number of points to touch the times, on a spiritual level its restraint

contrasted with the rather frenzied appeal that
political nationalism was having elsewhere in the
empire. Born of compromise and good-will, the
Brünn program stood out, for example, in comparison with the German Pfingstprogramm (Whitsuntide
program) of 1899. This program was worked out by
a number of opposition parties in the Austrian
parliament, including the German People's Party,
the German Progressive Party, the Union of
Constitutional Aristocrats, the Christian-Social
Union and the Free Democratic Union, who all
feared the growing numerical superiority of the
Slavs. What they wanted in this program was a
preservation of German culture with as few concessions as possible to the Slavs.[82]

The Brünn program satisfied the older
elements in the party, but it failed to convince
several of the party's younger members. This
was true especially of Karl Renner and Otto
Bauer,[83] who were convinced that the nationalities question would someday have to be solved at
a much more intricate level than that found in
the Brünn program. As it was, both Renner and
Bauer were critical of the program's general
nature and its somewhat dated view of nationalism. Between 1900 and 1907, first Renner and
then Bauer attempted to overcome these deficiencies by making the party's position on the
nationalities question both more subtle and more
intricate.[84] The more involved view of nationalism was a precondition of internationalism.[85]
But the nationalism that they had in mind was of
a unique variety, one which was closely identified with culture and one which depended upon
personality.

The personality principle, as Renner presented it, represented a departure from nearly all
previous thinking on the question of nationalism.
The principle was not new to the party, for it
had already emerged, at least in an elementary
form, at the Brünn party congress. There, the
South Slav delegate from Trieste, Etbin Kristan,
had stated the idea as a part of his own halting
attempt to describe the course that nationalism
had taken in the empire. In his speech, Kristan

argued that the migrations taking place in the
empire had made it impossible for anyone to
continue to define nationalism exclusively in
territorial terms, which is what the Brünn
congress, erroneously in Kristan's view, had tried
to do. Changing circumstances, he contended, were
making nationalism, first of all, something that
was really quite personal and, besides, something
really quite divorced from location. Trying to
summarize his idea, he told the other delegates:
"The principle of a free society finds its
parallel in the separation of the idea of nation
from that of territory."[86] What Kristan did, of
course, was to present to the congress a highly
original concept, one that insisted that nationality was not a static concept but something that
was actually mobile, a possession that every man
carried with him without ever relinquishing from
one place to another. It was obvious in 1899
that he had made a point that was beyond the com-
prehension of most. Yet in embryo, it was the
very same concept that Renner was to develop with
much greater acumen in the years that followed.

In works published between 1899 and 1902,
Renner undertook one of the most sweeping re-
appraisals ever done of the phenomenon of nationalism. To start with, he made a clear distinction
between the state and the nation;[87] a distinction
that was predicated upon his view that the trend
of the times had reversed itself and was now
running in favor of larger political entities
and against the nation-state.[88] In those
countries that included several nationalities,
he argued, the institution of the state has to be
seen as the very embodiment of the principle of
unity. Because this was true, the state alone,
he argued, has the right to possess sovereignty.
But, by the same token, in a democratic polity
the state represents the will of the various
groups that compose it, including the nationalities, each of which possess certain rights.[89]

After outlining his approach in his earlier
works,[90] Renner proceeded in 1902 to publish his
most significant study of the nationalities
question, Der Kampf der österreichischen Nationen

um den Staat.[91] His thesis in this book rested upon the assumption that each and every nationality in Austria possessed a right to its own cultural development. That development was conceivable but only within the context of a reorganized Austrian state and it would only be possible if the principle of organization which was accepted in Austria in 1900, the territorial principle (the territorial division of the state according to its traditional crownlands)[92] was completely abandoned.[93] The crownlands, as they were called, would have to be eliminated because too often they had become the means by which one nationality had come to dominate another.[94] In place of what was, Renner proposed to establish a two-dimensional system,[95] one that was ethnic to solve the nationalities question, and one that was economic to solve the social question. To solve Austria's current dilemmas, Renner declared: "We must organize the country according to two principles. We must put a double network on the map, an economic and an ethnic one. We must cut across the functions of the state. We must separate national and political affairs, we must organize the population twice, one nationally and one according to administrative requirements."[96]

What Renner wanted to do was to reorganize Austria not once, but twice. In order to do this the old administrative system based upon the seventeen crownlands would have to be eliminated. Renner proposed to substitute for them a completely new plan, one that would conform more truly to the personality principle.[97] Because he had now identified the personality principle with nationality, he translated this to mean that every nation would have to be given the administrative means to develop culturally.[98] The practical means by which this goal would be achieved was for each nationality to form central, intermediate and local national bodies (Kreise),[99] some of which would be large, some small. Each of these bodies, regardless of size, would exercise a maximum amount of autonomy,[100] and was to be composed, as far as possible, of a homogenous national population.[101] Thus, by dismantling the older system and raising up a newer one, Renner hoped to guarantee to each of the nationalities in Austria exclusive control of its own cultural life.

Within the system that Renner wanted to create, each of the eight national groups composing the Cisleithanian portion of the empire was to be granted its own national chamber or university, through which it could control its own educational system. Only by doing this, Renner reasoned, would each nationality be in a position to protect its own cultural identity.[102] The eight national chambers that would have to be created were to be fully representative bodies, popularly elected, with the suffrage limited to those of the same nationality. For example, only Czechs, living in their various national areas dotting the empire, would be empowered to vote in elections for the Czech national chamber.[103] The elections for these chambers would be crucial ones, for they would bind together each one of the national groups living in Austria, organically, if not territorially. Beyond this, the eight national chambers would be given certain legislative powers, just enough to allow them to tax in support of their separate linguistic and cultural programs.[104] If jurisdictional disputes arose, they would be settled by a court of arbitration that Renner further suggested would have to be set up.[105]

Along side of this ethnic system, Renner wanted to create yet another to deal with economic disparities. For this second system, Renner proposed to divide Austria both geographically and economically. What he envisioned, in this instance, was still another federal system that would deal with the normal economic functions of government and leave out all those matters that were clearly cultural. The older crownlands would again have to give way, this time to a two-tiered system of Gubernia. The base for this second system would be formed by the creation of eight local Gubernia,[106] each of which would be autonomous in economic matters. On top of these local Gubernia, there would be a higher tier made up of four super-Gubernia, which would take on primary responsibility for the solution of economic and social problems. The four particular Gubernia would cover the Alpine lands, the Sudeten lands, the Carpathian lands and the Littoral lands, with their capitals respectively at Vienna, Prague, Lemberg and Trieste.[107] As in the case of the eight local Gubernia, these more powerful Gubernia would be forbidden to touch upon cultural considerations.[108]

The two-dimensional federal system that Renner intended to create for the solution of Austria's linguistic and economic problems would be supervised from above by a powerful central government that would operate both as a constitutional monarchy and as a democracy.[109] The powers that this government would have would be wide-ranging and would allow it to decide social and economic policy, to administer justice and to conduct foreign, military and financial affairs.[110]

In overall terms, Renner's design was essentially a highly imaginative attempt on his part to divorce the nationalities question from the realm of politics, so that the state might again function in some kind of normal way. Because this was his aim all along, the ethnic phase of his program, which he continued to sophisticate right down until 1914, became the best known part of his work.[111] As soon as they were published, Renner's ideas won a certain currency.[112] Although his ideas were never endorsed by a party congress, he succeeded in capturing support for his proposals both inside and outside of the party.[113] The growing acceptance that his ideas received in some quarters was counterbalanced, as it turned out, by some rather pointed criticisms elsewhere. His critics normally opposed him for one of two reasons: either because his thinking was too abstract or because he underestimated the exact proportions of nationalism both within and outside of the party.[114] His major difficulties stemmed from his refusal to go beyond cultural considerations and to consider the more radical possibility of national self-determination. This failure alienated a number of Slavs in the party who felt that his proposals were not sufficiently sweeping.[115]

Renner and the party were usually in accord but on one conspicuous point they parted company, that being the matter of dualism. In Renner's view, Austria and Hungary would continue to be connected and he predicted a time when the solution he suggested for the west would be applied in the east.[116] The party did not go along with Renner. In its view, separatism was an inevitability and Austria would never be a viable state until that separation was achieved.

During the 1890's, the party said virtually nothing about Austria's continued connection with Hungary. What broke its silence in 1897 and 1898 was the controversy that developed over the decennial economic negotiations between Austria and Hungary, a controversy that dated back to 1867. The Ausgleich of 1867 had created two independent states, Austria and Hungary, where the old Austrian empire had once been. Austria and Hungary continued to be linked after 1867 but only by a common crown, foreign policy, army and tariff.[117] According to the agreement signed in 1867, representatives from the two halves of the monarchy had to meet every ten years to work out the common expenses that each state agreed to bear. In 1867, the Austrians had assumed 68½% of those common expenses, while the Hungarians had taken over only 31½%. By 1897, pressure had built inside of the Austrian parliament in favor of a revision of that original formula, pressure which the Hungarians deftly tried to avoid. Finally in 1898, after months of negotiating, the Hungarians agreed to take on a somewhat greater burden and to accept a total of 33 3/4% of the empire's common expenses. The agreement represented a partial victory for the Austrians but it disappointed several political parties largely because it fell short of the 42 per cent that the Austrians had at first demanded.[118] When the agreement came to a vote, it provoked so much opposition in parliament that the prime minister, Thun, was finally forced to make it a law by using

Article 14, thus bypassing the recalcitrant parliament.[119] The incident turned Austrian socialism against dualism and against the type of economic tribute which the party maintained the <u>Ausgleich</u> agreement forced the Austrians to pay to the Hungarians.[120]

While the party contributed to the opposition that was raised against Austria's most recent decennial agreement with the Hungarians, it was not until 1903 that the party took an official position on the question of dualism. In the meantime, the party's views were largely given shape by Austerlitz who kept attacking dualism and all of its implications. According to Austerlitz, the link between Austria and Hungary was a purely artificial one that was lacking in linguistic, cultural and even historical justification. It was true, he admitted, that the Austrians and the Hungarians exchanged, preferentially, manufactured goods for foodstuffs; but, he argued, as vital as that link was, it was simply not enough to justify the continued connection of the two states. Dualism, he declared, had lost its meaning. It existed only because it helped the dynasty to maintain the illusion that Austria was some kind of great power.[121] What was needed, Austerlitz maintained, was a complete separation. For a while, at least the party was divided, but in time opinion in the party began to drift toward Austerlitz's arguments.[122]

After years of open debate, the party finally settled the issue at its 1903 general congress by coming out in favor of separation. At the congress, Austerlitz repeated the arguments that many had heard before. Dualism, he said, was an antiquated political form. It was an empty system, he maintained, that was costing Austria too much economically for it to be retained.[123] In the debate that followed, the congress was almost unanimous in supporting Austerlitz. One of the few skeptics was the Viennese representative Leopold Winarsky, who warned the congress that if the dualistic connection was cut, it might lead to the total disintegration of the empire.[124] Ellenbogen thought that the possibility was very remote,[125] and not even the Czech party leader, Němec, could imagine that it would happen. After all, Němec told the congress, the idea had to be incongruous since Austria was bound by the fact that the Czech and German workers of Bohemia had more in common than the Germans of northern Bohemia and the Alpine lands; and as long as that link persisted, Austria would continue to exist.[126] After this, Austerlitz presented a resolution to the delegates which came to the conclusion that the future development of Austria depended upon her cutting her connection with Hungary, a conclusion that met with the unanimous approval of the congress.[127]

By 1903, the party had made its position on the nationalities question clear. The party wanted to see the Austrian state continue.[128] But it wanted that state freed of its burdensome ties with Hungary and transformed by means of cultural autonomy. At an official level, that autonomy was defined territorially; but increasingly the party took over the idea proposed by Renner that nationality was a part of man's personality and therefore could be carried with any man from one portion of the empire to another.[129] For many years, the personality principle was looked upon philosophically as a kind of guarantee of survival for those nationalities which found themselves either isolated or surrounded by a hostile majority. It seemed as if, for many, the personality principle held out the hope that men might still retain their cultural identity even at those moments when they were outnumbered. Whatever appeal the idea of personality might have had at this time, it was less a matter of its possibility and more a consequence of its promise that made it attractive. And, in a very real sense, this particular psychological consideration was still strong when Bauer picked up the idea of personality and refined it even more in the years before World War I.

In many ways, Bauer was the product of those years just prior to the war that witnessed an intensification of national feelings.[130] Bauer intercepted that mood and tried to harness it in such a way as to make it conform to some of the preconceived ideas which the party had. Later on, at the end of World War I, Bauer admitted that nationalism did have a political character and that this quality had carried the peoples of eastern Europe all the way to national self-determination.[131] But for the period before 1914, he accepted the somewhat circumscribed ideas of Renner which had defined nationalism exclusively in terms of the personality principle and the idea of cultural autonomy. While Bauer accepted Renner's thinking in this regard, he was highly critical of Renner elsewhere, not so much for what was said but what had not been said. In his own study, <u>Die Nationalitätenfrage und die Sozialdemokratie</u>, published in 1907, Bauer not only took up Renner, but went beyond him to deepen the party's commitment to the personality principle.[132]

According to Bauer, both the Brünn program and the proposals set forth by Renner were incomplete largely because they failed to take into account social and economic realities. In Bauer's estimate of things, nationalism and socialism were both compatible and complementary. The lone reason why this had not been discovered before was that the bourgeoisie had used nationalism in a selfish way to block social and economic progress.[133] As Bauer analyzed it, every nationality possessed a national character, a quality that was subject to constant change and which was equivalent to a living, breathing life force. This force was, in turn, the essential part of a nation's culture, an inheritance, a cultural inheritance that had evolved only over long centuries.[134] This force was identified by Bauer as a nation's character and was, in the main, a "reflection of the history of a nation."[135]

One of the distinguishing features of capitalism, Bauer added, was that it kept the working class from the cultural traditions possessed by the various nations. Given this fact, the struggle put up by the working class for political and social reforms, for shorter hours and higher wages, for freedom of the press and assembly, for the right to form unions and for free education, was really an attempt by the various national working classes to gain admission to their own cultural communities.[136] With the coming of socialism, Bauer argued, the whole nation,[137] including the working class, would be absorbed into the cultural life of each and every people. The completion of this process had been made possible because industry had so increased productivity that labor could now be raised up.[138] And the whole process would be speeded up once the means of production passed into the hands of the working class.[139]

Bauer was so completely sure of his position that he stood up to the criticism of many including Karl Kautsky. Kautsky condemned Bauer for defining culture as something that was exclusively national.[140] Bauer retorted by rejecting as unreal Kautsky's assumption that what the proletariat was struggling for was a culture that was based exclusively on the interests and the attitudes of the working class.[141] While Bauer was not able to satisfy Kautsky, whose concept of internationalism came out of an earlier era, he did, for the moment at least, win over many who were convinced that he was in contact with the basic line of development that nationalism was following in central and eastern Europe.[142] If the age was forcing upon some a more realistic approach to the nationalities question, it was also asking that something be done about the problem of poverty in society; and here as elsewhere, the party was to come up with an answer which was typically piece-meal in its approach.

Chapter V

THE SEARCH FOR A SOCIAL POLICY

Speaking to the eighth congress of the Austrian Social-Democratic Labor Party in 1899, the veteran party leader Josef Hannich observed that Austrian socialism possessed two souls, one that lived in the present and one that lived for the future.[1] Living in the present for Austrian Social Democracy meant, of course, doing something about the relatively low standard of living of the industrial working class, the same class that the party purported to speak for. In the early years of the party, the view was widely held that poverty would not cease until the time came when capitalism disappeared.[2] But, as it was, neither the trade unions nor a majority within the party were really willing to wait for that to happen. What they wanted was to eliminate pauperism and to improve the workers' standard of living. So, while the party viewed the coming of socialism as a benefit, it paid much more attention at its founding congress, and in the years thereafter, to the type of legislation that would establish more decent working conditions and much higher wages.[3] In so doing, the party reinforced its own moderate tendency to meet immediate problems with short-term or piece-meal solutions, a propensity which, as has been stated before, marked the general approach that Austrian Social Democracy took toward larger issues.

At the time of Hainfeld, Austria had already put into effect significant social legislation; legislation which had been introduced by socially-conscious Catholic and conservative political leaders in the 1880's. The scope of that legislation had been so broad that Adler himself conceded before the 1891 congress of the Second International that Austria possessed, at least on paper, one of the most progressive systems of social legislation then known to Europe.[4] But, the party's attitude toward the legislation of the 1880's (legislation that had shortened the workday for women, regulated the amount of child labor, created a corps of factory inspectors, founded a program of health and accident insurance for most factory workers, as well as introducing other changes[5]) was, to say the least, an ambiguous one.

In general, the party favored the legislation because of its humanitarian orientation and because the trade unions had asked for it.[6] But beyond this, the party seemed to vacillate in its feelings between its own desire for reform and the interpretation that its intellectual elite had given to these reforms. For according to Kautsky and others, these reforms, and the support they had received in the working class, could not be understood except against the perspective of historical and social developments. As Kautsky explained it, the struggle by the working class against the bourgeoisie and exploitation, no matter what the results, was good, not because it improved the workers' standard of living in the short run but because it sharpened the class consciousness of the workers and developed within them a greater degree of revolutionary zeal.[7] This was so, according to Kautsky, because the efforts of the workers within capitalism, regardless of whether the workers were conscious of it or not, were really directed toward the creation of a new society, one in which there would be no private ownership, and not toward, even though it might seem to be the case, the reform of then existing society.[8] This view, which was the orthodox one, was expressed at Hainfeld by Adolf Braun. While he praised social reform, Braun was committed enough to ideology to remind those who created the party in 1889 that the conditions that confronted the working class could not possibly be improved until such a time as the means of production, now owned by the capitalists, had passed into the hands of the working class.[9]

At Hainfeld, the party approved a plank on social reform that reflected its own inner conflict over ideology and practicality. The preamble to the party's resolution attacked

Taaffe's attempt to reach out to the working class with social reforms. The proletariat, the resolution began, would never be deceived that the rich and powerful classes in Austria actually cared about the masses, nor would it be lulled by the idea that the mass of men would one day be free from exploitation. But, once the resolution got beyond this point, it turned completely around. For it went on to demand from Taaffe an immediate improvement in the system of health and accident insurance, an expansion of factory inspection, greater freedom of association, the eight-hour day, the prohibition of night-work, more child labor laws, and the introduction of Sunday as a day of rest.[10] The resolution concluded with the demand that the whole system be rounded out by the introduction of survivors' benefits and old-age benefits.[11] In placing its emphasis where it did, the party not only followed Adler, it also supported the Second International, which to the dismay of the anarchists still in it, had likewise come out in favor of social reform.[12]

Because of the emphasis that it placed upon piece-meal reform, it was virtually inevitable that Austrian socialism would at some time gravitate toward a partial acceptance of the existing order inside Austria. In a sense, the party was pulled further in this direction by the trade unions which confronted the results of poverty much more closely than it did itself.[13] In the minds of many labor leaders, the misfortunes of the working class tended to dissolve the importance of ideology; and what these labor leaders wanted was more immediate relief. It is true that the labor legislation of the 1880's had reduced the workday for women and children;[14] nevertheless, the workday was still long for most factory workers during the 1890's.[15] For example, between 1889 and 1899 in Vienna, the length of the workday remained fixed at ten hours. The unions were, of course unrelenting in their attempts to bring down that total, to the degree that in and around the year 1900, 30 per cent of all the strikes in the monarchy were for shorter hours.[16] The goal of the trade unions was that set by the Second International, the eight-hour day,[17] but the working class in Austria did not even come close to its goal; in fact, as late as 1906, half of the industrial workers there were still working shifts lasting longer than ten hours.[18]

The overall picture of labor conditions at this time was far from good, although one of the worst abuses of the industrial revolution, child labor, had been eliminated by restrictive legislation. Left behind in this development were tens of thousands of workers who had known nothing but factory work since they were six or eight years of age.[19] By contrast, factory inspection, which had been compulsory for most of the larger industries, was still spotty, primarily because the corps of factory inspectors was still so limited.[20] Even more frightening for the working class were the fluctuations in production that occurred around 1900 and which tended to force wages up and then down. In general, wages grew steadily through the 1890's and continued to do so after 1900, although after this date they failed for several years to keep up with prices. The worst period came immediately after 1900 when the average wage of industrial workers increased by 21 per cent, while food prices climbed anywhere from 30 to 50 per cent.[21] To most observers, the grimmest scenes were not to be found in factories but in the mining districts of Bohemia and Moravia. There, a large number of pitworkers had arrived only recently from the rural portions of Galicia and Slovakia and their lot was often desperate. Already debilitated, their general condition was compounded by illiteracy, illness, alcoholism and slum-like housing.[22]

The trade unions fought to limit the effects of unemployment, under-employment, poor working conditions and wage inequities but they were not particularly successful in the 1890's, primarily because their organizations were weak. Before 1914, in relative terms, Austria had the highest percentage of unionized labor of any country in Europe after Germany and England.[23] Yet, statistically, the number of workers enrolled in most unions in the 1890's remained too low for the unions to be truly effective. In the metallurgical and mining industries in the middle of the 1890's, the percentage of organized workers never rose above six percent and the figures were worse for the textile industry, Austria's largest, where only 7,000 of the 400,000 workers had joined unions.[24] Ten years later, the comparable figures were higher with 12 per cent of the textile workers, 25 per cent of the metal workers and 33 percent of the leather workers in Austria unionized.[25] The unions relied more heavily upon collective bargaining than strikes to achieve their aims. But when they did strike, their power was increased by the fact that they attracted large numbers of non-unionized workers away from their jobs. In the period before 1903, that is prior to the big upsurge in trade union membership that took place around 1904 and 1905, during strikes the unions were able to draw half of those employed in any industry from their jobs; and after 1903, the total was closer to two thirds.[26]

Outside of the factories, in the cities proper, the social question, as it was called in the 19th century, had progressively taken on the character of overcrowded housing, widespread vagrancy and on occasion hunger. The poor conditions that existed at the time were noticed by many, including Adolf Hitler, who once commented that "There was hardly any other German city where social questions could have been better studied than in Vienna."[27] Housing conditions, which were the worst aspect of rapid industrialization, were especially bad, with 43 per cent of Vienna's population in 1900 forced into flats no larger than one or two rooms.[28] Accidents and disease contributed to the somewhat chronic poverty of the era, although here relief was available, in part, in the form of health and accident programs which the government had made compulsory for industrial and commercial workers in 1889.[29] As the size of the working class grew in the 1890's, so did these programs, which came to cover some 2 million wage workers after 1900.[30] Still, complaints were heard from within the Krankenkassen that the payments were inadequate and that the programs were a failure as a stable form of relief. As far as most Krankenkassen officials were concerned, the programs could best be improved if the state took over the payments that the workers had been forced to contribute.[31]

While conditions were far from satisfactory, the working class in Austria did apparently have a higher standard of living in 1899 than in 1889.[32] These gains were largely the result of the better wages paid by industry, gains which the trade unions tried to hold on to and increase once their organizational strength improved. Still, in the 1890's, the Austrian working class was without real power: first, because of the organizational weakness of the unions; and, second, because it was without political representation. In this situation, the working class had to depend upon the curial parliament for legislation beneficial to it, legislation that was not forthcoming in the 1890's. For, after more than a decade of reforming zeal, the mood of the 1880's, in parliament, gave way to a feeling in favor of retrenchment as the lower house progressively disassociated itself from the cause of reform. The pieces of legislation affecting the working class passed by parliament in the 1890's were few. In 1891, parliament provided tax relief for builders who put up workers' housing and the following year it permitted the trade unions to organize across provincial lines.[33] But after this, the cause of social reform lost its priority to the more pressing issues of political reform and the nationalities question. Except for a bill that regulated work on Sundays and holidays in 1895 and another that affected the payment of miners' salaries in 1896, parliament was silent on social reform until after the turn of the century.[34] For a while, Pernerstorfer seemed to be the only Austrian deputy in the middle of the 1890's who was even concerned for further social legislation.[35]

Even the Social Democrats seemed preoccupied

in the middle of the 1890's with political and organizational problems and somehow less concerned about social reform. Now, as in the past, it was the trade unions which pressured the party into renewing its campaign for the type of legislation that would provide the working class with a greater degree of social security. The concern that the labor movement felt was expressed by Jakob Reumann at the 1896 congress of the Austrian trade unions. There, Reumann produced a detailed study proving that the existing system of health and accident insurance in Austria was inadequate to meet the needs of the working class.[36] To ameliorate conditions, he proposed to the congress a 13-point program of reform. The program, prepared ahead of time by the Austrian Trade Union Commission, summed up the basic expectations of the labor movement in Austria. The resolution's preamble condemned the capitalist system for the moral and physical degeneration of the working class but made it plain that the labor movement expected restitution. Among the demands of labor were the ones that favored the eight-hour day, the abolition of night-work, equal pay for women, the expansion of factory inspection, the extension of health and accident insurance, the introduction of old age and survivors' benefits and government subsidies for employment agencies administered by the trade unions.[37] In an extraordinary move, the resolution was adopted unanimously without debate, a vote which indicated the absolute unanimity of the Austrian labor movement on social reform.[38] The passage of the resolution, with its evolutionary overtones, represented the most extreme demand that the Austrian trade union congresses were to make before 1914. For the next few years, the effect of this resolution upon the party was to be salutary, for the party could hardly ignore what constituted the basic claims that the Austrian labor movement was making on the Austrian government.

The pressure that the trade unions were able to exert on the party was proven a year later at the party's 1897 congress when Leo Verkauf presented to the leaders of the party the demands that the trade-union congress had previously put forward.39 Taking up where the trade unions had left off, Verkauf attacked the entire system of social security as it then existed in Austria as baneful and inadequate. Prompted by the leaders of the trade unions, the congress adopted a resolution that called upon the newly elected Social-Democratic faction in parliament to use its influence to achieve the type and the kind of legislation that had been outlined at the time of Hainfeld and at a number of trade-union congresses after that.40 By passing the resolution, the party committed itself, as never before, to the type of legislative action that would have provided for only a gradual change in the society that Austria had produced by the 1890's. This time, unlike Hainfeld, there was no attempt to portray social reform as a sop or to qualify what the party was about to do; its commitment to reform had become unequivocal. As a result of the party's moderating position, two years later at the next party congress, Hannich could read off a whole list of proposals that the party faction had presented to the lower house, including a plan to increase compensation for industrial accidents, a design for expanded factory inspection, a suggestion for improving working conditions in retail stores and a demand that old age and survivors' benefits be introduced immediately. In spite of the party's efforts in the later 1890's, which followed the demands set forth by the trade unions, parliament refused to entertain any of the party's proposals.41 A short while later, Verkauf reported to the trade unions what everyone already knew, that the Austrian parliament had virtually ceased to function and that the prospects for social reform had darkened.42

Seen from a somewhat different perspective, the changing attitude of the party toward social reform was reflected in the way that it responded to the municipal reform proposals that Lueger had implemented in Vienna after 1896. The antagonism between the Social Democrats and the Christian Socialists had become more pronounced not only because the two parties had an overlapping interest in the working class but because the Christian Socialists had directed a great deal of anti-Semitic propaganda against the Social Democrats.[43] In spite of the emotions that separated the two parties, the Social Democrats were unable to find fault with Lueger's program, a program that had municipalized the lighting and transportation systems, created employment agencies and expanded hospital and medical care in the imperial capital.[44] In fact, by the late 1890's, the Social Democrats had ceased all criticism of the principles behind Lueger's master-plan, just as they had dropped all opposition to the social legislation that Taaffe had sponsored in the 1880's. In both instances, the party's criticisms were now exclusively directed at the administration of these programs and not to their origins.

From the late 1880's on, Austrian Social Democracy had pursued a policy of peaceful change without putting a label to what it had done. That ten-year period, during which ideology had played less and less of a function, came to an end in 1898 as a result of the controversy that revisionism engendered within the European socialist community. The first startling effect that it was to have for Austrian Social Democracy was that the policies it had been following no longer seemed to be ideologically correct.

Revisionism originated with the writings of the German socialist Eduard Bernstein.[45] Before revisionism died out as a conscious force sometime before World War I, Bernstein produced a gigantic debate in socialist circles over whether the movement was actually following the line of development that Marx had laid down for it. The controversy began when the empirical-minded Bernstein disproved a number of basic Marxian assumptions by arguing, somewhat pointedly, that there was not sufficient evidence from social development to warrant their acceptance. Among the assumptions that Bernstein attacked was the Marxian belief that capitalism would collapse from its own structural weaknesses and Marx's famous <u>Verelendungstheorie</u> which assumed that in the last days of capitalism the working class would be subject to both increasing poverty and pauperization. Bernstein gathered together enough empirical evidence to cast serious doubt upon the credibility of both of these basic Marxian views.[46] Once he argued against them, Bernstein stirred a controversy within German Social Democracy that was still unresolved when it began to spread to other parties, including the Austrian. Bernstein raised the controversy to new levels when he told the German party that its practice did not conform to its theory, that it was pursuing reform within the capitalist system almost as if it expected capitalism to live on, while anticipating at the same moment, somewhat abstractly, the collapse of the system. As far as Bernstein could see the German party was so deeply committed to reform and to an improvement in the workers' standard of living that it had lost sight of its revolutionary goals. In doing this, Bernstein maintained, the party, whether it admitted it or not, had accepted the assumption that it was possible to reform the capitalist system from within and had rejected the idea of some kind of ultimate or sudden revolutionary experience.[47] Finally, he advised his party at last to set aside the more meaningless phrases of the past and to concentrate instead upon the immediate goals of social reform and responsible government in Germany.[48]

As soon as Bernstein made his attacks public, he was repudiated by both the center and the left, headed by Kautsky and Rosa Luxemburg respectively, in his own party.[49] The first of several clashes between Bernstein and the opposition took place in 1898 at the German party congress held in Stuttgart. Just before the congress opened, Bernstein succeeded in widening the conflict so as to include the Austrians by publishing in the German party organ <u>Vorwärts</u> an article which praised the methods of Austrian socialism as both gradualistic and opportunistic.[50] Adler was shocked by the assertions which he took as blame, even though Bernstein had obviously intended them as praise. This blow coupled with Adler's own growing fear that Bernstein was about to destroy the ideological unity of the European socialist movement drove Adler into an immediate alliance with Kautsky and Luxemburg.[51] He made the move, even though in truth, his own philosophical position was not all that far removed from that of the German Revisionist.

In October, 1898, Adler made his first reply to Bernstein by denying that European socialism had lost sight of its revolutionary goals. He declared:

> No one in the party in Germany or anywhere else would be so thoughtless as to take, 'the expansion of the political and economic rights of the workers' as the lone focus of their efforts. Anyone who has thought about it at all, and this is whether the catastrophe [the collapse of capitalism] is near or far, puts his energies to work not only to win a slow rise in the standard of living and the political rights of the workers, as if this was his only goal, but also works as if the catastrophe was about to come at any moment.[52]

Adler's admission that he had worked to improve, step-by-step, the lot of the worker and his inference that he had done nothing to bring about revolution seemed if anything to prove Bernstein's contention about Austrian Social Democracy. Actually, Adler's attempt to refute Bernstein had turned out badly, for it had led him into a number of philosophical inconsistencies. For the moment, those inconsistencies were lost in the controversy that swirled around Bernstein, but they would not get past Kautsky a few years later when he examined more minutely Adler's position on revisionism. All in all, Adler's first parry with Bernstein was less of an attempt to meet him on logical ground and more of a product of his own belief that the ideological unity of European socialism ought to be maintained. He made his attack, not because he was a believing Marxist, but because he was convinced that a common set of ideals were psychologically-speaking an imperative for European socialism.

A few months after this, Adler replied again to Bernstein, this time in a review of Bernstein's book, <u>Die Voraussetzungen des Sozialismus und die Aufgabe der Sozialdemokratie</u>, which he produced for the <u>Arbeiter-Zeitung</u>. Displaying a greater knowledge of Marxism than at any time before or after, Adler attacked Bernstein for his rejection of economic determinism and for his dismissal of socialism as a cultural consideration rather than as historical necessity. According to Adler, Bernstein had completely lost contact with historical development as it had been defined by Marx and this loss had caused Bernstein to deny that capitalism would inevitably have to end and that an entirely new social system would inevitably have to replace it.[53] The support that Adler expressed for Kautsky and Luxemburg and the opposition that he voiced to Bernstein made Adler appear much more orthodox in 1898 and 1899 than he actually was. All of this occurred at a time when, under the pressure that had resulted from revisionism, theory was taking on more importance than ever before. From a tactical point of view, Adler had done the right thing when he aligned himself with Kautsky; but in personal terms, the position he had taken was an artificial one. For Adler was not a leftist, but a rightist and when he snapped back to that position after 1899, it shocked Kautsky who believed that Adler had now placed himself much too close to Bernstein.

In the period between 1889 and 1901, the unity of the Austrian Social-Democratic party had been threatened on several occasions by the divisive influence of nationalism, but it had never been endangered by deep ideological differences. Now, as of the turn of the century, that was no longer to be the case, for, in 1901, ideological concerns, which had always before been minor, suddenly became vitally significant. The disputes that arose over ideology in this era threatened both the party and the friendship that Adler and Kautsky had for one another. The specific differences that emerged in 1901 between Adler and Kautsky did not so much involve the practices of the party but rather the ideological explanations that should have been given to those practices. Once Kautsky began to examine those practices he became convinced that the party had drifted, ideologically speaking, to the right and he tried earnestly to arrest that process before it brought Austrian Social Democracy abreast of revisionism.

The first public indication that the two leaders had opposed each other came in September, 1901. In that month, Adler published an article in the Arbeiter-Zeitung that called for major changes in the party's Hainfeld program. To the chagrin of Kautsky and some of the leading intellectuals in the European socialist movement, Adler insisted that the Hainfeld program had been devised to meet conditions existing in 1889 but that the document had now become obsolete.[54] Without spelling out his meaning, Adler went on to declare that a number of changes had occurred in the social and economic life of the empire since 1889 and that the Hainfeld program would have to be revised in accordance with them. Again, without specifying too much, Adler proclaimed that what had happened over the course of that decade made it imperative that the party take a more serious look at the process that had been outlined much earlier in the century by Marx's Verelendungstheorie. Adler knew that Bernstein had laid the theory open to doubt, but he declared that the issue here had nothing to do with Bernstein's criticism.[55] The important question, he implied, was whether the workers had actually suffered a decline in their standard of living over the last ten years or not. Dismissing, by implication, both Bernstein and Kautsky, Adler concluded that pragmatically his party would have to continue to work, as it had before, for both the spiritual and material betterment of the working class.[56]

Evidently motivated by the finer intellectual distinctions that the revisionist controversy had forced most thinking socialists to conceive, Adler had turned, entirely on his own, to an appraisal of the capitalist system. He found there two trends at work at the same time. To begin with, he noted that it was in the nature of capitalism to exploit the working class and subject it to pauperization. But, he pointed out, there was a simultaneous tendency on the part of the proletariat to develop the means that would not only check that exploitation but actually overcome it and this was exactly the type of power that the proletariat had developed in the 1890's. In order to give his opinion more legitimacy, Adler insisted that the position he had taken was the one that Marx had imparted in the Communist Manifesto, although Adler failed to cite any specific portions of that work. What Adler was trying to do was easy to discern even though it was presented with a good deal of philosophical evasiveness. He had already come to the conclusion that the growing organizational strength of Austrian Social Democracy had been the single most significant development of the 1890's and he wanted to include that fact in a new party program.[57]

Adler's writings brought immediate rebuttals from both the center and left in Central Europe. Criticism of his stand developed within the Austrian, German and Polish parties because he had done one of two things or both. First of all, in the view of many, he had softened his party's traditional interpretation of capitalism by suggesting openly that its tendency to exploit might be mitigated and, secondly, many concluded that the changes he had hinted at had taken too much from Bernstein's recent criticism of Marxism. Besides, everything that Adler had to say publicly up to this point seemed to be touched by the propensity of revisionism to concentrate more and more on the present and less and less on the future. As far as the orthodox, or rather near-orthodox, were concerned, Adler was just too close to Bernstein in 1901; so much so, in fact, that at a later date Otto Bauer was led to admit that he could hear the "weak echo" of revisionism coursing its way through Adler's suggestion for change.[58]

What underlined the conflict that was about to become public at the 1901 congress of the party held in Vienna between Adler and his principal challenger, Kautsky, was the different interpretations that the two men had given to the events of the 1890's. To Adler those events had run counter to the Verelendungstheorie, whereas to Kautsky, they confirmed it. The issue was complicated by the fact that it had now become a matter of importance to be orthodox, as it had not been before, and, as a result, Adler had to be embarrassed especially when it turned out that his views coincided with those of Bernstein on the matter of pauperization.[59] It was clear in 1901 that the Austrian party, which had all but ignored Marxist theory in the past, now found itself in a dilemma. The dilemma was especially difficult for Adler, who was now called upon in 1901 to make fine intellectual distinctions in order to defend his stand, nuances that often enough contradicted orthodoxy.[60]

As soon as the revisionist controversy broke in the Austrian party, it gave Leopold Winarsky, one of the more subtle of the party's theoreticians, an opportunity to take on Bernstein, and by obvious inference, Adler as well. Winarsky directed his attacks in the party press against Bernstein, but his criticism of the German Revisionist only seemed to veil slightly the insinuations in his writings that Adler had absorbed far too much of the revisionist outlook. Without hesitating long, Winarsky began to consider the central issue that had developed during the debate, the question of pauperization. Winarsky concluded that Bernstein had come to the conclusion that the process of pauperization within capitalism was only relative by looking at only a portion of the actual evidence. Segments of the working class, Winarsky noted, had gained under capitalism, but the success of a few, he argued, had obscured for Bernstein and those who thought like him the basic fact that the overwhelming proportion of the proletariat had been dragged down to a lower economic standard as a consequence of capitalist exploitation. Because this trend was present in capitalism and would continue, Winarsky, who now represented what orthodox opinion there was in the Austrian party, opposed any change in the Hainfeld program. In particular, he declared that he would resist any attempt to change that portion of the party's original declaration which had described pauperization as a hard and unyielding process that could not possibly be reversed.61

Kautsky followed Winarsky's rather pointed criticisms in the party press with his own. He confessed that he had been unable to understand the reasoning behind the proposed changes in the party's program of 1889. The principles that had been included in the party program at the time of Hainfeld were just as valid, he maintained, as they had been at the time when they were first written. Kautsky admitted that in line with changing conditions party programs sometimes needed to be revised. But, he added, such was not the case here; nothing had happened in Austria that would warrant change in the party program. Worse still, he went on, many of the changes being contemplated, not all of which had been made public yet but all which Kautsky knew of, were simply too close to Bernstein to be acceptable.62 He readily accepted, he said, Adler's public statements that the changes were in no way indebted to Bernstein, but, he warned, others would not come to that conclusion largely because too many of the changes seemed to follow from Bernstein's criticism of Marx.63

Growing even more critical, Kautsky charged that the committee the party had set up to work over these changes had gone too far. He was particularly incensed because the committee had decided to drop from the new document that it had prepared that denunciation of capitalism which had been written in 1889 and which had insisted that "the possessors of the capacity to work, the working class, are thereby cast into the role of slaves vis-à-vis the owners of the means of production, the capitalist class."64 Kautsky objected that the new draft had deleted the section on enslavement and had substituted for it a much weaker statement to the effect that "the possessors of the capacity to work, the working class, became [within capitalism] in growing measure dependent upon the possessors of the means of production."[65] This new phrasing implied a softer line on capitalism, a condition that Adler was willing to accept, but which Kautsky was not.[66] While Adler and Kautsky may have argued over the nature of capitalism, the real issue that divided them was the question of whether the working class had experienced a rising or declining standard of living in the 1890's. Adler maintained that it had risen and Kautsky that it had not.[67] At any other time in the history of the party, the issue would have been much smaller, but once it became embroiled with revisionism the whole controversy was magnified by the impact of ideology.

Up until the 1901 congress of the Austrian party, Adler had not bothered to defend himself against his detractors,[68] to the extent that he even allowed them to place him uncomfortably close to Bernstein.[69] The reason why he permitted this did not become clear until the day before the party congress was scheduled to open. Writing in the Arbeiter-Zeitung, Adler singled out the party bureaucracy, calling it the most important force that there was in the rise of Austrian Social Democracy.[70] He deliberately picked out the thousands of Vertrauensmänner in the party for praise, not only because he needed their support in his upcoming struggle with Kautsky, but because he was genuinely convinced of their importance to the movement.[71] To have assumed, as Winarsky and Kautsky had, that the condition of the working class was not improving would have meant that the administrative work of these men during the 1890's had accomplished next to nothing. The only way that Adler had of telling them that they had contributed to a general improvement in conditions was to soften his line on capitalism and to admit that reform had indeed taken place. He had to do this, even though it meant alienating some of the more theoretically-inclined members of the international socialist movement.

On the first day of the congress, Adler finally made public the full change in the Hainfeld program that he had worked up with

Daszyński, Ellenbogen, Franz Schuhmeier and Herbert Steiner.[72] Now on the offensive, Adler was particularly blunt in presenting the new party program to the delegates. He told them that the Hainfeld program was outdated and that the new one represented the views of the overwhelming majority in the party.[73] He admitted that a number of sentences in the draft proposal had stirred controversy but, he went on, the proposals, taken as a whole, accurately described conditions as they existed in 1901.[74] Once he got past his introductory remarks, Adler took up some of the questions that had been posed by Marx's Verelendungstheorie. Defending himself intensely for the first time, Adler quickly quoted from Engels' critique of the German Erfurt program of 1891, pointing out that Engels had once declared that, "It is not true that the misery of the proletariat always becomes greater. It is possible that the growth of an organization can establish a dam against the growth of misery; what definitely does grow, however, is the insecurity that the proletariat feels about existence."[75]

Once having defended himself, Adler next turned to the opposition to ask, rhetorically, whether they believed Engels had been a Bernsteinian or not.[76] Brushing aside the question of pauperization for the moment, Adler next suggested to the delegates that from a tactical point of view Austrian Social Democracy would have failed in its attempt to reach out to the masses if it had told the mass of men in society that pauperization was both inevitable and irreversible. In point of fact, he admitted that the standard of living of the workers had not risen as fast as that of the bourgeoisie, but he found it inconceivable that anyone would say that it was not better in 1901 than it had been in 1889.[77]

Before Kautsky delivered his rebuttal, the congress listened to the remarks of the Viennese trade-union official, Jakob Brod. Brod set an extreme tone for Kautsky by accusing Adler of spreading the ideas of Bernstein and the commission that had been set up to undertake the changes in the party program of having lost sight of the teachings of Marx.[78] In contrast to Brod's overly frank presentation, Kautsky was actually quite circumspect. In part, his caution was an outgrowth of his own realization that a majority of delegates had already made up their minds. Kautsky repeated himself by telling the congress that he did not intend to open up a new revisionist controversy and that he had not been able to find the influence of Bernstein in the new party program. But, he added, he felt that others would. Broadening his attack, Kautsky told the delegates that the commission had made a serious mistake when it had diminished the idea of proletarian poverty and that it had erred when it weakened the party's stand on the oppressive character of capitalist society. To illustrate the changes that had been made, Kautsky pointed to the sentence in the new draft proposal that spoke of existing conditions; it read, "the standard of living of ever-deepening strata of the working people contrasts more and more with the rapidly rising productivity of their own work and the expansion of the wealth they themselves create."[79]

Kautsky argued that this sentence was too mild, that it lacked a cutting edge and that, like most of the key sentences in the new draft, it did not sufficiently indict capitalism.[80] He preferred the wording in the old Hainfeld program which had first established the party's uncompromising opposition to capitalism and then stated it in unequivocal terms.[81] For a moment, Kautsky's criticism seemed to touch the delegates, but the spell he created was quickly broken as one after another of Adler's lieutenants, including Ellenbogen and Němec, backed the party leader.[82] By the time the vote had been taken, opposition to the new party program had all but evaporated and it was accepted with only three negative votes.[83] It was evident from what Kautsky had said that he really did not intend to push his disagreement with Adler any further than he had in 1901. Instead, he agreed to accept whatever decision the congress came to.[84]

Nevertheless, the differences between Adler and Kautsky lived on after the congress to emerge once again, unexpectedly, at the 1904 congress of the Second International.

The 1904 congress of the Second International was marked by an extraordinary feud between the German and French parties over the fate of revisionist theory. The Germans, led by Bebel and Kautsky, wanted the International to condemn revisionism, just as the German party had done recently at its Dresden party congress. The Germans soon found, however, that they were being blocked by the French party leader Jean Jaurès, who did not want to see an outright rejection of revisionism by the International.[85] In an effort to end the dispute, Adler and the Belgian party leader Émile Vandervelde pushed forward a compromise that would have left the position of the Second International on revisionism very ill defined. They did this by editing the original proposal which the Germans had laid before the congress to such an extent that the word revisionism was completely left out.[86] Eventually, the compromise put by Adler and Vandervelde was defeated and the congress came out against revisionism, but not before Adler had stirred memories of his older feud with Kautsky. In the strained atmosphere of the congress, Adler heard himself referred to by his friend, August Bebel, as "a revisionist in disguise," an allegation that the Russian party leader George Plekhanov also repeated.[87] Stunned by the charges, Adler could only express his own surprise to the congress that Bebel and Plekhanov could ever conceive of him as "a revisionist in disguise."[88]

A few months after the congress, Kautsky, evidently satisfied by the decision of the International, finally brought the controversy between Adler and himself to an end. During an exchange of letters, Adler expressed the fear that ideological differences had damaged their friendship. Kautsky assured Adler that their friendship was larger than any of the differences that had divided them. At the same time, he told Adler that Bebel's reference to him as a revisionist had largely been a joke and, in an off-handed way, insisted that if everyone was as well acquainted with Marx as Adler was there would never have been a revisionist controversy to begin with.[89]

The ideological battle between Adler and Kautsky over the meaning of the Viennese party program of 1901 tended to obscure many of the more profound changes that had been written into that document. Gone from the new Viennese party program were many of the ambiguities about social reform that had been included at the time of Hainfeld. The new party program was as straightforward as it could be, calling for a number of social reforms including a comprehensive system of social-security legislation.[90] Speaking to the party's commitment, Jakob Reumann told the party congress in 1901 that it is the function of the state to care for the sick and the injured, the widowed and the orphaned in society. He talked about state action in such a way as to suggest that he was oblivious to the theoretical implications of what he was saying. Indeed, the whole debate on social reform indicated that a majority of the delegates, who were more practical than ideological, had not even been aware of the subtle theoretical differences that had loomed so large for both Adler and Kautsky in 1901.[91]

The endorsement that the new party program gave to social reform, along with the optimism produced during Körber's first few months in office, gave rise to some expectations that parliament might act on behalf of social reform. The party's hopes were realized in 1901 and 1902 when parliament passed legislation which regulated child labor and the duration of the workday in the mines and provided workers in the building trades with greater protection from accidents.[92] But, after this, the Austrian parliament stopped voting social and economic legislation and proposals like those of the Social-Democratic deputy, Franz Schuhmeier, to reduce the legal workday in Austria to eight hours never even emerged from committee.[93]

Even though the party did not gain the legislation that it expected, it still used parliament to defend the interests of the working class. It did this, for example, in February, 1902, when it charged Körber with responsibility for the violence in Trieste where street demonstrations had left several workers killed and more than a score injured,94 and again five months later, this time after police had fired upon a crowd of strikers in Lemberg.95 The party's most determined attempt to change things came in October, 1901, when it presented to parliament a mass petition that favored the introduction of unemployment insurance and old-age and survivors' benefits. The petition included almost 700,000 signatures and was supported by 480 different municipal officials, 1,200 trade-union locals and 480 <u>Krankenkassen</u> assemblies.96 As forceful as it was, the petition failed to affect parliament's mood and thereafter all hope for social reform died away.97

While Austria's political processes were noticeably slowed during this period, her economy continued to grow rapidly. In the decade after 1903, her industrial revolution intensified as the number of new industries founded jumped 41 per cent and coal and iron production increased 54 and 90 percent respectively.98 The steady expansion of industry after 1900 contributed to even greater unrest in the party than before; for many felt that a much higher percentage of the new wealth that had been created should have gone to the working class.99

The party's growing disenchantment with social and economic conditions found expression at the party's 1903 general congress held in Vienna. The man who summed up the party's feelings at this point was the Social Democratic deputy from Brünn, Ferdinand Eldersch. Eldersch accused Körber of refusing to respond to the needs of the mass of Austrians.100 He even went so far as to suggest that it would be better if the party gave up on parliament and worked through the trade unions. Perhaps, he reasoned, the unions might be able to draw from the employers concessions which the government had so far refused to exact from them.[101] The congress failed to take up Eldersch's suggestion primarily because it diverged so completely from the party's long-standing commitment to state action.[102] Instead, the congress simply passed a resolution that laid the blame for the failures of the curial system to Körber and to his administration.[103]

The failure of Austria's curial system to function after 1900 was, in a sense, a disappointment for Austrian Social Democracy. It was a disappointment because just as it turned reformist, and even Fabian in tone, the Austrian parliament lost its ability to reform. Paralyzed by the struggle between Germans and Czechs, Austria's curial parliament was steadily worn down as an effective instrument for reform. When it, at last, became obvious to the emperor and to other political parties that reform was doomed unless parliament itself was reformed, it was only then that others began to join the Austrian socialists in a clear call for a more democratic system. When this happened, it finally opened up the possibility for universal manhood suffrage in Austria.

Chapter VI

THE ACHIEVEMENT OF ELECTORAL REFORM

By 1905, Austrian Social Democracy had developed to the point where it was in a position to affect the outcome of events in Austria. But, while it exercised real power through the trade unions and its own party apparatus, that power lay, for the most part, outside of parliament. The only way that the party had of expanding its power, of applying real political pressure in 1905, was through the cause of electoral reform. Realizing this, the party did what was obvious; it identified itself with the cause of electoral reform more thoroughly than any other political party in the empire.[1] What gave the party, beginning in 1905, an opportunity to move from the periphery to the very center of Austrian political life was the steady erosion of public confidence in the curial parliament.[2] In the main, that decline was the work of the Young Czechs, who tormented the lower house of the Austrian parliament with their incessant obstructions between 1900 and 1905 to such an extent that the house seemed close to death at a number of points.[3]

The vacuum that was thus created was filled by the Social Democrats and like-minded political parties, all of whom agreed that Austria would achieve political stability only after the franchise had been opened up and only after the masses had been introduced to the suffrage. While these arguments were being put forward, Article 42 of the house's standing rules of procedure continued to license the activity of the Young Czechs who successfully prevented whole sessions from accomplishing anything. The Social Democrats viewed these obstructions somewhat coldly. They themselves never engaged in the practice of obstruction; that was left to Karel Kramař and the Young Czechs. But the Social Democrats did see an advantage in the way that the curial parliament was being paralyzed as of 1905 because at least it opened up the possibility of a more democratic franchise.[4]

The party had lost its desire to see the curial system saved, primarily because the system had steadily reduced the ability of Austrian Social Democracy to translate its popular following into any meaningful kind of political power or political representation.[5] In spite of this, the party, guided by its own peaceful disposition, continued to believe in reform and to eschew street demonstrations, boycotts, revolution and other forms of direct action.[6] In part, its continued faith in a more representative system of government was sustained by its successful showing during the imperial elections of 1901. Of the 5,753,462 votes cast in the five different curiae in 1901, a figure that included hundreds of thousands of plural voters, the Social Democrats emerged with the largest total; 799,461. They were followed by the Young Czechs with 525,558 votes. Yet, by the curial system, where the number of mandates assigned did not necessarily reflect the popular vote, the Young Czechs came out as the largest single political party in parliament, with 53 deputies, and the Social Democrats as one of the smallest, with only ten.[7] What mitigated the party's disappointment from 1901 to 1905 was not only its hope for future franchise reform, but its own peculiar sense of fatalism, a feeling that had been very much present at the 1901 congress of the party when it had virtually "excommunicated" Kautsky for demanding too much from it.[8] The party had grown Fabian in spirit and its overriding sense of caution prevented it from acting precipitously even in 1905 when Körber's government gave way to that of Baron Paul Gautsch.[9]

Gautsch assumed office in January, 1905. When he did he promised Austria a quieter period of politics, and, as if trying to confirm that mood, he did not even mention electoral reform in his first speech to parliament. The change in governments did, however, have its effect upon parliament, which finally began to function in a much more normal way. The various political parties, evidently fearful for the existence of parliament, gave up on obstruction, thus allowing the house to move from one piece of legislation to another.[10] After passing the budget, for the first time in years, and approving a military recruitment bill, the house disbanded for its summer recess.[11] Before it reconvened, the empire found itself in political ferment, the result of events taking place in Russia and Hungary.[12] The outbreak of revolution in Russia in 1905 won both the sympathy and the support of Austrian Social Democracy, but the full impact of Russian developments was not actually felt until the following September when a constitutional crisis in Hungary along side of what was happening in Russia, turned out to be the prelude to electoral reform inside of Austria.

In the summer of 1905, political unrest in Hungary rebounded to affect the cause of electoral reform in Austria. For almost half a century, growing national sentiment in the Hungarian parliament had been leading the Hungarians to resist the political ties that had bound together the two halves of the monarchy. That steadily increasing feeling manifested itself in 1905 in a major electoral victory for Francis Kossuth, the son of Louis Kossuth, and his nationalistic party. Kossuth failed to become prime minister in the spring of 1905 even though he had a majority in the house, only because he was unable to come to an agreement with the emperor, Franz Joseph. Unable to find the right man, Hungary went without a prime minister until June, when the emperor finally named Baron Geza Fejerváry to head a minority government. In an obvious effort to undermine the numerical strength of their opponents, the nationalists in the house, Josef Kristoffy, Fejerváry's minister of the interior, proposed to open up the franchise to the lower classes and to eliminate Hungary's restrictive suffrage. Kristoffy hoped that an extension of the suffrage would overwhelm the nationalists, who, in a sense, held their majority artificially from a very limited electorate. In conference with the emperor, Fejerváry backed the proposal of his minister of the interior but Gautsch opposed it strenuously, fearing, as he did, the political effect that it would have in Austria. On September 10, Gautsch again stated his opposition to electoral reform inside of Hungary, a move that led almost immediately to the collapse of Fejerváry's government and Kristoffy's plan for electoral reform. As rumors and facts circulated freely in the press, Gautsch was condemned for having destroyed Fejerváry's government and for having undermined the chances for franchise reform in both Hungary and Austria.[13]

The spread of both rumors and news involving electoral reform encouraged not only the Social Democrats but other parties that were desirous of political change. The Social Democrats began street demonstrations in September and began attacking Gautsch in the press as "an enemy of the people."[14] Sensing that the government was now on the defensive, the party's central executive committee immediately called a Reichskonferenz in order to coordinate the party's policy. The conference was ultimately attended by some 64 representatives from the various national sections of the party.[15] The conference met on September 24 and issued a manifesto that was so vitriolic that it was obvious that, in spirit, the party had already moved much further to the left. The manifesto was accepted with cries in favor of pushing the struggle against Gautsch into the streets. The conference ended on a somewhat ominous note with the normally moderate trade-union leader, Josef Tomschek, vowing that there would be no public order in Austria until universal manhood suffrage had actually been achieved.[16]

Parliament, meanwhile, reconvened on September 16, the whole empire in turmoil. On the second day of the new session the usually placid Pernerstorfer all but threatened the government with revolution, warning it that unless the issue of the franchise was settled the revolutionary flames now burning in Russia, as he put it, would spread to Austria as well.[17] Meanwhile, Gautsch's government was itself overwhelmed by seven different motions of urgency, each one of which demanded the immediate introduction of universal manhood suffrage. Defending himself before the house, Gautsch denied that he was in any way an opponent of franchise reform; instead, he said, he had always supported the idea of extending the suffrage, although, he implied, not to the point of universalizing it.[18] In spite of the sympathy that he had expressed for reform, Gautsch refused to consider the tabling of such legislation even as pressure mounted inside of parliament from the Young Czechs and Christian Socialists and outside of parliament from the Social Democrats for precisely that move.[19]

While Gautsch hesitated in the early part of October, Ignaz Daszyński, the party leader in the lower house, joined with a number of other party leaders to force on the house a motion of urgency calling upon the government to prepare a reform bill. The motion, on October 6, failed to receive the two-thirds majority that it needed, since it was a procedural matter, but the final vote was 155 in favor to 114 against. While more than a third of the house had abstained on the vote, the idea was now generally accepted in the empire that the house had committed itself to reform, even if the government had not.[20] For the most part, events had already outstripped Gautsch's indecision; for just at the very moment when the house registered its approval of reform, the emperor also decided that Austria would have to have the bill.[21]

Through October, the liberals in parliament continued to pressure the government against the hesitancy of Gautsch and the conservatives. Opposition to an extension of the suffrage inside parliament was centered among aristocratic deputies and in certain bourgeois political parties,[22] while on the outside it was encouraged by the heir to the throne, Franz Ferdinand, who was thoroughly opposed to any reform. The conservatives were genuinely fearful that a reform of the franchise would bring either the Social Democrats to power or mob rule or both, fears which Otto Czernin and other conservative spokesmen kept expressing.[23] On the liberal side, the cause of electoral reform was aided in mid-October when Victor Adler was suddenly elected to parliament in a by-election.[24] After so many defeats, Adler's victory seemed, if anything, to symbolize the fact that, at least for the time being, political initiative inside of Austria had passed to the liberals and the socialists.

At the end of October, right in the midst of Austria's raging debate over the electoral reform, the Social Democrats held one of their regular party congresses.[25] Adler opened the congress with a speech that exhorted the delegates to "revolutionary" action. Just what he meant by this term soon became apparent, for instead of turning, at this vital moment, to Marx, he fell back on Lassalle. He recalled for the delegates those passages in Lassalle's work where Lassalle had pointed out that the proletariat would never achieve the right to vote until it had devoted all of its organizational energies to the cause of political change and political revolution,[26] i.e., to the winning of the franchise.

After inflammatory speeches by Pernerstorfer, who attacked parliament for its prolonged inactivity, and by the party secretary, Ferdinand Skaret, who condemned Gautsch for his failure to bring in a reform bill,[27] the congress settled back to listen to a more dispassionate speech by Ellenbogen on the unhappy state of the Austrian economy. While he spoke, he was handed a note by Němec. His husky voice ringing out, Ellenbogen announced to the delegates that the revolution in Russia had won out and that the Czar had granted the Russian people a constitution.[28] The news caused a wild scene among the delegates; spontaneously the Czechs and Poles broke into "The Red Flag" and the Germans into "The Marseillaise"; and with it all there were repeated cries for mass demonstrations and a general strike.[29] In short order, the delegates translated their enthusiasm into a resolution calling for the adoption of universal manhood suffrage,[30] a move which underscored the congress's emotional acceptance of Ellenbogen's earlier statement to the effect that "we have had enough of the old Austria."[31] The inspiration that the revolution in Russia had now produced seemed, if anything, to have gripped the party and pushed it toward even more resolute action. In the atmosphere that was thus created, Adler, to the surprise of many, reversed himself and came out in favor of a "general strike" as long as, he said, it was limited to a period no longer than twenty-four hours.[32]

Breaking with his previous sense of caution, Adler told the delegates that the time had come for a strike, but it would have to be one in which the masses participated to the fullest possible extent. Tempering his approach as he went along, Adler steadily toned down the congress's emotions by drawing a number of overly fine distinctions for the delegates. He reminded his audience that the party had faced a very similar situation in 1893 but that it had retreated from a collision with the government. This time, he declared, the balance of power had shifted and the party would not hesitate to move out and actually challenge the government. The party, he insisted, would have to give up docility, for the proletariat now needed the franchise. Unless the masses were given the right to vote at this particular moment in Austria's history, Adler argued, Austria would continue her decline, social reform would be lost, national hatreds would deepen and the standard of living of the workers would stagnate. More than this, Adler argued on, one had to take into account the therapeutic effects, the new sense of life, that the reform would have for the empire as a whole.[33]

In pushing for direct action, Adler was careful not to convey to the delegates either a sense of recklessness or irresponsibility. In his speeches and in the resolution that he put to the congress, he sobered the hot-heads by informing the congress that the party was out neither to destroy the state nor to cripple the economy. Instead, Adler drew a close distinction for the delegates between a general strike, which was by its nature both anarchistic and destructive, and what he described as a <u>Massenstreik</u>, a strike which would be much more circumspect and which would aim at the achievement of a more specific political goal.[34] It is highly doubtful that a majority within the party, or for that matter, in the government, really understood the fine distinctions that Adler was making. Fewer still were ready to accept the cautious moderation that Adler had tried to impose by his speech. As it was, the fall of 1905 was not, in fact, a time for subtle distinctions.

The course that the party was now prepared to follow was really not unique. If the idea of revolution had been lost to the European socialist movement as of 1905, and it had, the idea of making use of a general strike to achieve a limited political or economic goal had indeed replaced it. Since the 1890's, the idea had become much more accepted especially after several general strikes had been invoked. In 1902, for example, the Belgian labor movement had staged a general strike to secure universal manhood suffrage, and in 1903, the Dutch trade unions had gone out in an attempt to block anti-strike legislation from passing parliament. Closer to 1905, in 1904, Swedish workers had conducted a mass demonstration in favor of an extension of the franchise that had also turned into a general strike. By 1905, the idea of a general strike, which in the 1890's had been condemned by the Second International because of its anarchistic and syndicalistic connotations, had been accepted by most socialists.[35] The idea had spread so far that in 1904 at the Amsterdam congress of the Second International, the idea of a general strike, shunned before, was now approved, with qualifications, by almost 90 per cent of the delegates that attended.

The congress restricted the use of the general strike by rejecting as too extreme the idea that it should be used to shut down a country's economy. Instead, after some hesitation, it voted a much tamer resolution, one which sanctioned the use of a general strike as long as it was conducted in a highly disciplined manner and as long as its goal could not be achieved in any other way.[36] Adler had operated in October, 1905, totally within the spirit of that resolution when he had suggested that his party impose a general strike upon Austria. But, while he may have approved of the idea in part, his own hesitancy about its implementation was revealed not only in his desire to limit it time-wise but also in his overly subtle and overly cerebral distinction between what was a general strike and what constituted a <u>Massenstreik</u>.[37] The checks that Adler tried to place on the party's enthusiasm at the time of the congress were, in actuality, swept away by declarations, by one labor leader after another, in favor of a general strike.[38] So, plans for the strike moved along, even though it was evident that the Trade-Union Commission and certain party leaders were not happy about the amount of the spontaneity involved or the fact that the real initiative for the strike had passed into the hands of some of the more radical <u>Vertrauensmänner</u> in the party.[39]

Meanwhile, street demonstrations had broken out toward the last of October. Almost immediately, they led to bloody clashes between police and groups of demonstrators.[40] In spite of the violence, the demonstrations continued right into November, reaching a high point between November 2 and 5 in both Vienna and Prague. For the most part, the party's trained <u>Vertrauensmänner</u> kept control, but the massive scale of the demonstrations along with the high-pitched feelings of the moment made for some violence. By the end of the first week of demonstrations, the toll was two dead and nearly 100 workers wounded, most of them by police fire. In Prague, where street fighting had broken out between workers and regular troops, barricades had gone up in the streets.[41] With public order seemingly now in the balance, Franz Joseph finally convinced Gautsch to bring in a reform bill.[42] On November 4, with demonstrations still taking place, Gautsch released the news that the government was now ready to draft a reform bill. The news, far from dampening the demonstrations, only encouraged them down to November 6.[43] After this, they abated, but with the Social Democrats announcing plans for a gigantic demonstration of their own on November 28.[44]

In the interval, the Social Democrats continued to exert pressure upon the government, this time from a different source. On November 9, the socialist-dominated railway workers' union began working to rule, a move which, in effect, imposed a slow-down on rail traffic throughout the western part of the monarchy. Officially, the "strike" was for higher wages but in truth it served as another warning to Gautsch, who was by now aware that the Social Democrats could embarrass him both politically and economically.[45] Two days later, on November 11, Gautsch gave in and announced that a reform bill was being prepared.[46] Once again, the news only tended to encourage the Social Democrats, who, on November 28, came as close as they would ever come to a general strike. On that day, the party sponsored mass demonstrations in almost every industrial town and city in the western part of the monarchy. In Vienna itself, more than 250,000 workers, marching in absolute silence, filed past the parliament building; in the industrial areas of northern and western Bohemia some 260,000 workers attended dozens of protest rallies and in Prague a total of 100,000 people participated in a mass rally on behalf of universal manhood suffrage. Demonstrations of a similar sort took place in Brünn, Linz, Graz, Laibach, Trieste, Lemberg and Cracow as well as in scores of other towns, with actual violence occurring only in Austerlitz (Slavkov), where two demonstrators were killed and 30 wounded.[47] All together, the Social Democrats poured almost a million workers into the street; and their powerful display, coupled with a similar show by the Christian Socialists on November 27, was enough to force Gautsch to announce that he would bring in a bill in favor of universal manhood suffrage sometime early in 1906.[48]

On November 30, two days after his party had staged what was, in effect, a general strike,

Adler rose in parliament to declare that the movement toward reform had become irrevocable and that it would "overwhelm [the opponents of reform] if they did not go along with it."[49] Now convinced of Gautsch's sincerity, Adler went on to warn the conservatives and the opponents of reform that those who wanted reform would resist to the last any attempt on their part to blunt its impact by either proportional representation or plural voting.[50] The unusually inflammatory tone of Adler's very first speech to parliament seemed to set a precedent for the kind of invective that other Social Democrats were to use in December. In the following weeks, Hybeš, his tone hysterical, denounced both the aristocracy and the middle class for their opposition to the bill,[51] and Daszyński, rather uncharacteristically, delivered an extraordinarily profane attack upon the old regime in Austria.[52] The vehemence that the leaders of the party displayed in parliament had two goals. It was designed to move the party's campaign out of the streets and back into the house and to cover up, at the same time, a rather serious split in the trade-union movement that threatened to weaken the unity of Austrian socialism at a very critical stage.

The divisions that now threatened the trade unions were an outgrowth of the tensions that had been dividing Germans from Czechs ever since the 1890's. The crisis that had originated in 1897 and had led to the creation of a separate Czech trade-union commission had, in a sense, been laid aside in 1900 only to reemerge in 1905, right during the party's struggle for a reform of the franchise. These new difficulties began when the Czech trade-union commission demanded that it be recognized, both inside and outside of Austria, as a separate and distinct institution representing the economic interests of the Czech working class. Pushing hard, the Czech separatists in June, 1905, carried their appeal to the International Trade-Union Congress, meeting in Amsterdam, only to be rebuffed by the delegates, who overwhelmingly voted down their request.[53] Disappointed here, the Czech commission turned next to press its claims against the Austrian

Trade-Union Commission. Through the fall of 1905, the commission worked feverishly to come up with a compromise that would satisfy the Czechs, but compromise proved elusive. Stymied, the commission next called an extraordinary congress of the Austrian trade unions and set the congress for December.[54] The move was, in reality, a hasty one, for just as the party was about to act as an organized pressure-group, a schism had opened up that threatened the unity of both the trade unions and the party, a division that was soon to be exaggerated by the congress.[55]

No sooner had the first session of the congress begun than Czech spokesmen, both from the party and the trade unions, were demanding that the Czech trade-union commission be made an equal partner of the older Trade Union Commission based in Vienna. At first, Adler tried to smooth over the controversy with an extraordinary plea for party solidarity, and he was backed in his efforts by a number of Czech trade-union leaders.[56] But, in spite of the well-intentioned, the congress dissolved into a match between the trade-union secretary, Hueber, and the Czech party leader, Němec. Němec restated the Czech position but his arguments were immediately countered by Hueber, who was furious at the Czechs to begin with.[57] Voting by industry, a procedure which automatically benefitted the numerically-superior Germans, the congress rejected the Czech demands by an overwhelming majority.[58] Even worse, the congress actually widened the differences between the Germans and the Czechs by involving the Czech party in, what had been up to this point, only a trade-union matter. That move, in itself, diminished whatever chance there had been in December, 1905 for a reconciliation.[59] After this, the unity of the Austrian labor movement hung by a thin administrative line. What prevented that unity from collapsing totally was the outside pressure that arose from the electoral reform campaign, for neither side wanted to see the bill's chances jeopardized by the movement's disunity.

Two months after this, on February 23, 1906,

Gautsch brought in his bill at long last. The aim of his bill was to create as delicate a balance as possible among the various social groups, national elements and urban and rural interests in the empire.[60] In overriding terms, the bill was an attempt to satisfy all the vested interests in Austria at exactly the same time.[61] But, as it turned out, it alienated a far greater number of deputies than it satisfied.[62] The proposed bill divided the chamber of deputies into two antagonistic factions. The right and the center opposed it because it would have meant an end to all privilege while the left supported it enthusiastically, the left tending to support any bill as long as it was reformist in nature. The right, primarily the Polish Club, the Pan-Germans and the representatives of the upper middle class, had set themselves ahead of time against any reform.[63] In the middle, the German Populist deputies and the German Progressive Party both favored reform, but they rejected Gautsch's bill because it would have left the Germans a minority in the new house, thus reversing their previous position.[64] The bill was accepted by the petty-bourgeois parties, the Christian Socialists and the Young Czechs, the Ruthenians and the Slovenes and the Social Democrats. The Slavs, to no one's surprise, backed the bill for the exact same reasons that the Germans opposed it.

The lone criticism that the Social Democrats had of the bill was the way in which it assigned its mandates.[65] Beyond this, the party was pleased by the bill and by the fact that reactionary trappings, which it feared might be a part of it, including literacy tests, plural voting and extended residency requirements, were, in fact, not present.[66] The day after the bill was tabled in the house the central executive committee of the party, obviously prejudiced in favor of the bill, called upon its <u>Vertrauensmänner</u> to organize a campaign against the opponents of the bill.[67] The party had now aligned itself with the emperor and with Gautsch in defense of the bill against the expected German and conservative opposition to it, the party now in the strange position of being, in essence, a government party.[68]

The bill went through first reading in the house on March 7, 1906. Presenting the bill to the house was Gautsch's minister of the interior, Count Artur Bylandt.[69] His presentation touched off a bitter debate that occupied the house for a number of weeks. Early in the debate, Adler rose to defend the government and its bill. Adler told the house that the lower classes in Austria had waited long enough for electoral reform and that their patience had, as of now, run out. Reversing himself slightly, Adler then went on to ridicule some of the bill's shortcomings, including the fact that it had set the voting age at 24, instead of 20, the one-year residence requirement that it had set up for voting and its obvious failure to extend the suffrage to women.[70] At the same time, in an attack on Gautsch, he criticized Gautsch for his attempt to bring about a reform of the house's standing rules of procedure. Originally, Gautsch had asked for a reform of the house's standing rules so he could insure both the safety and continuity of the larger reform that he had proposed. Gautsch wanted to limit obstruction, arguing that the new parliament's viability would be undermined if it was not protected against obstruction in a way that the old house had not been.[71]

Rejecting Gautsch's logic, Adler argued, somewhat shortsightedly, that Gautsch's proposal, here, should be defeated since obstruction was only a symptom of the ills of the old curial system, a symptom that presumably would not return once the franchise had been opened up to the masses and to their representatives.[72] Then, reversing himself in his speech, Adler declared that in spite of the bill's shortcomings and the legislative paraphenalia accompanying it, "the Social Democrats welcomed the submission of the bill on electoral reform, just as it is."[73] Almost as quickly, he changed his tone once again, this time with a vicious diatribe against capitalism, one that seemed to be designed to frighten away rather than attract what middle-class backing there was for the reform bill.[74] In part, Adler had been goaded into an extreme stand by the conservative Tyrolean deputy Karl von Grabmayr. Grabmayr had suggested during the debate that Gautsch's bill was dead, a suggestion that Adler adamently denied.[75] After two more weeks of extremely partisan debate, the house finally agreed to create a 49-man electoral reform committee that was to work out the details of the legislation,[76] doing, in effect, what the Social Democrats had advocated all along.[77]

After the house recessed, responsibility for the bill's development passed to the electoral reform committee, which continued in session through the spring of 1906. The membership of the committee closely reflected the overall composition of the house and included a highly strident Polish faction which kept insisting that Galicia's special status within the empire be recognized by the grant of 110 seats in the new house.[78] The Poles were so resolute that on May 2, 1906, Gautsch resigned, having been defeated, in effect, in the committee by the Poles and their conservative allies on the issue of the distribution of mandates.[79] Gautsch was succeeded by Prince Konrad Hohenlohe, the governor of Trieste. The appointment of Hohenlohe by Franz Joseph was an obvious attempt on the part of the emperor to intimidate the right-wing opposition to the bill, especially since Hohenlohe had a reputation as a reformer and had been known in both liberal and socialist circles as the "red prince".[80]

Hohenlohe, as if to confirm his stand, kept Gautsch's cabinet, already committed to reform, completely intact. If there were any doubts at all about Hohenlohe's liberalism after this, Hohenlohe dispelled them immediately. Speaking to a reassembled parliament, on May 15, Hohenlohe committed his government to immediate electoral reform, saying that the suffrage would have to be expanded for the good of the Austrian state.[81] Beyond this, Hohenlohe left Gautsch's proposal unchanged. The only modification that he made was a proposal to increase the number of mandates assigned. With this change Hohenlohe hoped to overcome the impasse that had developed earlier in the committee over the distribution of house seats, an impasse which had stalled any progress on the bill since March.[82] Hohenlohe had been called upon, in the first place, to bring the reform bill through to completion and it had been expected that he would do so. Suddenly, at the end of May, Hohenlohe resigned, leaving the bill's fate in doubt. Hohenlohe had been forced to step down when he refused to accede to the emperor's demand that he accept the idea of a separate tariff area for Hungary. Caught between the Hungarians and the Austrians, the emperor, this time, had sacrificed Hohenlohe and perhaps the bill. For his part, Hohenlohe had simply refused to allow the Ausgleich to take precedence over the need for electoral reform.[83]

The socialists were frankly disturbed by Hohenlohe's departure, as were the liberals and some of the emperor's closest advisors.[84] The collapse of two successive governments, both dedicated to the bill, within the span of a few weeks had not produced an air of public confidence. Worse still, popular dissatisfaction with these delays had once again manifested itself in the streets, although, this time it never reached the heights that it had during the previous November. In the midst of this governmental crisis, Franz Joseph turned to a career civil servant, Dr. Max Beck, to be his new prime minister.[85] Beck took office with neither Gautsch's experience nor Hohenlohe's reputation. What he did bring with him was a capacity for compromise and a respect for constitutional government. Once in power, Beck immediately endeared himself to the left and the center by creating a new coalition government that included the leaders of the largest political parties in the lower house.[86]

Beck's conscientious attempt to create for himself a clear parliamentary majority was not only a blow for responsible government, it also strengthened his own position, which, at the beginning, was somewhat uncertain. Supported in parliament, he also had the unqualified backing of the emperor when on June 7, 1906 he undertook to push Gautsch's original reform bill through to completion.[87] Beck's subtle maneuvering at the beginning of the summer was at first not appreciated by the Social Democrats. The party had grown impatient over the delays of the last few weeks and was once again threatening to impose a general strike upon the country.[88] Speaking before a working-class audience in Favoriten, Adler told the crowd of the party's growing frustration with the matter.[89] In still another speech, he told his audience that the electoral reform committee had not approved of a single paragraph in the bill even though it had been working at it for months.[90] As June moved on, the Social Democrats applied even more pressure. The Arbeiter-Zeitung announced that if the committee did not get on with its work that the party would call a three-day general strike.[91] Building upon the momentum that the party press had helped to mount, Schuhmeier threatened Vienna with a strike of unprecedented impact and his inflammatory statements drew a big response from his working-class audience.[92] By the end of June, it appeared as if the Social Democrats would initiate another general strike, although as before the trade-union commission seemed reluctant even if the masses did not.[93]

In July, the lower house of parliament finally recessed for the summer, leaving the electoral reform committee, now more active, to finish up on the details of the bill.[94] Once the committee began to work its way through the bill, the Social Democrats reduced some of the pressure by allowing their strike threat to lapse. Meanwhile, the job of representing the Social Democrats had passed to Victor Adler, the lone socialist on the 49-man electoral reform committee. During the month of June Adler had spent his time on the committee defending the fact that the Social Democrats had moved back into the streets against those who had insisted that only the rabble was behind the reform bill.[95] Pushing his defense, Adler denounced those who had held up the bill against the will of the emperor and the great mass of Austrians.[96] At the same time,

Adler took advantage of the mass rallies sponsored by the party in June to warn both the aristocratic and bourgeois opponents of reform that unless the impasse on the committee was broken, the Viennese working-class would begin a three-day general strike.[97]

Prodded from above by the emperor and Beck and from below by the Social Democrats, the committee finally began to work out the details of the bill through July and August. Meanwhile, Beck kept admonishing the committee to complete its work, a move by his government which helped Adler to tone down the sentiment in favor of a general strike that still existed within the party.[98] When the committee completed the bill on September 13, a delighted Adler expressed his relief to the committee that the principle of universal manhood suffrage had never once been threatened.[99] The very last problem for the committee had been solved when Beck agreed to increase the number of seats in the new house to 516;[100] otherwise, the bill remained anatomically similar to the one that Gautsch had introduced the previous winter. Speaking outside of parliament to a mass assembly in Margareten, Pernerstorfer declared, in celebration, that the opponents of reform had now lost the initiative. From here on in, he insisted, the force of public opinion would carry the bill on through to completion.[101]

The bill went through second reading on November 7. In the house, Adler defended the bill against its opponents, conservatives who insisted that the house had been intimidated into accepting the bill by the street mobs. Adler denied that this was so. He told the house that the cause of electoral reform had its own driving force, that it was a historical necessity, and that it was this spirit which was about to realize itself in the form of universal manhood suffrage. Turning to the bill itself, Adler, almost from habit, denounced it because it had failed to provide for female suffrage and because the residency requirement for voting had been kept at one year.[102] But, he said, even though the bill was not all that the party expected, Austrian socialism would accept it as a workable compromise. The party was accepting it, he added, in the hope that it would prevent Austria from following the kind of disastrous governmental policies that she had pursued in the past.[103]

After this, conservative opponents of the bill succeeded in stalling it for a short while, but it finally passed the house on December 1, on third reading, 194-63,[104] with a large number of abstentions. Once the house had voted it, the bill still had to get by a reluctant upper chamber before it could become law. The Herrenhaus had opposed the bill instinctively from the beginning, a feeling which expressed itself in the special commission which the upper house had chosen to consider the reform bill. For a while it appeared as if the committee would emasculate the bill with a provision for plural voting and that the house would demand that the emperor accept numerus clauses (which would have placed a ceiling on the number of seats open in the upper house) as its price for passing the reform. When the commission met on December 10, it did so among reports that it was about to demand a double vote for all men over thirty-five.[105] The rumors so incensed the Social Democrats that they threatened yet another general strike in mid-December,[106] although this time the threat seemed even more rhetorical than before.[107]

The proposal by the lords for plural voting so incensed public sentiment in Austria that the upper house backed away from the idea.[108] On December 21, the upper house passed the bill, but only after the crown had agreed to relinquish forever its prerogative of increasing the number of seats in the upper house. After this, the number of seats in the upper house was set between 150 and 170, thus assuring the house that its conservative character would never be overcome.[109] At long last, the emperor gave imperial sanction to the bill in January, 1907, making it law.[110] In parliament, his life's work now secured, Adler jubilantly predicted that the absorption of the working class into the politics of the empire would surely give to Austria a new kind of life.[111]

Adler had now convinced himself that the achievement of political democracy in Austria would soon mean the coming of the welfare state. Looking past the election campaign that was about to begin, Adler told a working-class audience in December, 1906 that it was now time for the working class, as he said, to pick up the weapon that the party had forged for them and use it. The working class would still struggle, he admonished them, but a metamorphosis had indeed occurred and the struggle henceforth would be for social reform instead of political change.[112]

Immediately after the bill became law, the Social Democrats began to plan for the imperial elections scheduled for May. During the campaign, they concentrated their attacks upon the various German and Czech bourgeois parties and the Christian Socialists out of fear that they might draw working class votes away from them.[113] Adler summarized the party's general approach to the electorate when he reminded a working-class audience that it had been the Social Democrats, alone of the parties, who had devoted themselves to a gradual improvement in the workers' standard of living.[114] The Social Democrats conducted their campaign in a highly disciplined and sophisticated manner, although some internal friction did develop. The most serious clash took place in Vienna where the Czech party organization demanded that Victor Adler step down as the party candidate in *Favoriten*, in favor of a Czech, so as to permit the Czech workers in Vienna a representative in parliament. Adler rejected the request, arguing that he stood for the working class as a whole and not for any one nationality. Another clash, of somewhat lesser note, occurred in Lemberg, where the Polish party leader Daszyński refused to back the candidacy of the Ruthenian party leader Hankiewicz for a house seat.[115] Apart from this, the Social Democrats waged a professional campaign, emerging from the first round of elections on May 14 with the largest number of seats any party had, 58 in all, with

113 other candidates standing in the run-offs.[116]

Actually, the party's showing in the second round of elections was not as favorable as in the first, primarily because the various German and Czech bourgeois parties usually formed electoral alliances on the second ballot against the socialists. In spite of this, the party did manage in 1907 to pick up 29 more seats, increasing its overall total to 87. In the ensuing months, the party added two more seats by winning by-elections in both the Tyrol and Silesia.[117] Even more encouraging was the total vote that the party received in 1907. Out of the 4,676,636 voters who were at the polls in 1907, 1,040,100 or 23 percent of them, voted for socialists candidates; this, even though the party took only 17 percent of the seats in the house.[118] The party made its largest gains in the principal industrial centers of the empire, winning 40 percent of the popular vote in the German and Czech-speaking areas of Bohemia, 40 percent of the vote in Vienna and 30 percent of the votes cast in the Czech-speaking areas of Moravia.[119] And for a while, the Social Democrats even emerged as the largest party in the new house,[120] a distinction that they lost shortly thereafter when the Christian Socialists and Catholic Conservatives joined to form a new political grouping consisting of some 96 deputies.[121]

The elections of 1907, which had given a decided advantage to the parties of the left and center, meant that real representative government was now a prospect for Austria.[122] Beck expected this to happen, and in an attempt both to bring this about and to strengthen his government's hand in the upcoming decennial talks with the Hungarians, he put together a majority government made up of representatives from the Christian Socialist and Czech, German and Polish agrarian parties. Although his new government was not stable, and excluded the socialists, Beck's move was widely accepted as one that would soon lead to a system of ministerial responsibility.[123] The Social Democrats approved of the move toward constitutional government, even though it meant that the Christian Socialists were now to share in power.124 Meanwhile, the presence of the Social Democrats in parliament was recognized by a number of key committee appointments, including two appointments to Austria's Ausgleich delegation.125 The policies of the Social-Democratic club in parliament were shaped by a twelve-man central committee composed of the party's various national leaders. Among those on the committee were its chairman, Victor Adler, and Pernerstorfer, the Czech party leaders Němec and Soukup, the Italian party leader Valentino Pittoni, with Otto Bauer serving as the faction's parliamentary secretary. The club itself was composed of fifty Germans, twenty-four Czechs, six Poles, five Italians and two Ruthenians.126

As soon as parliament was back in session, the Social Democrats were once again pushing for the type of reform they had been advocating when they had essentially been outside of parliament. Wanting the tempo of reform to continue, they put forward proposals calling for the immediate introduction of female suffrage, the lowering of the voting age to 21, the elimination of all residency requirements for the vote and the formulation of a universal system of old-age pensions and insurance for invalids.127 Austria's new house failed to act on these proposals but it did prove that it was viable by passing the budget, instead of having it imposed by Article 14, and by working out a rather uncontentious decennial agreement with the Hungarians that contained a number of clauses distinctly favorable to the Austrians.128 The passage of this legislation not only proved that parliament could now act but it added lustre to Beck's reputation as the most consummate politician that Austria had yet produced. His stock with the left, already high, rose even more when he presented to parliament a brand new Old-Age and Invalid Insurance act, the details of which were to be worked out by a special committee of the house.129

Up to the actual achievement of the suffrage in 1907, the Social Democrats had passed themselves off as irreconcilable opponents of the existing political order in Austria. Their propaganda often rejected the curial system, the system of capitalism that supported it and rule by the aristocracy and the upper middle-class, which, the party maintained, followed from the first two. The party had been forced, during this stage of its development, to stand apart from politics, all the while growing in strength and therefore in moderation. As far removed as it had been from the center of power in Austria, Social Democracy had still been bound to the empire's fate. The link that connected it to Austria's future and at times to Austria's present was its own commitment to the concept of parliament government and to the exercise of political power by democratic means. The party had grown long before this from a few thousand men to the point in 1907 where it had now absorbed the political loyalties of a full quarter of the Austrian population. The party, under Adler and Pernerstorfer, had chosen a highly peaceful path to power and the results had been most satisfying. It had patience and, in part, it had won out, in 1907.

Half-jokingly, in 1907, Adler told representatives of the party that Franz Joseph and he had achieved universal manhood suffrage together for Austria.[130] In a real sense, the comment symbolized the hope of both the party and the emperor that the empire would live on now intact, with its basic political institutions democratized.[131] What had happened was that the Social Democrats, while remaining liberal, had become a prop of empire. But, in the next few years, both the party and the emperor were to be disappointed, Austrian Social Democracy before the emperor; for after 1907, national sentiment would lead to the disintegration of that coalition which had been known as Austrian Social Democracy, a process that foreshadowed by only a few short years the eventual disintegration of the empire.

Chapter VII

THE DISINTEGRATION OF AUSTRIAN SOCIAL DEMOCRACY

Austrian Social Democracy originated in the late 1880's as a coalition of German and Czech socialist parties. It remained essentially a coalition for nearly twenty years until 1907 when it began to divide under the pressure of growing national identification.[1] The split that developed divided the movement so decisively that it was no longer possible, after 1911, to speak of a unified Social-Democratic movement in Austria. The immediate cause of the collapse of the German-Czech alliance that had formed the real essence of Austrian Social Democracy was the campaign that was waged by the Austrian Trade-Union Commission, dominated by the Germans, and the leaders of the Czech party for the loyalty of the Czech working class. The final result of that conflict was the almost complete separation of the Czech Social-Democratic party and most of the Czech trade unions from the remainder of Austria's Little International. The origins of these divisions, and of Czech separatism itself, can be traced back to the 1890's and to the continuous demands of the Czechs at that time for an autonomous status within the larger party to which they were allied.

In 1896 and 1897, the Czechs managed to impose upon the party a compromise which allowed them to set up what they had always, in fact, desired and that was an autonomous political organization, free of both Vienna and the Germans. In these years, Czech particularism had been strong enough to see the establishment of a political party organized along federal lines but it had not been powerful enough to continue the momentum and separate the Czech trade unions from the highly centralized trade-union structure which the Austrian Trade-Union Commission had already brought into existence prior to this time. Recognizing that, even with an appeal to national sentiments, it could not attract the bulk of the

Czech workers away from the larger commission, the Prague commission, after 1900, began to move in the direction of complete cooperation with the Austrian Trade-Union Commission.[2] This turn, directed away from nationalism and toward international cooperation, was the work of Josef Roušar, the secretary for the Prague commission, whose earlier defiance had now given way to greater realism.

The crisis that was to follow these years of cooperation came in two distinctive waves. The first broke in 1904 and 1905, and the second in 1910 and 1911. The first produced a sense of instability, the second actual division. Roušar's illness and death in 1904 opened the Prague commission to more militant and aggressive elements, who wanted a much more independent policy toward Vienna.[3] As suspicions increased throughout 1904, minor differences surfaced that were soon exaggerated by both the Prague and Viennese commissions. The Czechs' first move was to demand that a Czech representative be placed on the Workers' Advisory Council that had been created within the Ministry of Commerce. The council had been set up in 1898 at the urgings of the then liberal party leader Josef Baernreither. In theory, the council had the power to recommend legislation to improve the working class's standard of living although in practice its recommendations were largely ignored.[4] In spite of its low status, a representative of the Austrian Trade-Union Commission always sat on the council, and the Czechs wanted equal representation, a proposition which the Austrian Trade-Union Commission rejected because it would have improved the position of the Prague commission both in the view of the government and the working class.[5] This rift was followed all too quickly by the division of the commercial workers into two competing unions, one German and one Czech,[6] a split that foreshadowed the eventual division of most of Austria's industrial and commercial unions in the years to come.

The growing alienation of the Prague commission, so evident in 1904, manifested itself again in May 1905, this time in the form of new claims which Roušar's successor, Emmanuel Škatula, made directly to Karl Legien, the chairman of the International Commission of Trade-Union Secretaries. Škatula, demonstrating the depth of national feelings that had overtaken the Prague commission, insisted that the International would have to recognize the Prague commission immediately if the Czech working class was going to be saved from the program of Germanisation which the Austrian Trade-Union Commission was conducting among Czech workers.[7] Škatula's plea was made public at a time when the Prague commission had already declared its unilateral right to be recognized as an independent national trade-union commission representing the aspirations of the Czech working class.[8] This unprecedented claim by the Czechs put to both the International and the Austrian Trade-Union Commission was a direct outgrowth of Czech fears that they were about to fall under the complete domination of the Germans within the Austrian trade-union movement. The Prague commission had already decided that it had to stop this process by attracting as many Czech unions as it could away from the Austrian Trade-Union Commission and to its own jurisdiction,[9] thus its own fight for greater recognition.

The Prague commission, which now, as never before, threatened the leadership that the Austrian Trade-Union Commission had always given to the working class, turned for redress to the International Commission of Trade-Union Secretaries which was scheduled to meet in Amsterdam in June. There Němec and Hueber confronted each other again over the question of just how much power Czech particularism was to have in Austria. Appearing as the political representative of the Prague commission, Němec put forward the commission's claims with a clarity and a frankness that few had heard before. The Czechs, he said, constituted a separate people and a separate and distinct nation and in order to preserve their unique national heritage the Czech working class would have to be removed from the authority of the Austrian Trade-Union Commission, which, he went on, was nothing more than an agent for German interests in the empire.[10] Němec's speech, as it turned out, was so indelicate that it immediately gave the edge to Hueber, who quickly denounced Němec for petty-bourgeois nationalism. On the offensive, Hueber denied that the commission possessed a national bias, and insisted that it represented, with real equality, all the nationalities that it served.[11] Němec did not try to answer Hueber; instead he noted that the party had been led to decentralize and that he expected the trade unions to do the same.[12] Hueber replied by arguing that the economic interests of the working class differed in kind from their political interests and to divide the trade unions along national lines would only weaken Austrian labor before the capitalists and industrialists.[13] Backed in the debate by Legien and during the voting by other trade-union secretaries, Hueber easily won as the conference unanimously turned down the Prague application for recognition as an independent Czech trade-union commission inside Austria.[14] After this, Němec returned to Austria where he condemned anew, in Pravo lidu, what he called the insidious process of Germanisation that had almost overtaken the Czech working class.[15]

Despite the differences that had grown up between them in 1904 and 1905, both the Germans and the Czechs wanted to maintain the movement's unity, especially through the campaign for electoral reform. Accordingly on October 15, 1905, the two commissions met on neutral ground in Brünn in order to come to some kind of an agreement. The atmosphere at the conference was strained to the full. Němec repeated the demands that the Germans had heard the previous spring at Amsterdam. The Czechs were really not capable of imposing their will at this time, but as the other Czech representative, Josef Steiner, told the Germans, the Czechs would do so just as soon as they could.[16] Hueber, meanwhile, speaking for the Austrian Trade-Union Commission, refused any concessions, telling the Czechs that "we [the commission] will never accept the idea of national trade unions because the idea is opposed to our own international outlook."[17] In essence

what the conference proved was that a stalemate
had developed which was only covered for the
moment by the much larger issue of electoral
reform.[18] Given the exigencies of the moment and
the fact that they were in need of one another,
the two commissions tried once again for a
rapprochement, this time in December. The stage
was the extraordinary congress which the Austrian
Trade-Union Commission had called for December to
consider the issue of a separate Czech trade-
union commission. Once again, the Czechs were
defeated badly as one industrial union after
another, with their powerful German majorities,
voted against independence.[19]

    Before that vote had been taken, the
Austrian Trade-Union Commission had met the
demands of the Czechs by falling back upon the
decisions of the International Conference of
Trade-Union Secretaries, which had not only defeated the Czech request but had actually gone on
to advocate an even greater degree of centralization than the Czechs had known up to that
time.[20] Karl Vaněk, the leading Czech trade
unionist in Brünn and a man still loyal to Vienna,
tried to explain to the commission that the
desire for autonomy among the Czechs would always
grow in proportion to the degree of centralization
that was being introduced from above;[21] but it
was in vain. The leaders of the Austrian Trade-
Union Commission did not understand that greater
bureaucratization and greater efficiency had
given life to Czech fears that they were about to
be absorbed, a process which the leaders of the
Czech party in the congress kept calling Germanisation.[22] In 1905, the Czechs did not possess
either the financial resources or the inclination
to separate, but they intended to do so, Steiner
told the Germans, just as soon as they had the
numbers and the means.[23] Unable to have their
way, the Czechs began to soften their demands and
to ask for a compromise. A month earlier, at
the party's general congress, the Czechs had
informed the movement that they would compromise
if need be. There, another Czech spokesman,
Franz Soukup had told the others in the party that
because of their desire for real proletarian

unity, the Czechs would not push their claims. In return, he noted, the Czechs expected that the question of a separate Czech trade-union commission would be settled soon either by direct negotiations between the Prague commission and the Austrian Trade-Union Commission or by a decision arrived at by an extraordinary congress of the general party.[24]

For the while the question of an independent Czech trade-union commission was submerged by the much larger struggle for electoral reform. As it was, the reprieve the party received in December was over a few months later. For in 1906, a number of unions, most conspicuously the shoemakers, split nationally, dividing Germans and Czechs as never before in the history of the labor movement.[25] The full impact of these divisions was cushioned by the unparalleled growth of the Austrian trade unions through to 1907. In an era of rising prosperity and increasing wages, trade-union membership under the Austrian Trade-Union Commission rose from 189,000 in 1904 to 448,000 in 1906. These numerical increases were paralleled by rising revenues, mostly from dues, that went into the treasury of the Austrian Trade-Union Commission, and from where it was doled out, usually with strings attached, to the locals.[26] The Prague commission positively resented both the increased financial power that its rival had now accumulated and the fact that the vast majority of Czech workers joined the Austrian Trade-Union Commission primarily because of the benefits that it could supply. Indeed, the number of workers adhering to the Vienna-based commission soon passed the half million mark with some 180,000 of them Czechs.[27] The Prague commission, meanwhile, grew past 34,000 in the same period, a third of them adherents from the recent split in the shoemakers' union.[28] Yet, even with these gains, five out of every six Czech workers unionized in 1907 still subscribed to the Austrian Trade-Union Commission, and, in the view of the Prague commission, to its German majority and policies.

In the period from 1905 to 1907, both the

central executive of the Czech party and the
Prague commission became increasingly concerned
for the allegiance of the tens of thousands of
organized Czech industrial workers, especially
since many of them were still organized into
locals which adhered only nominally to the Austrian
Trade-Union Commission and which could, therefore,
presumably, be rather easily detached.[29] The
Austrian Trade-Union Commission was conscious of
the independence that these locals had shown before this and it tried to lessen the appeal which
the Czech party and the Prague commission had for
them by tightening its administration and by
holding out to the Czech locals the prospect of
even more economic benefits than they had previously received. The commission's first big
move in this direction came in 1905 when it reorganized the industrial unions and strengthened
the power of the Landesgewerkschaftskommissionen,
the intermediary trade-union bodies in the
provinces.[30] The tightening-up of the tradeunion apparatus brought to an end the semiautonomous status of many of the unions, among
others the union of commerical clerks, as well as
many of the locals that the Czechs had already
set up.[31]

The success of these organizational changes,
just as the earlier victory of centralization in
the party in the 1890's, proved to be the party's
undoing. For just as before, this tightening up
tended to compound the fears of the Czechs that
they were about to be absorbed into an essentially
German organization. Those fears, in themselves,
drove their feelings beyond a desire for autonomy
and to the point where separation became for them
a very real alternative. The new administrative
system introduced by the Austrian Trade-Union
Commission proved difficult for relative moderates
among the Czechs, such as Vaněk, to accept. But
beyond this, it frightened Němec and other more
nationally-conscious Czechs, who saw in the
changes yet another means by which the Germans
would exercise even greater hegemony over the
organized Czech working class in Austria. Of the
two, Vaněk represented the sentimental and
administrative link that bound most of the orga-

nized Czech working class in Austria to the Trade-Union Commission. Yet, even he was critical of the fact that the commission had not sought to include Czech, Polish or Italian labor leaders in the commission even though taken together the minorities constituted a full forty per cent of the organized labor force in Austria. In an age of growing national consciousness that type of policy, Vaněk warned, could easily produce its own reaction.[32]

The Prague commission responded to the new organizational changes introduced by the Austrian Trade-Union Commission with an all-out campaign to increase the number of Czech locals that accepted its authority. The campaign extended not only to the Czech working-class districts of Bohemia and Moravia but spread to the mixed language areas of Silesia, Upper Austria and Lower Austria. Its aim was to create as many Czech locals as possible, each with a nucleus of fifty members or more.[33] The administrative struggle that the two commissions engaged in actually lasted for a number of years. The Czech challenge was never enough to destroy the unified character of most of the industrial unions, but it did create so much animosity between Germans and Czechs that it tended to divide the big unions psychologically years before the actual split took place. Through it all, the leaders of the Czech party continued to demand that their own unique status as a nation be, in fact, recognized by the trade unions. And Němec continued to argue that if that recognition was granted it would strengthen the Austrian trade-union movement as a whole because it would make international cooperation more voluntary and less a matter of compulsion.[34]

In the latter part of 1908 and into 1909, the Prague commission achieved its greatest success to date by splitting the metalworkers' union along national lines. The Germans and the Czechs in the union had been quarreling with each other for years. Finally, the Czechs pulled out and linked up with the Prague commission in February, 1909.[35] The attraction of Czech nationalism had now split one of Austria's oldest unions, with the effect of it being to lame almost all trade-union activity within the entire union. The union's branches in Bohemia were a case in point. Immediately before the break, the union counted some 7,580 workers in Bohemia. Of that total, 4,875 went over to the newly-formed Czech union, another 1,692 continued to support the older union while the remainder left the trade-union completely.[36] In spite of the obvious drawbacks to union activity, the Prague commission refused to lessen the pressure on the industrial unions that it had been exerting all along in favor of separation. Through 1908 and 1909, it nibbled away, detaching one local after another, until at the end of this era it had attracted more than 10,000 Czech workers away from the major industrial unions.[37]

Victor Adler watched the growth of Czech separatism through 1908 and 1909 with real apprehension. While the actual number of workers lost to the central unions had not been great, Adler feared that a precedent had been set, anticipating that major dissolutions might result. Even worse, as far as Adler was concerned, was the added worry that the controversy might expand and threaten the entire movement, a movement whose internal cohesion had already been shaken by years of national discontent. In a letter which he wrote to Hueber, Adler, in fact, foresaw much of the division that was about to strike the movement in 1910.[38]

In March, 1910, the rancor and disputes over national identification that had been coursing their way through the movement finally found expression in a crisis that would only end in the complete collapse of Austrian Social Democracy. The crisis that was about to destroy the alliance between the Germans and the Czechs that had formed Austrian Social Democracy for so long started when the Czech party finally stepped into the situation existing in the trade unions. It began with a unilateral declaration by the leaders of the Prague commission, backed by the central committee of the Czech party, to the effect that it, and it alone, would henceforth represent the interests of the organized Czech working class in Austria.[39] The Czech party, in an atmosphere of increased militancy, now directed its total administration to the task of removing the whole Czech working class from the jurisdiction of the Austrian Trade-Union Commission and of bringing it over to the Prague commission. In a memorandum signed by Němec, Soukup, Steiner and Rudolf Tayerle, the Czech party executive justified its extraordinary action as a proper and necessary one designed to fit "historic necessity".[40]

In actual fact, the economic and administrative feuds over the years between the Austrian Trade-Union Commission and the Prague commission had never been enough, in themselves, to encourage the cause of Czech separatism. Separatism became a real possibility in 1910 only after the Czech party intruded on its own behalf, giving to Czech separatism much more of a political than an economic complexion. The Czech party executive had over the course of time been adding up its resentments against the Germans and it was these resentments rather than economic concerns which had really brought on the crisis. For example, at their own party congresses in 1907 and 1908, the Czechs had passed resolutions condemning the Germans for their continual refusal to accommodate Czech demands for an immediate change in the party's Brünn program and for the failure of the Germans to support the cause of Czech language rights in Lower Austria.[41] German apathy on these matters, which was at first more cultural than political, had only increased the degree of national sensitivity that the Czechs had felt. All of this made the Czechs even more aware of the trade unions, which the party leaders feared the Germans were about to dominate once more, culturally, organizationally and economically. For their part the Germans responded with indifference, constantly calling, in reply to the Czechs, for more and more international cooperation,[42] a phrase which the Czechs interpreted as just another code word for Germanisation. These differences of mind only added to the divisions in the general party which had already reached such a point that it could truly be said that no general party existed. The party's general executive, for example, had conspicuously failed to call a general congress in 1907 or in any of the ensuing years even though the party statutes specifically provided that one had to be called every two years.[43] The result of this was that the party congress of 1905 turned out to be the last one that Austrian Social Democracy ever held.

Actually, neither the Germans nor the Czechs wanted a party congress where their differences would have been played up. Above all, the Czechs did not want to enter a congress where they were the minority, and the Germans seemed desirous of evading those issues that would make a final break inevitable. Already divided, the general party drifted after this, with one after another of its central organs falling into disuse. For not only were regular party congresses not called, but its guiding institution, its general executive, failed to function any further as a representative body.[44]

The cracking process that went on, so obvious as far as the central organs were concerned, soon revealed itself in parliament as well. During the first session of parliament after the elections of 1907, the German and the Czech deputies, who formed the real nucleus of Social-Democratic strength in the lower house, came up with a common policy and voted with one another without exception.[45] But during the next session, the Czechs balked at full cooperation, with one of them, the renegade, Franz Modráček, even breaking party discipline in order to participate in an obstruction.[46] All of these strains formed the vital prelude to the more spectacular break that was to begin in March, 1910; as it turned out, the final one in the history of the Austrian Social Democracy.

In the spring of 1910, the conflict between the Germans and the Czechs, which had already so many different facets, shifted from the realm of politics back to the trade unions. Only this time, the scene of the conflict was to be the

Moravian unions rather than those in Bohemia. Up until 1910, the Moravian unions, both the German and the Czech, had remained largely outside of the trade-union disputes of the last half decade. This was especially true of the Czech unions in Moravia which had been shielded from these conflicts by their leaders, Karl Vaněk and Vlastimil Tusar, both of whom had maintained a steadfast loyalty during these crucial years to the Austrian Trade-Union Commission. Simultaneous with the Czech party announcement that it favored independence for the trade unions, Vaněk and Tusar were subjected to extraordinary pressure from both their own <u>Vertrauensmänner</u> and the Czech party itself to establish yet another independent Czech trade-union commission based this time upon Brünn.[47] Vaněk was among the first to give in, followed in time by Tusar. Writing in the Czech party-newspaper, <u>Rovnost</u>, Vaněk explained his shift in loyalties by arguing that in a democracy the type of trade-union organization accepted must be the result of the will of the majority,[48] and the majority by this time had already gone over to separatism.

Vaněk's defection was the key to the entire future success of the separatist movement. Without him, the Czech party would never have been able to rip the remaining Czech unions away from the jurisdiction of the Austrian Trade-Union Commission. After this, defections became contagious and with them, the Prague commission, after so many years of trying, finally began to develop both the numerical and the financial strength to set itself up independently.[49] It was now able to create the type of administrative and fiscal structure which it had not been able to form before 1910. Vaněk's defection, which keyed the whole thing, was not the outgrowth of either expediency or fatalism. In large measure he had been convinced by separatist propaganda which maintained that the Czech working class had suffered under the Austrian Trade-Union Commission and that the Czechs would be far better off if they were on their own.[50] In an attempt to justify his stand in a published article, Vaněk pointed out that the Austrian Trade-Union

Commission had always used its tremendous economic strength to keep the local Czech unions in line. The commission would hold out or distribute money, for strikes and other purposes, depending upon whether the local had or had not complied with the policies of the commission.[51] Vaněk argued that this particular kind of paternalism had always increased resentment among Czech labor leaders, especially in areas like Moravia, where the Czech unions were at least as strong as the German.[52]

Having removed a portion of the Czech trade-union apparatus from the authority of the Austrian Trade-Union Commission, the Czech party, in conjunction with the Czech trade-union commission in Prague, moved to consolidate its administrative hold on the movement by declaring that in the future the Czech party and the Czech trade unions would henceforth be united by common organizational ties. The declaration was, in itself, one more step in the direction of independence for the Czech Social-Democratic movement, a cyclical return to the position it held in 1888 and 1889, just prior to the formation of the Austrian Social-Democratic party. The Czechs were no longer, as they had been, the junior partners in that alliance. Their organizational and financial strength had grown by 1910 to the extent that they could now guarantee their own independent existence. For example, by 1909, the Czech party had already founded more than 2,400 locals in the western half of the monarchy, in Silesia, Lower Austria and Upper Austria as well as in Bohemia and Moravia. By 1910, this set-up included some 130,000 dues-paying party members, a total comparable to what the Germans had. Along side of the party, the Czechs had built up an imposing press that poured out hundreds of thousands of publications every year.[53] With a growing cohesiveness, the Czechs had reached the point where, according to Otto Bauer, they were no longer willing to accept German leadership in any area, and most especially in the trade unions.[54]

The separatist victory in Moravia seemed at

first to have stunned both sides, neither one of whom was able to respond with a next step. Otto Bauer took advantage of the situation to put forward a number of proposals which he hoped would bring to an end the growing differences between the Germans and the Czechs. In his pamphlet, <u>Krieg oder Friede in den Gewerkschaften?</u> Bauer came out in favor of an immediate division of the trade unions along national lines and for a reorganization of the trade-union apparatus according to a federal formula.[55] What he did, in essence, was to offer again the formula that had saved the party in 1897, this time to the trade unions.[56]

In his pamphlet, Bauer reminded both the Germans and the Czechs that their continual emotional responses to one another were lessening the chances for compromise and that it would be better if they both began to make concessions here and now. To begin with, Bauer, argued, the organization of the trade unions exclusively along industrial lines and without any attention to nationality would have to be ended. The only way that the industrial unions could be saved would be to grant to each nationality within them the widest amount of self-administration compatible with the continued efficiency of the unions. A rapprochement was conceivable, Bauer counselled, but only if the Austrian Trade-Union Commission would immediately rewrite the statutes governing the internal workings of the various industrial unions and only if the Czechs responded by dissolving their separate trade-union organizations.[57] As it was, Bauer's suggestions were too magnanimous for either side to accept. The Czechs refused to consider them unless they were guaranteed complete autonomy for their unions ahead of time,[58] and the Austrian Trade-Union Commission dismissed them as specious and impossible.[59]

The pitiless way in which both the Germans and the Czechs rejected Bauer's efforts at reconciliation indicated, of course, just how much animosity had actually grown up between the two groups. Those feelings were extended even further in the latter part of 1910 when the indefatigable Czechs successfully split the textile, chemical and leather workers' unions, drawing tens of thousands more Czech workers to their own side.[60] Despite these successes, the actual balance toward the end of 1910 was, nonetheless, still with the Austrian Trade-Union Commission, what with 100,000 Czechs remaining in the central unions. Through 1911 and 1912, however, the shift was definitely toward the national unions and by the end of this period the majority of Czech workers had gone over to the Prague and Brünn commissions.[61] The divisions that asserted themselves in the trade unions soon affected other areas as well, especially as the cooperatives also began to divide between Germans and Czechs.[62] The tensions that had been developing between the Germans and the Czechs within the party, the trade unions and the cooperatives expressed themselves immediately after this in the lower house of parliament over the famous Stanek affair. In 1910, František Stanek, a representative for the Czech Agrarian party in the lower house, proposed to the house's budget committee the grant of a 100,000 Kronen subsidy for the support of a private Czech school in the city of Vienna. Months later when the proposal reached the floor, the German Social Democrats voted against it, the Czechs for it, and the Poles and Italians abstained, trying to stay away from the conflict between the Germans and the Czechs.[63]

The issue centered on the fate of hundreds of thousands of Czechs who had emigrated to Vienna, many of whom wanting to maintain their identity as a cultural minority.[64] Explaining why the Germans had voted against the appropriations, Bauer told the Czechs, in line with his own and Renner's writings,[65] that the Germans were not, generally speaking, opposed to the establishment of schools for minorities. But, in this instance they had voted against the bill because implicit in Stanek's proposal was the suggestion that the principle of cultural autonomy would have to be extended to every single minority, no matter how small, wherever it happened to be in the empire. Under these conditions, the principle of cultural autonomy would have to be applied universally no matter how impractical certain instances might seem. There was no need for this, Bauer said. There had to be limits to the application of the principle, and just as there had to be limits to the principle of cultural autonomy, practicality dictated that there had to be a beginning for the principle of cultural assimilation.[66]

The hostility that separated the Germans and the Czechs in the trade unions,[67] the cooperatives and in parliament was ventilated next before the International Socialist Congress meeting in the summer of 1910 in Copenhagen. There, with all desire for reconciliation gone, the Germans instead sought a moral victory over the ever recalcitrant Czechs. The Czechs, led by Němec, Vaněk, Tusar, Soukup and Tayerle, entered the congress as an independent delegation from Bohemia,[68] separating themselves from the group that had represented them in all previous congresses of the Second International. As it was, friction developed between the separatists and the Austrian delegation even before the first plenary session. It began with a move in the credentials committee by the Czech separatists to unseat the Czech centralists, led by Franz Jura, who had attended the congress as an integral part of the Austrian delegation.[69] The separatists were concerned about the presence of the Czech centralists because they represented a serious challenge to their own claim that they alone spoke for the interests of the Czech working class in Austria.[70] Speaking before the International Socialist Bureau on the point of admitting the centralists, Adler, who had remained relatively silent on the matter of Czech separatism up to now, turned to denounce separatism and Nemec, in particular, as an unprincipled politician. In absolute support of the Austrian Trade-Union Commission, Adler argued before the bureau that the commission had always represented the 300,000 Germans, the 118,000 Czechs and 20,000 Poles within it solely on economic grounds and never in regard to nationality. Beyond this, he went on, despite the claim of the separatists to the contrary, the commission still did represent the majority of the Czech workers,[71] a fact which was, of course, true at this particular time. Adler's opening attack in front of the bureau was only the beginning of a long series of humiliations which the Czechs would be forced to take at Copenhagen. In the plenary sessions of the congress, the Germans advanced a carefully-worded resolution which described the necessity for the existence of only one single, overriding trade-union organization within each country and which went on to condemn any attempt to break up the unity of any trade union by means of an appeal to nationalistic feelings.[72] The first speaker to back the proposals was the Russian Social-Democrat, George Plekhanov, who, reminded of the difficulties in his party, warned the separatists that the course that they had travelled up to now was, in his words, suicidal.[73] Němec was extremely subdued throughout the long debate. At first, the only reply that he offered was that the International had never been adequately informed on the conditions that existed in Austria and that a great deal of misinformation had been let out to the delegates. Growing weary and confessional as he went along, Němec finally told the congress that the steadily tightening administrative structure thrown up by the Austrian Trade-Union Commission and the regular inability of the Czechs to come up with a real source of revenue had, in fact, been the wellsprings of Czech separatism.[74] After these somewhat unintentioned revelations, Jura rose in the congress with his own telling criticism to the effect that the Czech workers had actually never wanted separatism,[75] but that it had been imposed on them by the leaders of the Czech party, most of whom had deliberately aimed at the division of the trade unions along national lines.[76]

The Czech separatists were not, however, quieted by this criticism. Instead, they replied with a resolution of their own that described the controversy between the Germans and the Czechs in Austria as a purely internal one and asked that the International consider it in that light. The resolution was quickly defeated, 185-9.

Almost immediately, the congress followed up its action by passing the resolution that the Germans had presented that favored only one commission for each country, 222-5, a vote that had the effect of condemning separatism.[77] The Germans emerged from the congress with a considerable triumph. They had humiliated the Czechs before the entire socialist community in Europe. The International had obviously not solved the problem,[78] but after its implied condemnation of separatism, it did order both sides to begin negotiations designed to end their particular differences.

Both the Germans and the Czechs had now been ordered by the International to moderate their approaches and to proceed to negotiate in "a spirit of socialist brotherhood."[79] Pravo lidu went along immediately. It indicated, right away, that the Czechs were now looking to the Germans for some kind of opening toward which both sides would be able to proceed.[80] The Czechs softened their approach on several occasions after this, evidently hoping to create a more conciliatory mood. Their first major move away from a hard line came when the Czechs suddenly expressed their approval of the ideas which Bauer had advanced some six months earlier for a solution to the difficulties in the trade unions.[81] Beyond this, the Czechs gave more direct evidence of their change in attitude at the sixth Austrian Trade-Union Congress held in October, 1910. Vaněk told the delegates at the congress in a frank concession that "we [the Czechs] want to take into account the decisions that the International has made."[82]

At the same time that they continued to criticize the Germans through both September and October, the Czechs kept letting out conciliatory statements.[83] These leads, which were interspersed through the propaganda of the Czechs, were either misread or misunderstood by Victor Adler, who continued to act as if the Czechs were uncompromising when, in fact, they had actually been chastened by the criticism of the International. Immediately after returning from Copenhagen, Adler's speeches and writings were punctuated by an inflexible attitude toward the Czechs, a stance that seemed highly inappropriate for a party leader who, in an earlier age, had made his reputation as a compromiser.84 Unable or unwilling to recognize the opening that the Czechs had created, Adler continued to insist that the separatists had removed any chance for real agreement by their personal attacks upon him and others.85 Adler had not only been hurt by the criticism that the Czech Social-Democratic press had directed against him, it had apparently taken from him all desire for an actual accommodation. For example, at the very same time when Vaněk had expressed an indirect hope that negotiations could take place, Adler was not only condemning the separatists but was also interpreting to the trade unions the decision of the International in much harsher terms than it had originally been stated.86

Adler's refusal to compromise with the separatists did not entirely cover up what sentiment there was in the German party for a real rapprochement.87 What good-will there was left was tapped on both sides in November when a unity conference was called to reach some kind of a compromise. The unity conference met not because the Germans and Czechs wanted it but because it had been suggested by the International. The representatives who attended its sessions were drawn from among the centralists and the separatists in the trade unions and the Germans and the Czechs in the party. The Austrian Trade-Union Commission was represented by Hueber, Jura and Franz Domes, while the Prague commission sent Tayerle, Tusar and Rudolf Jaros. The German party selected Adler and Josef Seliger, while the Czechs picked Němec and Soukup. The conference was headed by the Polish party leader Hermann Diamand and the Slovene delegate Etbin Kristan, both of whom were to serve in the situation as mediators.88

The Czechs expressed an early interest in reconciliation but that desire was not strong enough to move them away from their previous inflexible insistence upon the national division of the trade unions. They even insisted that they would have to have, in any event, international recognition for both their party and their trade unions.[89] Instead of answering the Czechs on these points, Adler came back with his own proposal for the creation of a number of common organizational ties between the German and Czechs.[90] It was clear that neither side had really talked to the other during the first session of the conference, but both sides did agree to a second meeting.

Hueber opened the conference's second session with the announcement to the effect that the Austrian Trade-Union Commission had now agreed to extend official recognition to the unions that the separatists had already established. But, that recognition was contingent upon the Czechs accepting a common policy on strikes, boycotts, wages and lockouts, most of which would have been determined by the Austrian Trade-Union Commission. Along with the above, Hueber called upon the Czechs to surrender all the mixed language areas to the commission's jurisdiction and to cease all further agitation for separatism. The Czechs, for their part, did not even try to reply. They quit the conference, agreeing only to go over the proposals. Three months later, in March, 1911, the unity conference held its third and final session. By now, the two sides had stopped talking to one another and the conference soon fell apart. The end of this attempted reconciliation marked the final collapse of that alliance between Germans and Czechs which had formed the essence of Austrian Social Democracy. When that coalition ended Austrian Social Democracy as it had been known for nearly a quarter of a century likewise ceased to exist.

The collapse of the talks lasting from November to March placed the Czechs completely outside of the general party which now consisted of the German party and the much smaller Polish, Czech centralist, Slovene and Italian parties. After this, the separatists were excluded from almost every level of the party's organizations.

In March, the Austrian Trade-Union Commission called a <u>Reichskonferenz</u> to announce that it would no longer negotiate with any of the separate Czech trade-union organizations.[91] The separatists reacted by expelling those who were still loyal to the general party, the Czech centralists, from the positions they held in the Czech party. The Czech centralists responded to their ouster by reconstituting themselves as the Czech Social-Democratic Labor Party,[92] and by declaring their outright allegiance to the general party and to the cause of international trade-union solidarity.[93]

The Czech separatists had now been divorced from the general party both politically and economically and they carried that realization, in full, into the elections of 1911. In the elections, they stood candidates quite independent from those offered by the general party. While the separatists had been isolated from the other socialist parties, they did gain support outside of the party, most noticeably from bourgeois journalists and writers like Eduard Beneš.[94] As for the separatists themselves, they moved quickly in the direction of the middle-class support that they had received. The shift was most obvious in Moravia where the separatists soon entered a number of electoral alliances with Czech bourgeois parties, breaking with the general party's long-standing commitment to the political idea of proletarian exclusiveness.[95] These early alliances laid the foundation for the so-called Moravian accords of the summer of 1911 which saw Vlastimil Tusar join the presidium of a group of Czech parties, including the Agrarian, People's Clerical and Social-Democratic parties, all of whom united in order to push for as full and complete an extension of the Czech school system as was possible.[96]

The steady movement of the separatists away from the socialist camp and toward an even greater degree of national identification constituted, in effect, the prelude to the rather acidulous electoral campaign which the two socialist parties in Austria were about to wage. The most immediate result of years of animosity and distrust was, of course, a divided and diminished effort for the socialists in both Bohemia and Moravia. That division revealed itself in five key electoral districts where the interests of the centralists and the separatists met head-on. In the twenty-first Bohemian electoral district, which included Jungbunzlau (Mladá Boleslav), the Czech separatists and the Czech centralists each ran candidates without one affecting the other's vote total. But, the clash between the two did prove damaging in the industrial and coal mining district of Mährisch-Ostrau (Ostrava), where the Czech centralists drew off enough votes on the first round to deny the seat to a Czech separatist, who did, however, win it on the second round. The same factious story was repeated in ridings in Jamnitz (Jamnice) and Brünn. Simultaneously, in the twenty-second electoral district, which centered on the Moravian textile center of Prossnitz (Prostějou), the two Social-Democratic candidates actually succeeded in eliminating one another.[97] In the final analysis, the threat posed by the centralists to the separatists turned out to be marginal since the separatist candidates amassed some 350,000 votes and the centralists only 20,000.[98]

The divisions, now widening, within the once unified Austrian Social-Democratic movement were mirrored in particular in the new parliament, with the Social Democrats splitting immediately after the elections into three separate clubs. The first was made up of some forty-four Germans, three Italians and one Ruthenian, the second of twenty-five Czech deputies and the third included eight Poles and one Czech centralist.[99]

The feelings stirred by the elections along with the refusal after this of the Czechs to cooperate with the other two clubs in parliament led to a final and irrevocable break between the Germans and the Czechs. The Germans, in 1911, decided at their Innsbruck party congress to expel permanently the Czechs from the general party. In a speech to the congress, Adler recommended that the Czech centralists, actually the Czech

Social-Democratic Labor Party, be formally admitted to the general party on an equal footing with the other autonomous national parties.[100] The Germans approved of the move at their party congress,[101] followed by the Poles in the same year and the South Slavs in 1912. The Czech centralists, headed by Edmund Burian and Viktor Stein, were accordingly inducted into the party on June 20, 1912,[102] with the Czech separatists protesting the move. The Czechoslovakian party secretary, Anton Bruha, in a formal protest denied that the general executive had the power to admit the centralists. Adler dismissed Bruha's complaint, telling the separatists that the decision had been made and that it had been binding upon them.[103] The separatists responded by quitting the party, but not before Němec attacked the Germans as nationalists masquerading as Marxists whose only real concern was to perpetuate the essentially German character of the Austrian state.[104]

At the moment of the last break, the Germans still held the idea that Czech greed had started the whole crisis. Their position was made clear when Friedrich Adler, Victor Adler's son, now a party leader on his own, condemned the Czechs for their partisanship, and Karl Renner asserted that the Czechs alone had been responsible for reducing the movement's international sense.[105] The only man who seemed to reach beyond the criticism of the moment was Otto Bauer. In spite of his backing for the policy of the German party, Bauer continued to offer suggestions for compromise. The mending process, he insisted, would have to begin immediately and it would have to start with the Czech centralists and separatists getting together again.[106] Very few on either side were willing to follow these suggestions. For the most part, the Germans tended to accept Adler's fatalistic assertion to the effect that, "We must wait until separatism has run its course. The change when it does come must come from the Czechs and not from any outside force. ...We cannot help our Czech comrades in overcoming separatism; they must do it alone. Anything we try to do will only provoke them more."[107]

After this, the conflict between the Germans and the Czechs seemed to die away. In the main, the two sides were just too exhausted to continue it. The origins of separatism go back into the period before 1907. In actuality, the Germans and the Czechs never had talked to one another. What dialogue there had been in the past had been based upon their common desire to advance themselves politically by means of universal manhood suffrage. Once this goal was achieved, what divided them increasingly replaced what had once united them. And what divided them was their differing conceptions of organization. The Czechs had always conceived of themselves as different and they had always wanted to protect that difference by means of autonomy. The Germans, however, had always thought in terms of centralization. When the party grew more centralized it only encouraged Czech autonomy. When the trade unions became more highly centralized it only provoked a greater reaction in the form of Czech separatism. This last crisis might have been settled by compromise except that Adler had passed beyond that stage. Perhaps the criticism of Němec and the Czechs had been too harsh, for it seemed to inure Adler, who in an earlier age had been more willing to moderate his views. The only man who stood out as a potential arbiter in the dispute was Bauer, who really represented an older tradition in the party, but whose views failed to secure the backing they needed in both parties. After twenty years, the ability of Austrian Social Democracy to compromise and to resolve problems step-by-step had been lost to ideology. But, logically when one considered the past, it was not socialist doctrine that paralyzed the tendency of the party to moderation, for ideology in that sense had never had a strong grip upon the party; rather it was the force of nationalism and national identification which brought that coalition known as Austrian Social Democracy to an end in 1911 and 1912.

Chapter VIII

THE COMING OF WORLD WAR I

During the years 1905 to 1908, it was not unusual for people to speak of the revitalization of the Cisleithanian half of the Austro-Hungarian monarchy just as though it had experienced a kind of rebirth. In the view of a number of prominent historians of the time, most especially Heinrich Friedjung and Richard Charmatz, new and more modern forces had arisen and begun to circulate in Austria. According to them, the signs of this new vitality were everywhere: in Austria's growing industrial strength, in her new democratic suffrage and even in her more robust foreign policy, her renewed <u>Drang nach dem Süden</u> which had led to her unqualified absorption of the area of Bosnia and Herzegovina.[1] All of these events, which seemed for the moment to have rejuvenated Austria, were transformed almost immediately into outright misfortune. The democratization of the franchise, which was supposed to spur the process of reform, only gave greater voice to national hatreds in the empire. The economic prosperity of the period before 1907 ultimately gave way to depression and dislocation. And even worse, from Austria's point of view, the annexation of Bosnia and Herzegovina only encouraged among the peoples of the Balkans the desire for a united Slav state, the one unrequited aspiration that the Austrian empire would not be able to handle.[2] In a period of uncertainty, Austrian Social Democracy still believed that the western half of the monarchy could be revived by well-placed political and social reforms and that the Austrian government could be turned from an overly aggressive stand in the Balkans.

Into 1908 and 1909, the Social Democrats continued to believe that the full impact of universal manhood suffrage had yet to be felt in Austria and that the potential of parliament as a law-making body had not even been realized. They persisted in this belief even past Beck's resignation in November, 1908, and his replacement by Baron Richard von Bienerth.[3] Still, when Beck stepped down, it had to be a loss, for both Beck and the Social Democrats had looked to parliament to accomplish what they had wanted. Through his years in office, Beck had collaborated with the Social Democrats on a number of occasions and a real feeling had developed between them. That feeling persisted in spite of the fact that the coalition government which Beck had formed was definitely anti-socialist in outlook and in character.[4] In time, the party systematically reduced its attacks upon the government especially as Beck pushed the Electoral Reform Bill and the Ausgleich agreements of 1907 through parliament and then sought a legislative solution for the nationalities question.[5] This, and along with it his plan for the introduction of a system of social-security legislation,[6] had not only improved the position of parliament, in general, it had also created a climate within which reform seemed much more acceptable. After this, parliament continued the initiative that Beck had introduced to it by passing the budget right into 1909, proving that it had taken over effective control of fiscal matters from the executive branch of government.[7] When Beck finally resigned, the differences between them over Bosnia and Herzegovina did not prevent the Arbeiter-Zeitung from complimenting Beck on his moderate, middle-of-the-road policies.[8] After this, the party continued to support the institution of parliament as intensely as ever, a growing attachment that was confirmed one month after Beck's resignation when one of the party's leading spokesmen Engelbert Pernerstorfer was elected vice-president of the lower house.[9]

From 1905 to 1909, the Austrian parliament had functioned as a normal parliamentary institution but after this it failed to maintain its own initiative. Beginning in 1909, it lapsed into inactivity, paralyzed as it had been before 1905 by deliberate obstruction and turmoil. In this instance, the planned obstructions were the work of the newly-formed Slavic Union.[10] The Union had come into existence as a result of the annexation of Bosnia and Herzegovina and brought together into one parliamentary union Czechs, South Slavs and Ruthenians, all of whom united in the belief that Slavic interests in the empire would be safeguarded more vigorously than in the past.[11] Time and again, the Union moved to paralyze parliament and Bienerth's government whenever it felt slighted on questions such as the role of the Czechs in Bohemia or the use of Slavic languages in the civil service.[12] Throughout 1908 and 1909, Bienerth committed himself to fulfilling the legislative plan that his predecessor, Beck, had already laid out. He even reappointed the coalition that had supported Beck so faithfully while he had been in office.[13] But Bienerth's determined attempt to carry through the legislation that had been conceived by Beck's previous cabinet, legislation that was reformist in nature, was stymied by the Slavic Union which kept insisting upon obstruction. The unexpected revival of obstructionism in 1909 necessarily limited the ability of parliament to enact further reform and constituted a setback for Bienerth, the members of his coalition, including the Christian Socialists, and the Social Democrats.

As the number of obstructions increased, the Social Democrats reacted by reviving von Gautsch's previous demand for a reform of the house's orders of procedures, a reform that Adler had once minimized as unnecessary for a democratically elected house.[14] The disappointment that the Social Democrats felt was increased shortly after this when Bienerth responded to the obstructionist tactics that the Czechs had been using by dissolving the session that had been sitting. As far as Adler was concerned both the Slavic Union and Bienerth had acted extremely and both were equally guilty of destroying the elan that parliament had built up over the last few years.[15] With parliament unable to function, the party increased its response by ordering mass demonstrations against the Slavic Union through the summer and fall of 1909, but the demonstrations did nothing to affect the morale of the obstructionists.[16] The parliamentary crisis that had begun early in 1909 climaxed on December 15 when a handful of Czech deputies turned the deliberations of the lower house into chaos with no less than 37 different motions of urgency. The government coalition with the support of the Social Democrats now moved hastily to save the house from total collapse. Together they defeated the obstruction with an all-night session and on the next day came out with a major proposal to change the house's standing rules of procedure. By December 18, the Social-Democratic leaders in the house, working with the leaders of the coalition, had so altered the standing rules of procedure that obstruction now seemed less threatening.[17] The new ruling, supported by both the government deputies and the Social Democrats, granted to the president of the house more power over the length of debates, thus reducing the effect that obstruction could have upon the legislative process.[18]

The reform was viewed by many as still more proof of the resiliency of parliament, a view which Renner interpreted skeptically. He was convinced that the Austrian parliament was again in decline,[19] and that the process, once it set in, could not be arrested.[20] In the months that followed, his pessimism would be proven correct. Into 1910, the lower house was characterized by a degree of ineptitude that was reminiscent of the old curial parliament. The collapse of parliamentary activity necessarily demoralized the party and the trade unions, both of whom had been carried along by the expectations of reform through legislation. Now, that faith no longer seemed appropriate. The growing disenchantment that the unions now felt about the political process found expression at the Sixth Congress of the Austrian Trade Unions held in 1910. There, Anton Schrammel, the long-time labor leader from Aussig, stated openly that the labor movement had become increasingly uneasy over the failure of parliament to enact welfare legislation.[21] The major result of this growing sense of pessimism was that the movement's long-standing belief in the efficacy of political democracy now began to decline.

For almost two decades, the leaders of the party had sustained the movement's faith with visions that had not materialized. The result of all of this was that political democracy no longer seemed to be the road that it once had been for the social and economic transformation of Austrian society. Friedrich Adler was especially concerned that the resulting disappointment would cause the working class to turn away from political activity, a consequence that he feared especially since it had taken so many years to awaken the working class's political consciousness. The younger Adler readily admitted that the disillusionment had penetrated deeply, but he warned the party that if the workers deserted parliament it would return the institution to the upper classes and Austria would be back to where she had been, politically, in the 1890's.[22]

At the same time that Friedrich Adler had advocated stronger working class support for parliament, he could not help but wonder himself if the movement had not placed too much faith in parliament over the years.[23] The doubts that he expressed were compounded in 1911 when the imperial elections showed that the steady gain that the party had experienced at the polls since 1897 had now come to an end and that the party's vote total had levelled off from 1907 to 1911. While the party held its vote total, its total number of seats fell from 89 to 82, in part, as a consequence of its own divisions. Yet, even with the division between the Germans and Czechs, the party remained the second largest in the house, ahead of the German Nationalists and behind the Christian Socialists.[24] The party tended to blame the coalitions that had been formed against it at the polls by other parties for its losses,[25] a fact that only accounted, in part, of course, for its loss of seats.

After years without real legislative gain, Bienerth's coalition finally became so unstable that he was forced to resign in the middle of 1911, giving way to Baron Paul von Gautsch.[26] Gautsch's government remained in office for only a few months before it was replaced by Austria's last pre-war cabinet established under the premiership of the highly conservative Count Karl von Stürgkh.[27] After an ephemeral attempt to bring the Germans and the Czechs to cooperate and thus to get parliament functioning again,[28] Stürgkh allowed parliament to lapse into inaction. He did this by proroguing one session of parliament after another as a response to the new techniques of the obstructionists. With the collapse of parliament and the onset of the Balkan wars, Stürgkh shifted his government's legislative focus away from reform and toward defense.[29] As the months passed, Stürgkh all but eclipsed parliament by issuing the legislation he needed under Article 14 of the constitution, doing without a parliamentary vote most of the time. As Bauer saw by 1913, Austria had returned to absolutism and could only be brought back if the house's standing rules of procedure were drastically altered,[30] which they never were.

By 1913, nothing could have saved parliament. Between the nationalities who used it as a battle-ground and Stürgkh who increasingly ignored it, parliament ceased to function. Proof of this came between 1912 and 1914 when Stürgkh made use of Article 14 to circumvent parliament more than 120 times, a total that may be compared with the period from 1897 to 1904, when a number of premiers confronted with similar circumstances made use of Article 14 only 76 times among them.[31]

With parliament obviously in decline, the party had to admit that it was no longer capable of winning even minor reforms for the working class.[32] It was this realization that formed the essence of Otto Bauer's speech to the German party congress held in 1912 in Vienna. There, Bauer openly admitted that the chance for further reform had been lost, even though he declared in some rage, "we have waited long enough for truly relevant social reform in Austria."[33] What he had in mind, of course, was the social-security package that Beck had presented to parliament in November 1908 which had still not emerged from committee some four years later.[34]

Austrian Social Democracy was genuinely
alarmed by these developments. Over the years,
it had steadily modified its stand toward the
prevailing political system and had progressively
moved from the far left of the political spectrum
to the near center on the assumption that it would
eventually gain what it desired by parliamentary
means, if it could only sustain its own belief
in étatisme. Victor Adler had drawn this idea
from Ferdinand Lassalle and had passed it on to
his followers at almost every one of the movement's levels. The support that the party had
given to the cause of electoral reform before
1907 and to the maintenance of the integrity of
parliament after 1907 had, indeed, all been motivated by the expectation that a popularly-elected
lower house would begin the progressive redistribution of wealth that the socialists had
anticipated all of this time. If expectation
gave way to impatience and moderation to extremism
after 1907, it was due primarily to the fact that
the Austrian parliament had passed only fifteen
different pieces of social legislation, all of
them minor in their impact. By and large, they
were all of the kind that had shortened the workday for commercial workers or had outlawed the
use of phosphorous in the manufacture of matches
because phosphorous had been proven injurious to
health.[35] Absent, between 1907 and 1912, was the
kind of social-security legislation that would
have begun the process of redistribution.

As far as the Austrian Trade-Union Commission
was concerned, the laws that had been passed
were not wide enough in their scope. As the disappointment felt by the trade unions increased,
the moral hold that the party had once exercised
over them began to slip. In turn, the response
of the trade unions was really one of growing
disdain toward the party's parliamentary faction.[36] Ferdinand Hanusch summed up the declining feelings that the unions had for the party
at the Austrian Trade-Union Congress in 1913.
There, as if to undermine the party, he pointed
out that the old curial parliament, without a
single socialist deputy, had passed more social
legislation than the so-called people's parlia-

ment with its large Social-Democratic contingent.[37] The growing moral ascendency of the trade unions that emerged out of this situation had the result of placing Adler and the party in a distinctly subordinate role, a fact that most likely accounted for Adler's attack on Czech trade-union separatism, a tactic that seemed so far removed from his earlier tendency to compromise. By this time, he had, in a sense, become dependent upon the Austrian Trade-Union Commission and its more uncompromising attitude toward the separatists.

    The discontent expressed in the trade unions had an almost immediate effect upon the party, where extremists took advantage of the situation to demand a much more radical policy in parliament. Their demands were heard largely because sentiment within the party had now begun to turn away from the more moderate course that Victor Adler had advocated and toward a more anti-parliamentary attitude.[38] By November, 1913, feelings in favor of a more radical course had developed to such a degree that the German party leaders could not keep the issue from the agenda of the next party congress.[39] Not unexpectedly, the task of defending the integrity of parliament was taken up by Victor Adler, who admitted that parliament had fallen but who refused to countenance an attack upon it. In a speech that was obviously buoyed by his life-long faith in parliamentary democracy, Adler argued that the difficulties of parliament were only temporary and that it would soon reemerge, once again, as a dynamic force. As sanguine as ever about the potential of parliamentary democracy, Adler reminded his audience of Marx's wholehearted commitment to reform and of the gains that the working class had already made. In making the connection, he continued to combine political democracy and social democracy in such a way as to make them seem more indispensible to one another than ever.[40] A somewhat more realistic assessment of the situation came from Renner who told the congress that the party had been immobilized inside of parliament and that the initiative for gain for the working class had already passed to the trade unions and the co-operatives, the two organizations that had brought about real advances for the working class. With the movement's political consciousness less than it had been for some time, Victor Adler's leadership of the party suffered a rather serious setback when the congress voted to go over the use of obstruction under unusual or extraordinary circumstances.[41]

The frustration that had led the German party to this point was an outgrowth of its own basic realization that it had failed to improve the position of the working class. Indeed, the economic gains that had come to the workers were less the result of political pressure and more a product of the pressure exerted by the unions. For the most part, the demands of the working class still centered, as they had before, on the immediate issues of a shorter work week and a greater measure of social security.[42] In the euphoria that followed the political reforms of 1907, a good many workers were led to assume that old-age and unemployment benefits would soon be enacted.[43] As these expectations declined, the unions began to take more direct steps to secure the improvements that they had wanted. As wages began to replace the idea of welfare in the minds of the workers, the unions won better pay rates largely as a consequence of collective bargaining rather than as a result of strikes. Strikes had been more effective in the past because of the way that they had affected the non-strikers. Now, with larger memberships and growing financial resources, the major industrial unions focused on the more subtle aspects of contract negotiations.

As trade-union membership soared past 500,000 in 1907,[44] increased revenues gave the Austrian Trade-Union Commission an opportunity to supervise the type of welfare plans that it had once expected the party to win from the government.[45] The financial assistance that the trade unions provided to its members included not only unemployment benefits and burial allotments but support for widows, orphans, the sick and victims of industrial accidents as well. Between 1901 and 1909, the Austrian Trade-Union Commission expended nearly 40% of its total annual revenue on its various welfare programs,[46] a system that reminded many of the way that guilds had functioned in a previous age.

While collective bargaining had indeed become more common, the greater revenues of the Austrian Trade-Union Commission did allow it to support and sustain much more local strike activity than it had in the past. The renewal of strike activity, however, did not really come until after 1905, coincidental with a major advance in the economy. Before this, strike activity had been kept at a minimum. For example in 1901, there had been only 270 strikes in Austria, involving only 719 plants and the loss of only 157,744 workdays. These figures may be compared with strike activity in 1907 when strikes closed more than six thousand plants and more than two million workdays were actually lost.[47] The overall consequence of these strikes along with a series of new contracts gained largely from collective bargaining was a significant improvement in the workers' standard of living. These gains were reflected further in the progressive shortening of the workday in most of the major industries to ten hours and in metallurgy to only nine.[48] These changes were accompanied by a corresponding increase in real wages during the decade from 1902 to 1912. During that period, the average wages earned by mine, factory, transport and construction workers increased from 707 Kronen a year to 948 Kronen, that is by 34 per cent, with most of the gains going to factory workers.[49]

The labor situation after 1907, while it showed substantial improvement in a number of areas, was still beset by real misfortune. Alcoholism and tuberculosis continued to be prevalent in most working-class districts and the lack of proper housing was still a major social problem.[50] To add to these distresses, after 1907 a depression set in in Austria which threatened to wipe away, either in whole or in the part, many of the gains that the working class had picked up over the years. Most serious of all was the rising price of staple items after 1907, a price spiral that threatened the wage increases that the workers had only recently won in a number of industries. To Bauer, the depression of 1907 was just one more in a series of crises that had characterized capitalism during the nineteenth century,[51] but to the working class it meant a potential decline in its standard of living after more than a decade and a half of advance in real wages.

The trade unions were not in a position after 1907 to resist either the increase in prices or the instability that it brought, largely because their own effectiveness at the time had been undermined by declining membership and the organizational weaknesses produced by separatism. Membership in the trade unions fell to 482,279 in 1908 and then declined precipitously to 415,256 in 1909,[52] as a consequence of both rising unemployment and the force of separatism. After this, membership in the central industrial unions slipped again to 400,000 in 1910, inching back up to some 428,363 by 1912.[53] Through it all, the Austrian Trade-Union Commission did manage, however, to maintain the loyalty of some 70,000 Czech workers,[54] most of them in the mixed language areas of Silesia, western Bohemia and Lower Austria.

The underlying cause of the slowdown in the Austrian economy after 1907 was declining consumption, a situation that was accelerated by the reduced purchasing power of the working class in the years before 1914.[55] The Social Democrats were disturbed by this downward trend, especially when they compared it to the growing concentration of economic power in the hands of the upper middle class.[56] Beck's welfare bill of November, 1908, might have narrowed the distance between the upper and lower classes. But the arguments raised by the Social Democrats in favor of redistribution,[57] were always countered by the argument that such programs reduced the capital pool in Austria and thereby prevented further economic growth.[58] The failure of parliament to meet the possibilities suggested by Beck's plan for more social-security legislation disappointed the Social Democrats, in particular, the party, since its standing with the working class depended largely upon its ability to apply political pressure in this direction.[59]

The economic disabilities that weighed upon the working class were relieved only momentarily in 1911 by a good harvest, higher levels of industrial production and a more favorable trade balance for Austria,[60] but after this the depression renewed itself, threatening to claim all over again the economic advances that the workers had already made. The frustrations that the party felt in parliament over its inability to do anything about this crises led it to call for street demonstrations in 1909 against the so-called Teuerung, or rise in prices. These demonstrations, the largest in Austria since 1906, centered upon Vienna, Graz, Trieste, Brünn, Reichenberg, Gablonz (Jablonec nad Nisou) and Lemberg.[61] Even though these demonstrations failed to change things, the party continued to push them right into 1910. At the same time, the trade unions grasped just how serious the economic issue had become for the working class, and in an unusual foray into ideology, the labor leaders denounced the Teuerung as all a capitalist plot against the working class.[62]

The Social Democrats continued to stage mass demonstrations against the Teuerung and the governmental policies that supported it throughout 1910 and 1911, with Gautsch, in turn, denouncing the demonstrations as part of a plot.[63] The demonstrations that the party had mounted through the summer of 1911 finally culminated in a mass demonstration in September in front of the Rathaus in Vienna. That demonstration led to open clashes between the army and groups of workers that left three dead and scores wounded.[64] The deaths only enraged the Social Democrats who on October 4 called for emergency legislation from the government to halt the worst effects of Austria's inflation and depression.[65] Speaking before the lower house on the next day, Adler, using ideology, warned the possessing classes that the working class would not continue to tolerate this particular form of oppression.66 In spite of the threat, the party proved powerless to halt the effects of rising prices, and Austria's economic crisis, added to her political distress, created a sense of drift and disillusionment that seemed all but pervasive after 1911.

It was during these years of obvious crises that Austro-Marxism developed as a distinct philosophical school. As it was, it came too late to prevent Austrian Social Democracy from falling apart. This was especially so because most of its contributors were German and, for that reason, increasingly unacceptable to the Czechs while they were still in the party. If it was born too late to unite the party, it at least left Austrian socialism with much more of a Marxian tone than it had ever had in the past. In the years before World War I, Karl Renner, Otto Bauer, Max Adler and Friedrich Adler, all combined to give Austro-Marxism a unique intellectural flair.67 Renner's contributions to the school came before the war and focused primarily upon his own attempt to find a link between the ideas of socialist internationalism and his own belief in cultural nationalism.68 Bauer and the two Adlers, who were not related, made most of their contributions to Austro-Marxism after 1918, although their writings before 1914 very often reflected the more mature ideas that they were to express after the war.

The progressive addition of Marxian concepts to the body of socialist thought in Austria before 1914 took place only after Victor Adler's declining intellectual hold upon the party had actually passed away. Less and less was heard about Lassalle especially after Victor Adler's attempt in 1903 to present Lassalle's ideas to a younger generation of socialists as the equal of those of Marx.69 When the school of Austro-Marxism finally arose and finally intercepted the Marxist tradition, Marxism was, of course, a much tamer doctrine. The kind of Marxism that Austro-

Marxism absorbed after 1907 was both reformist and revisionist in mood. In a real sense, the innermost character of Austro-Marxism was expressed not by any of its principal contributors but by Adolf Braun, a man who, at least, had some distance on the movement. A former Lassallean, Braun condemned in Der Kampf, the party's leading theoretical organ founded in 1907, what he described as vulgar Marxism. Vulgar Marxism in his view was the philosophical assumption that Marxism was a static and irreducible body of thought incapable of adaptation and completely prejudiced against the possibility of reform within the capitalist system.[70] In many ways, Braun's description of what Marxism should not be fitted the mood of Austro-Marxism. For this otherwise discursive school of thought always proceeded from the assumption that Marxism was a dynamic force that could be adapted to the practical problems that confronted Austria before 1914. By its own estimate, Austro-Marxism was a part of the Marxist center, even though in reality it leaned to the right most of the time and even drew back from the precipitous idea of a general strike before 1914.[71]

Austro-Marxism first distinguished itself when Renner and Bauer both tried to come to terms with the growing phenomenon of nationalism. Many observers believed that their effort had actually carried them much too close to bourgeois nationalism,[72] that is that they had absorbed too much of it as they examined it. If they did, the price was too high, for in fact developments would soon outstrip what both of them had to say on the matter of nationalism. Of the two, Renner's views turned out to be atavistic, largely because they were more a product of Herder's type of cultural nationalism,[73] than a recognition of the more virulent kind of political and economic nationalism that had developed in central and eastern Europe by the late nineteenth century. What was conspicuous about his writings was Renner's refusal to see that there was a link between nationalism and political and social developments. That failure, in itself, robbed his ideas of their prescience and tended to weaken the intellectual ties that were supposed to exist between him and Austro-Marxism, a school that was, in the main, much more conscious of social and economic developments than he ever was.[74] If Austro-Marxism had an originator at all, it was Bauer rather than Renner. For it was Bauer who gave to the school its more modern sociological character, an emphasis which grew out of his effort to place both nationalism and the politics of the time in much more of a social and economic context. Bauer's more extensive pragmatism was really the product of his own realization that feelings of nationalism had penetrated the working class with an intensity that very few others were willing to admit.[75]

Bauer's vision of society rested first of all upon his commitment to political democracy, a view which saw parliament as the most likely means to social reform and political power for the working class.[76] Drawing upon working-class history in the nineteenth century, Bauer argued that the working class had passed through two separate and distinct phases using very different methods in each. The older method had been revolution, the newer democratic. The older and more anarchistic approach had been used while the working class was still a relatively small minority, being characterized by both violent insurrections and general strikes. This method had not brought about the gains the workers had asked for and by the end of the century both time and circumstances had made that particular approach absolete. No one knew this better, Bauer pointed out, than Engels himself who by this time had realized that "the time for a surprise attack on the part of a small conscious minority through revolution in order to gain domination over the unconscious majority had been passed."[77]

Newer methods had been opened up, Bauer insisted, but the growing transformation in society, a change that was being encouraged by economic growth. The tremendous increase in capitalist industry had pushed the working class into a second stage of development. For, in actuality, the growing size of the working class virtually guaranteed its eventual domination of the state by democratic means.[78] This development, according to Bauer, had taken place just as Marx had declared it would, for as Marx had predicted it was and would continue as "an independent movement of the overwhelming majority in the interests of the overwhelming majority."[79] Once this development reached its limits, Bauer predicted, bourgeois ownership of property would ultimately give way to a complete socialization of the means of producing things.[80] This whole process would in turn be carried along, Bauer concluded, by parliamentary means and would transpire in a very gradual way.[81] After the war, Bauer broadened his views by arguing in favor of the progressive nationalization of all heavy industry, accompanied by an adequate program of compensation for owners. Decisions within the nationalized sector of the economy in order to be truly democratic would have to be made in consultation with the trade unions, the cooperatives and special-interest groups representing the consumers.[82]

In spite of Bauer's contribution, the man who at last tied Austro-Marxism to the full body of Marxist thought, both orthodox and revisionist, depending upon the moment, was not Bauer but Max Adler. Max Adler was the most sophisticated thinker that Austrian Social Democracy produced in the period after 1900. Much more of a theoretician than either Renner or Bauer, Max Adler's principal concern with Marxism had become more obvious by 1910. Writing in that year in answer to a number of problems posed by George Plekhanov's <u>Grundfrage des Marxismus</u>, Max Adler addressed himself to the fundamental problem that occupied most of the humanistic followers of Marx, the function of the individual in the historical process. As far as Adler was concerned, the concept of historical materialism had been interpreted much too impersonally by others in the past. The concept, he went on, would have to be reworked so as to allow for a degree of individual involvement,[83] a belief that he derived at least in part from his reading of Kant. Proceeding from this premise, Adler's writings were basically an attempt to find some kind of middle ground between Marx's notion of social necessity and his own belief in the need for individual freedom.

Max Adler's determined bid to bring Marx and Kant together in a synthesis was the direct result of his own belief that social development had indeed produced a growing social awareness just as Marx said it would.[84] But, at the same time, Adler argued, social development had become so complex and so involved in the modern age that it had left a great deal more room for individual action and individual management than had previously been supposed.[85] Compared to the contribution of Max Adler to Austro-Marxism before 1914, Friedrich Adler's was much smaller. Still, he displayed a knowledge of Marxism in his writings and did help to identify Austrian Social Democracy much more thoroughly with Marxist tradition than it had been in the past.[86]

The emergence of Austro-Marxism as a clearly defined branch of neo-Marxism prior to 1914 was an indication of just how much intellectual energy there was in the party, but in and of itself, it barely affected the history of the party. By and large, the suggestions that it made seemed somehow removed from the major political, social and administrative problems that actually confronted the party. If anything, the unending weight of these problems had more than demoralized the party. Nothing demonstrated this process more than the way the party, after opposing the idea of war, gave into it in the summer of 1914. The sources of its acquiescence go back to 1908 and the absorption of Bosnia and Herzegovina, an act that stimulated the party into turning to foreign affairs, a field that it had actually kept away from up to then. The incorporation of Bosnia and Herzegovina in October, 1908,[87] brought a quick reply from the Social Democrats, who up to this time had masked their disinterest in foreign affairs by an occasional reference to the existence of imperialism. The first chance that the party had to speak to the government was immediately after the annexations when the Austrian and Hungarian _Ausgleich_ delegates met in October for

193

regular talks. Valenti Pittoni denounced the
annexations for the Social Democrats as, on base,
a violation of the rights of the Balkan peoples
to national self-determination.[88] During the
next session of parliament, Ignaz Daszyński
attacked the Austrian foreign minister, Count
Alois Aehrenthal, for having presented the house
with a <u>fait accompli</u> over Bosnia and Herzegovina
and for having done untold damage to Austria's
standing in international affairs. He concluded
his rather intemperate'speech by arguing that the
annexations were a direct result of the imperi-
alistic policies of Austria-Hungary and were
predicated on the silly assumption that somehow
little Serbia constituted a threat to the very
existence of the empire.[89] In an attempt to
embarrass Bienerth, who had succeeded Beck after
the events, the Social Democrats introduced a
motion of urgency calling upon the Austrian
government to prepare an immediate assessment of
Austria's foreign situation and to grant as soon
as possible a constitution to both Bosnia and
Herzegovina. The motion won a substantial
majority in the house, 265 to 155, but failed
because motions of this sort normally required a
two-thirds vote. The majority needed was lost
when the Christian Socialists voted against the
motion.[90] Still, the vote had indicated to the
government just how little support there was in
the house for a forward policy in the Balkans.

The Social Democrats were aware in 1908 that
the annexations had disturbed Serbia and shattered the idea of the formation of a South Slav
state in the Balkans. Moreover, the party
realized that the Austrian government was trying
to gain economic mastery over the two provinces
with its railway-building schemes.[91] Like most
of the opposition then, the Social Democrats were
conscious of the fateful character of the decision. Yet, their response to the annexations was,
if anything, a muffled one. The reason why this
came about was because Victor Adler had been
forced to hold back on his criticism for fear of
alienating the Poles in his own party. The Poles
were motivated by a hatred of the Russians that
cut so deep that they feared that any criticism

of Bienerth's government might strengthen the hand of Austria's principal rival in the Balkans, Czarist Russia. Adler, of course, had to give in. He did not dare alienate the Poles at a time when they were standing by the Germans during the Czech-party crisis.[92] The result was a measured attack upon the government that contrasted by its silence with the party's rather strident denunciation of militarism and imperialism in the Second International.

Victor Adler had always been one of the leading pacifists in the Second International,[93] and he succeeded in passing a somewhat similar attitude on to his party. Speaking to the Stuttgart Congress of the Second International in 1907, Adler reminded the delegates in attendance that an anti-militaristic attitude had long been one of the links that had bound the various sections of the Second International to one another.[94] At the very same congress, he helped to compose an Austro-Belgian resolution which condemned all aspects of militarism as well as its consequences for society.[95] Deploring the fact that this feeling was not widespread enough, Adler told the congress that the Second International would have to begin a campaign to educate the working class to the perils that militarism actually posed to modern society.[96] Three years later at the Copenhagen Congress of the Second International, Renner, standing in for Adler, helped to draw up a resolution that called upon the various sections of the International to do everything they could to prevent the outbreak of a major war in the event that one actually threatened.[97]

Down until 1912, the concern that the Second International manifested on occasion over the arms race, militarism and imperialism had somehow always seemed distant or unreal. But beginning in 1912, those issues suddenly took on a closer character with the beginning of the First Balkan War. The war itself was more than local in its impact. For not only did it absorb Serbia, Bulgaria, Montenegro, Greece and Turkey in open conflict, it also threatened at various stages to draw in Austria-Hungary, Russia, Italy and Germany.[98] In itself, the war occasioned fears that had not been felt in Europe for decades. Responding to those anxieties, Victor Adler and the French party leader Jaurès joined in calling for an extraordinary congress of the Second International, one that was finally held at Basel.[99] Adler wanted the congress primarily because the government of Austria-Hungary was on the verge of mobilizing her reserves,[100] an act which, had it come, would have focused world-wide attention upon the Austrian party and how it might deter the war.

The party had already acted in parliament to prevent, if it could, any further advance by Austria-Hungary into the Balkans. On October 22, Pernerstorfer, Pittoni and Adler all rose in the lower house to demand that Stürgkh's government make public a guarantee of its neutrality.[101] A few weeks later at their own party congress, the German Social Democrats reenforced their parliamentary stand with a call for peace and an immediate retreat from the Balkans.[102] As it was, these moves turned out to be the position that the party took when the Second International met.

The plenary sessions of the Basel congress produced a consensus but no real action. A motion was passed unanimously, but it did little except repeat the crux of the Stuttgart and Copenhagen resolutions which had called upon the working class in Europe to resist the pressure that governments were exerting for war.[103] Beyond these general instructions, the congress called upon the socialist parties of Austria and the Balkans to join in a common effort to forestall any Austrian attack upon Serbia.[104] At the congress, some, like the British party leader Kier Hardie, were convinced that the working class possessed the ability to prevent a major war from breaking out.[105] But others, Adler in particular, doubted it. As cautious as ever at the congress, Adler noted in reflection that "it really does not depend upon us Social Democrats whether there will or will not be war. And while it is true that the working class in almost every country is gaining strength daily... we should not overestimate our own capabilities."[106] In spite of Adler's sober comments, the congress was, generally speaking, optimistic. This was true, even though no practical proposals for implementing the stand that the congress had taken against war had come out of the deliberations. The idea of a general strike had come up but it had been passed over. Instead, most socialists somehow believed, in line with historical inevitability, that if a war did begin it would automatically mean the end for the ruling classes.[107]

Beyond all this, the Basel congress had the unexpected result of bringing the Germans and Czechs in Austria together for the last time before World War I. At Basel, Němec, Soukup and Adler all worked together closely on a number of proposals that the congress was ultimately to accept.[108] But after the congress, the two sides failed to maintain contact even as Austria-Hungary began to make threatening gestures toward Montenegro in 1913 and war once again faced both of the socialist parties in Austria.[109] When the Second Balkan War broke out among the states which had only recently defeated Turkey, the response of the Austrian socialists was even more halting than it had been in 1912.[110] Instead of taking direct action, the party hesitated, claiming that the war was the work of capitalism and insisting, just as Friedrich Austerlitz did, that the preservation of peace was the responsibility of the entire population and not of any one group.[111] The party now insisted on this point largely because it really did not want a general strike that might have meant ruin for its political and economic organizations.

A year after the Second Balkan War had been concluded, Franz Ferdinand, the heir to the Austrian throne was assassinated at Sarajevo on June 28, 1914.[112] At first, the full implications of the act were apparently lost to the Austrian population,[113] although Friedrich Austerlitz's lead article in the *Arbeiter-Zeitung* did have an ominous tone to it. More than most observers, Austerlitz realized that the death of Franz Ferdinand had created an entirely new situation for Austria-Hungary in the Balkans, one that would be interpreted, by some, as a threat to her existence. In what amounted to a major change of policy, Austerlitz dispensed with the party's usual condemnation of Austrian imperialism in the Balkans and instead attacked Russia for her intrigues.[114] In blaming Russia and her support for Serbia as the cause of the tensions in the Balkans, the party more than modified the critical tone that it had taken toward the government of Austria-Hungary up to then. However, at the same time, the <u>Arbeiter-Zeitung</u> did call upon the government to insure that it acted with restraint toward the Serbs.[115] That advice was, of course, lost to the more determined policy that both Vienna and Berlin settled upon over the course of the next four weeks.[116]

On July 23, nearly a month after the assassination, the Austrian government sent an ultimatum to Serbia that included a number of points which, in fact, abridged Serbia's sovereignty.[117] The note that Vienna sent was deliberately provocative. At its most intrusive point, it demanded that Austrian officials be allowed to investigate the murder on Serbian soil, if need be, and be permitted at the same time to participate in the trial of those accused. The Serbians were also ordered to put an end to all propaganda that was now being directed against the government of Austria-Hungary.[118] The response of the <u>Arbeiter-Zeitung</u> to the note was similar to that of other German papers in the empire, and that was highly patriotic. The government, the party insisted, had the right to defend itself against intrigue. But the paper separated itself from the others in condemning those sections of the ultimatum that threatened Serbia's sovereignty.[119]

The Serbs acceded to most of the Austrian demands, but they refused the more provocative ones. The Austrians replied by ordering a partial mobilization on July 27 and then total mobilization, an act tantamount to war, on July 28.[120] On the same day that war was declared, July 28, the governing body of the International, the International Socialist Bureau, met in Brussels to consider the crisis. No stenographic records were kept of the meeting, but from a number of accounts it was clear that in a depressed mood Victor Adler was forced to admit that the party had been paralyzed by both the general call-up and the government's declaration of martial law.[121] The Czechs did not attend the meeting, but Němec admitted that the Czechs had likewise grown fatalistic and would not resist the outbreak of the war.[122] At Brussels, Jaurès tried to convince Friedrich Adler that the Austrian party had a special moral responsibility to resist the war and to commence mass demonstrations against it, but he could not convince the younger Adler anymore than he could the older Adler that resistance was, in fact, sound.[123] Instead, what was left of Austrian Social Democracy, meaning the Germans and the Poles, acquiesced in the war: the Germans because they were carried away by a sudden feeling of patriotism and the Poles because of their hatred of Czarism and their expectation of a nation-state of their own.[124]

On August 4, the news came that the German Social Democrats in the Reichstag had voted for German war credits, acting in opposition to their stand in the Second International. After he heard the news, Victor Adler commented, "I know they had to vote for them; I don't know just how I can bring myself to say this, but it had to be done.... There is one thing that is worse than war and that is defeat."[125] The Austrian party, as it turned out, was spared a similar experience largely because Stürgkh assumed emergency powers in 1914 and prevented a vote on war credits from taking place in the now prorogued parliament.[126] Still, the party had failed to act even after it implied that it would in the Second International.[127] The party in 1914 chose caution. It did not try to challenge either the legal or military power of the state. Instead it turned its support to the war amid cries from its own leaders to keep the party's political and economic organizations intact and to resume the fight for social justice after the war was over.[128] Not too surprisingly, Austrian Social Democracy chose caution in the face of its greatest challenge, but then it had always been more a reformist than a revolutionary party, always more challenging in its ideas than in its actions.

CONCLUSION

The growth of Austrian Social Democracy from a small sect of some 15,000 members in 1889 to a major political force commanding the political allegiance of a full quarter of the Austrian population in 1907 is in itself a rather amazing story. To a large extent that growth was due to one man, Victor Adler. The role of the individual can never be as strong once a movement has been firmly established, but it can be very pronounced during the formative years of development and that was the role that Adler was destined to play. What he gave to Austrian Social Democracy was a certain tone, a certain air of moderation and restraint that was coupled with a driving desire for reform. So powerful was that force that it tended to drive dissident elements out of the ranks of Austrian Social Democracy. This was especially true of the anarchists, the radical socialists and the Vávra faction, all of whom were characterized by a complete unwillingness to compromise their rather extreme views. This was the case with Roušar and the dissident Czech trade unionists of the late 1890's, who in a matter of years gave up their intransigeance to return to a spirit of cooperation.

It was not that the moderates who controlled the party to the exclusion of the extremists were dogmatic. They were not. Rather they were a flexible lot for whom extremism of any kind, either ideological or tactical, did not have much appeal. The tendency of Austrian Social Democracy to compromise not only made it fit for a democratic society, it also guaranteed its own survival against considerable odds down until 1907. In an age when the various nationalities in Austria were growing apart and some of them were passing beyond cultural nationalism to the idea of self-determination, Austrian Social Democracy represented a pull in another direction. Instead of division, the movement was able to create unity largely as a result, it is true, of experimentation. When centralism failed within the party then a federal solution was sought for and found. When localism failed in the trade unions then centralism came to be adopted. It was little wonder that Renner believed that nationalism as a political force was coming to an end. He believed it of the outside world because it was in part true of the party.

The internal flexibility which Austrian Social Democracy displayed toward itself was turned outward on a number of occasions. Instead of isolating itsélf from the remainder of society, it sought to penetrate as many public institutions in the old Austrian state as was possible. Almost as soon as it was born it tried to move into and influence, if not control, such institutions as parliament, the cooperatives and the Krankenkassen assemblies, all in an attempt to widen its impact on public life.

For almost twenty years, from the Hainfeld declaration of 1889 to the time that it sided with Gautsch and Franz Joseph on the matter of franchise reform, it displayed a flexible character. That flexibility, which was the key to both its growth and survival, was, however, lost to it in the years after 1907. The loss was due to a number of factors, some of which might have been averted and some not. As Karl Kautsky found out in 1901, Austrian Social Democracy rarely permitted ideology to affect its course. Yet the party was trapped by an idea that limited its ability to maneuver. That idea was the idea of proletarian exclusiveness as laid down by the Second International. The party steadfastly refused to enter into alliances with other parties in the house and contantly refused electoral alliances at the polls. Instead, inflexibly it maintained its own separate identity as the party of the working class. At first, that policy was vital to its success especially at a time when it wanted to advertise its principles to the new emerging working-class electorate from 1897 to 1907. But, on those rare occasions when it did desert the idea of proletarian exclusiveness it led to significant tactical successes. Here, the way it helped the government's cause in the struggle for electoral reform and the manner in which it cooperated to limit the impact of obstruction in the lower house are two outstanding examples.

If the party had extended the principle of cooperation after 1907 to parties like the Christian Socialists and the Young Czechs, who represented the lower middle class and who wanted social-security legislation almost as much as the Social Democrats, the party might have won the legislative victory that it needed so badly in the years after 1907. As it was, the party was torn between its desire to stand apart from the government and to be clearly identified as an opposition party and its practical need to associate itself with a government that it needed to win social reform. Moreover, the idea of proletarian exclusiveness ultimately limited the party at the polls as well. There is no question that Austrian Social Democracy sought the vote of the working class, but it rarely went out of the way to draw in either the peasantry or the petty-bourgeoisie. The result was, of course, that its vote total began to level off after 1907 as it exhausted the voting potential of the working class.

The same sort of hesitancy and inflexibility characterized the crisis that emerged over separatism. It was not as if separatism was something new; the Czechs had always conceived of themselves as distinctive. The real problem was preventing Czech particularism from becoming what it had been in the 1870's and 1880's, a full-fledged feeling of separatism. The party had managed to contain that feeling ideologically in 1889 by means of compromise and organizationally in 1897 by doing the same. Yet after 1907 the trade unions seemed paralyzed, unable to adopt that sense of resignation and inevitability that had previously characterized the party's attitude toward the Czechs. In part, it may have been the commanding position of Hueber, especially as the unions came to dominate the party, and his unwillingness to see the elaborate edifice of the industrial unions dismantled by negotiations. But what the Trade-Union Commission refused to do by compromise, the Czechs accomplished by force, with the consequent loss of good will.

Throughout the last years of the party's history, the man who stood out as more in line with the early development of Austrian Social Democracy was Otto Bauer. His solution for the trade union dispute was simply to return to the federal solution of 1897 that had saved the party. If he had been listened to at the time the party and the movement would not have entered either the imperial elections of 1911 or the First World Was as splintered as it was. In the years before 1914 Bauer represented something that had been a part of the early history of Austrian Social Democracy and that was its sense of survival. Little wonder then in the crucial years after 1918 he emerged as the recognized leader of the German Social-Democratic movement in truncated Austria.

Austrian Social Democracy was born in the Austrian empire and in a sense died of the same disease as did the empire. Made intransigent by a lack of success, by overburdening feelings of national identification and then by the war, what was left of the movement divided even further as a result of the collapse of Austria-Hungary. If, in a real sense, it took on the problems and shared the fate of the larger society to which it had been joined over the years, at least the price it paid had the consequence of contributing to the political consciousness and the economic betterment of the Austrian working class.

NOTES

Chapter I: *The Advent of Social Democracy*

1. Herbert Steiner, *Die Arbeiterbewegung Österreichs 1867-1889* (Vienna, 1964), p.3; and Felix Czeike, *Liberale, Christlichsoziale und Sozialdemokratische Kommunalpolitik (1861-1934)* (Vienna, 1962), p. 56.
2. Heinrich Beer, "Eine Geschichte der österreichischen Gewerkschaften," *Der Kampf*, I (1908), 411.
3. See, for example, Engelbert Pernerstorfer, "Zum 13. März," *Arbeiter-Zeitung*, March 13, 1895, p. 2; *A-Z*, March 13, 1898, pp. 2-3; and Steiner, *op. cit.*, p. 3. The *Arbeiter-Zeitung* was the official newspaper of the Austrian Social-Democratic movement. Here and after cited as *A-Z*.
4. Confusion on this point continues to persist. In part, the problem lies in the fact that both Marx and Engels misread the sociological character of the Viennese revolution. In the course of time that misunderstanding was both perpetuated and accepted as true. For an examination of the various aspects of the problem here, see R. John Rath, *The Viennese Revolution of 1848* (Austin, Texas, 1957), pp. 128-129, 240; and A.J.P. Taylor, *The Habsburg Monarchy 1809-1918* (London, 1948), p. 58.
5. Rath, *op. cit.*, p. 240; and Beer, *op. cit.*, p. 411.
6. Rath, *op. cit.*, p. 241.
7. Max Beer, *The General History of Socialism and Social Struggles*, 2 vols. (New York, 1952), vol. II, pp. 47-48.
8. Rath, *op. cit.*, pp. 83, 162.
9. *Ibid.*, pp. 128-219, 240, 295-296.
10. Arthur J. May, *The Hapsburg Monarchy 1867-1914* (Cambridge, Massachusetts, 1960), p. 27; and Edouard Beneš, "Le mouvement ouvrier Tschéchoslovaque," *Le Monde Slave*, II (1918), 241.
11. William A. Jenks, *Austria Under the Iron*

Ring (Charlottesville, Virginia, 1965), p. 159.
12. Jiří Kořalka, "Über die Anfänge der sozialistischen Arbeiterbewegung in der Tschechoslowakei," *Zeitschrift für Geschichtswissenschaft,* IX (1961), 124; Steiner, *op. cit.*, p. 3; and Heinrich Beer, *op. cit.*, p. 412.
13. Max Beer, *op. cit.*, vol. II, p. 163; and Taylor, *op. cit.*, p. 179.
14. Koppel S. Pinson, *Modern Germany* (New York, 1954), pp. 196 ff; and Peter Gay, *The Dilemma of Democratic Socialism: Eduard Bernstein's Challenge to Marx* (New York, 1952), p. 78.
15. G.D.H. Cole, *A History of Socialist Thought,* 5 vols. (London, 1954-60), vol. II, pp. 79-80, and vol. III, part II, p. 524; Oswald Hillebrand, "Die erste sozialdemokratische Organisation in Oesterreich," *Der Kampf,* VI (1913) 350; and Ludwig Brügel, *Geschichte der österreichischen Sozialdemokratie,* 5 vols. (Vienna, 1922-1925), vol. I, p. 98. Here and after cited as Brügel, *Geschichte.*
16. Cole, *op. cit.*, vol. III, part II, p. 524; and Julius Bunzel (ed.), "Eine amtliche Darstellung der Anfänge der österreichischen Arbeiterbewegung," *Vierteljahrsschrift für Sozial-und Wirtschaftsgeschichte,* XII (1914), 284.
17. Bunzel, *ibid.*
18. Robert Preussler, "Erinnerungen aus der Arbeiterbewegung," *Der Kampf,* III (1910), 470. For a fuller discussion of developments in Bohemia, see Jiří Kořalka, "Über die Anfänge der Zusammenarbeit zwischen der Arbeiterbewegung in Deutschland und in den Böhmischen Landern," in Karl Obermann and Josef Polisensky (eds.), *Aus 500 Jahren deutsch-tschechoslowakischer Geschichte* (Berlin, 1958), pp. 311-316.
19. *Ibid.*; Julius Bunzel, *Die Anfänge der modernen Arbeiterbewegung in der Steiermark* (Leipzig, 1913), p. 12; and Julius Bunzel, *Die erste Lassallebewegung in Oesterreich* (Leipzig, 1914), pp. 1-2.
20. Bunzel, "Eine amtliche Darstellung," p. 285.
21. Taylor, *op. cit.*, p. 138; and May, *op. cit.*,

pp. 43-45.
22. William A. Jenks, *The Austrian Electoral Reform of 1907* (New York, 1950), pp. 14-16.
23. From the point of view of the workers, the right to organize had been granted by the liberals only nominally. For example, among other prohibitions the workers were forbidden to form centralized labor organizations; Bunzel, "Die Anfänge," p. 286; and Cole, *op. cit.*, vol. III, part II, p. 525.
24. Karl Höger, "Der Anfang," *A-Z*, January 1, 1905, p. 18.
25. Hans Mommsen, *Die Sozialdemokratie und die Nationalitätenfrage im habsburgerischen Vielvölkerstaat* (Vienna, 1963), p. 47. Oberwinder's knowledge of Lassallean principles was unsurpassed and he continued to hold a belief in their efficacy long after he ceased to take an active role in the movement. As an illustration of this point, see Heinrich Oberwinder, *Sozialismus und Sozialpolitik* (Berlin, 1887), pp. 6-46.
26. Mommsen, *op. cit.*, p. 47; and Jiři Kořalka, "Die deutschösterreichische nationale Frage in den Anfängen der sozialdemokratischen Partei," *Historica*, III (1961), 124-126.
27. Steiner, *op. cit.*, p. 8. The same sort of brotherly attitude also characterized the movement in Bohemia during its initial stages; Emil Strauss, *Geschichte der deutschen Sozialdemokratie Böhmens,* 2 vols. (Prague, 1925-26), vol. I, pp. 112-113. Here and after cited as Strauss, *Geschichte*.
28. Steiner, *op. cit.*, p. 12; a copy of the Hartung program may be found in Klaus Berchtold (ed.), *Österreichische Parteiprogramme 1868-1966* (Vienna, 1967), pp. 111-112.
29. Steiner, *op. cit.*, p. 13.
30. Heinrich Oberwinder, *Die Arbeiterbewegung in Oesterreich* (Vienna, 1875), p. 30; and Steiner, *op. cit.*, pp. 12-13, 15-16.
31. Kořalka, "Die deutsch-österreichische nationale Frage," p. 127; Brügel, *Geschichte,* vol. I, pp. 95-96; and Cole, *op. cit.*, vol. II, p. 237.
32. Kořalka, "Die deutsch-österreichische nationale Frage," pp. 126-128.

33. Steiner, *op. cit.*, pp. 12-13.
34. Kořalka, "Die deutsch-österreichische nationale Frage," p. 128.
35. Cole, *op. cit.*, vol. III, part II, pp. 525-526; and Julius Braunthal, *History of the International 1864-1914*, tr. by Henry Collins and Kenneth Mitchell (New York, 1967), vol. I, p. 212.
36. Anton Schäfer, "Aus der Geschichte der nordböhmischen Arbeiterbewegung," *Der Kampf*, III (1909), 85.
37. Benedikt Kautsky, *Geistige Strömungen im österreichischen Sozialismus* (Vienna, 1953), p. 4.
38. Braunthal, *op. cit.*, p. 117; and Oberwinder, *Die Arbeiterbewegung in Oesterreich*, p. 33.
39. Kořalka, "Über die Anfänge der sozialistischen Arbeiterbewegung," p. 124.
40. For an estimate of Social Democratic strength, see Braunthal, *op. cit.*, pp. 170-171.
41. Hans Fehlinger and Fritz Klenner, *Die österreichische Gewerkschaftsbewegung* (Vienna, 1948), p. 21; and Cole, *op. cit.*, vol. III, part II, pp. 524-525.
42. Charles A. Gulick *Austria from Habsburg to Hitler*, 2 vols. (Berkeley, 1948), vol. I, p. 21. Very similar demands were also heard in Reichenberg; Josef Hannich, *Erinnerungen* (Warnsdorf, 1910), p. 9.
43. Bunzel, "Eine amtliche Darstellung," pp. 287-288.
44. Braunthal, *op. cit.*, p. 212; and Engelbert Pernerstorfer, "Kleine Erinnerungen," *Der Kampf*, III (1910), 378. For a personal glimpse at the tribulations of Austrian socialism at the time and the effect that governmental repression had upon some of the leaders of the movement, see Heinrich Scheu, *Erinnerungen* (Vienna, 1912), pp. 30 ff.
45. Oberwinder, *Sozialismus und Sozialpolitik*, p. 93.
46. It is, of course, impossible to determine the number of organizations that were actually affiliated with the socialist movement - one estimate sets the figure at 197. These organizations centered upon Vienna enrolled thousands of workers in

numerous other industrial centers, including Wiener Neustadt, Korneuburg, Linz, Graz, Prague, Brünn, Reichenberg, Pressburg (Bratislava), Freiberg (Příbor), and Trieste; Braunthal, *op. cit.*, pp. 170-171; and Steiner, *op. cit.*, p. 16. Further evidence relating to this question is suggested in Brügel, *Geschichte,* vol. II, pp. 350-352.

47. Fehlinger and Klenner, *op. cit.*, p. 29; and Cole, *op. cit.*, vol. III, part II, p. 525.
48. Oberwinder, *Sozialismus und Sozialpolitik,* p. 95.
49. Eric Fischer, "The Negotiations for the National Ausgleich in Austria in 1871," *Journal of Central European Affairs,* III (1942), 138.
50. This was the exact same estimate that Lassalle made of the events of 1848, see Thilo Ramm (ed.), *Ferdinand Lassalle: Ausgewählte Texte* (Stuttgart, 1962), pp. 232-236.
51. Mommsen, *op. cit.*, pp. 58-59. Oberwinder seems to have been most impressed by Schäffle and his own expectation was that the minister of commerce would use the power of the state to initiate social change in the empire; on this point, see Oberwinder, *Sozialismus und Sozialpolitik,* pp. 97-99.
52. Emil Strauss, "Die nationale Frage in der Frühzeit der tschechischen Arbeiterbewegung," *Der Kampf,* XIV (1919), 254; Kořalka, "Über die Anfänge der sozialistischen Arbeiterbewegung," pp. 123-126; and Strauss, *Geschichte,* vol. I, p. 254.
53. Eberhard Wolfgramm, "Zur Erforschung der tschechoslowakischen Arbeiterbewegung bis 1918 in der tschechoslowakischen Geschichtswissenschaft," *Zeitschrift für Geschichtswissenschaft,* VIII (1960), 1230.
54. Strauss, "Die nationale Frage," pp. 254-255; and Mommsen, *op. cit.*, p. 81.
55. Mommsen, *op. cit.*, p. 84.
56. Strauss, "Die nationale Frage," p. 255.
57. One side of the conflict is explained in Oberwinder, *Die Arbeiterbewegung in Oesterreich,* pp. 74 ff.

58. Quoted in Steiner, *op. cit.*, p. 61.
59. *Ibid.*
60. The strange twists and turns of Kaler-Reinthal's career have been recorded in Benedikt Kautsky (ed.) *Erinnerungen und Erörterungen von Karl Kautsky* (The Hague, 1960), pp. 323-334.
61. On the matter of Kaler-Reinthal's personality, see Jacques Hannak, *Im Sturm eines Jahrhunderts* (Vienna, 1952), pp. 35-36.
62. Walter Göhring, *Der Gründungsparteitag der österreichischen Sozialdemokratie, Neudörfl 1874* (Vienna, 1974), pp. 11-17; Mommsen, *op. cit.*, p. 58; and Steiner, *op. cit.*, p. 62.
63. Steiner, *op. cit.*, pp. 95-99; and Wolfgramm, *op. cit.*, p. 1230.
64. A discussion of the program may be found in Steiner, *op. cit.*, pp. 99-100; a copy of the Neudörfl party program may be found in Berchtold, *op. cit.*, pp. 115-116. See also Eduard März, "Osterreich vor dem Neudörfler Parteitag. Die Politische und wirtschaftliche Entwicklung 1848-1974," in *Internationale Tagung der Historiker der Arbeiterbewegung. 100 Jahre sozialdemokratischer Parteitag* (1974), p. 21.
65. Pernerstorfer, "Kleine Erinnerungen," p. 379. The split between Oberwinder and Andreas Scheu was made irreparable in these years by Oberwinder's plan to support the liberals who had returned to power; on this particular point, see Benedikt Kautsky, *Erinnerungen*, pp. 309-313.
66. Heinrich Benedikt, *Die wirtschaftliche Entwicklung in der Franz-Joseph Zeit* (Vienna, 1958), p. 124; and Fehlinger and Klenner, *op. cit.*, p. 29.
67. Strauss, "Die nationale Frage," p. 256.
68. Mommsen, *op. cit.*, pp. 89-90.
69. Strauss, "Die nationale Frage," pp. 256-258; and Bauer's Introduction to Victor Adler, *Aufsätze, Reden und Briefe*, 11 parts (2nd ed., Vienna, 1929), part 6, pp. xii-xiii.
70. Mommsen, *op. cit.*, pp. 90-97.
71. Braunthal, *op. cit.*, p. 213; for a discussion of Most's years in Austria, see

Rudolph Rocker, *Johann Most: Das Leben eines Rebellen* (Berlin, 1924), pp. 21-30.
72. Quoted in Benedikt Kautsky, *Erinnerungen*, p. 363.
73. Quoted in Victor Adler, "Vor zehn Jahren," *A-Z*, December 25, 1898, p. 3; for a later assessment of Peukert, see Victor Adler, Peukerts Erinnerungen," *Der Kampf*, VII (1914), pp. 302-307. Peukert recorded his own memories of this period in Austria in his *Erinnerungen eines Proletariers aus der revolutionären Arbeiterbewegung* (Berlin, 1913).
74. Mommsen, *op. cit.*, p. 64.
75. Hannak, *op. cit.*, p. 43.
76. Quoted in Rocker, *op. cit.*, p. 173.
77. Karl Kautsky, "Die Gründung der *Gleichheit*," *A-Z*, December 25, 1906, p. 2.
78. Hannak, *op. cit.*, p. 44.
79. Jenks, *Austria Under the Iron Ring*, p. 161; and Braunthal, *The International*, p. 214.
80. Jenks, *Austria Under the Iron Ring*, pp. 160-161.
81. Brügel, *Geschichte*, vol. III, pp. 263, 312-314; for an interpretation of these events from the anarchist point of view, see August Krcal, *Blätter aus der Geschichte der Arbeiterbewegung Oesterreichs (1867-1894)*, (Zurich, 1913), pp. 33-34.
82. Viktor Adler, "Der Weg nach Hainfeld," *Der Kampf*, II (1909), 145.
83. Jenks, *Austria Under the Iron Ring*, pp.161-162.
84. *Ibid.*, pp. 162-178.
85. *Ibid.*, pp. 179, 185; and Brügel, *Geschichte*, vol. III, pp. 291-296.
86. James Joll, *The Second International 1889-1914* (London, 1955), p. 44.
87. *Ibid.*, Max Ermers, *Victor Adler* (Vienna, 1932), p. 109; and Jenks, *Austria Under the Iron Ring*, pp. 179-195.
88. For a contemporary appraisal of the situation leading up to the passage of the social legislation of the 1880's, see Francesco S. Nitti, *Catholic Socialism*, tr. by Mary Mackintosch (2nd ed., London, 1908), pp. 220-225.
89. Victor Adler, "Der Weg nach Hainfeld," p.

148; and Rocker, *op. cit.*, p. 172.
90. Victor Adler, "Der Weg nach Hainfeld," p. 148; and Benedikt Kautsky, *Erinnerungen*, pp. 363-364. Kautsky's close connection with this newspaper probably led him to overestimate the impact of Marxist ideas upon Austria at this time; on this matter, see footnote 94.
91. Paul Axelrod, "Adler und die russische Sozialdemokratie," *Der Kampf*, V (1912), 440.
92. Benedikt Kautsky, *Erinnerungen*, pp. 227, 231-232.
93. *Ibid.*, pp. 228-229, 313.
94. Kautsky's own views on the significance of Marxism in this period seem to conform more to a preconception than to the actual situation; *ibid.*, pp. 314-317, 332.
95. Rocker, *op. cit.*, p. 182.
96. Pernerstorfer, "Kleine Erinnerungen," p. 376.
97. Julie Braun-Vogelstein, *Ein Menschenleben: Heinrich Braun und sein Schicksal* (Tübingen, 1932), p. 32.
98. Julius Braunthal, *Victor und Friedrich Adler* (Vienna, 1965), pp. 25-26.
99. *Ibid.*, p. 26; and Pernerstorfer, "Kleine Erinnerungen," pp. 376-377. For more on Adler and Pernerstorfer, see Karl Renner, *An die Wende zweier Zeiten: Lebenserrinnerungen* (Vienna, 1946), vol. I, pp. 279-282.
100. Mommsen, *op. cit.*, p. 103.
101. On this matter, see Ermers, *op. cit.*, pp. 250-251; and Mommsen, *op. cit.*, p. 125.
102. Ermers, *op. cit.*, pp. 97-98.
103. Steiner, *op. cit.*, p. 260.
104. Taylor, *op. cit.*, pp. 161-162.
105. P.G.J. Pulzer, *The Rise of Political Anti-Semitism in Germany and Austria* (New York, 1964), p. 150.
106. *Ibid.*
107. Braun-Vogelstein, *op. cit.*, p. 36; and Mommsen, *op. cit.*, p. 104.
108. Braunthal, *Victor und Friedrich Adler*, p.36.
109. Adler's sincerity and earnestness impressed many observers in the 1880's; for example,

see Kautsky's letter to Friedrich Engels dated 7/22/1883 in Benedikt Kautsky (ed.), *Friedrich Engels' Briefwechsel mit Karl Kautsky* (Vienna, 1955), pp. 76-77. For some personal assessments of Adler, see Julius Braunthal, *In Search of the Millenium* (London, 1945), p. 52; and the comments of Otto Bauer quoted in Joll, *op. cit.*, p. 38.

110. Quoted in Ermers, *op. cit.*, p. 152. On the importance of political rights to Lassalle's schema, see Ferdinand Lassalle, *An die Arbeiter Berlins* (3rd. ed., Leipzig, 1872), pp. 15-16; Solo W. Baron, *Die politische Theorie Ferdinand Lassalles* (Leipzig, 1923), pp. 37-44; Thilo Ramm, *Ferdinand Lassalle als Rechts-und Sozialphilosoph* (Meisenheim, 1963), p. 47; for his discussion of the relationship between conscience and the progress of the working class, see Lassalle's *Gesammelte Reden und Schriften,* 12 vols. (Berlin, 1919), vol. II, pp. 215 ff.
111. Braunthal, *The International*, p. 215.
112. See the letter from Kautsky to Engels dated 3/8/1886 in Benedikt Kautsky, *Friedrich Engels' Briefwechsel,* p. 196.
113. Otto Bauer's *Introduction,* p. vii; and Karl Kautsky, "Die Gründung der *Gleichheit*," pp. 2-3.
114. Victor Adler, "Vor zehn Jahren," p. 3.
115. See, for example, the reference in Ermers, *op. cit.*, p. 169.
116. *Ibid.*, pp. 250-251.
117. *Ibid.*, p. 250.
118. Max Adler, "Zur Würdigung Victor Adlers," *Archiv für die Geschichte des Sozialismus und die Arbeiterbewegung,* XI (1925), 176.
119. Lassalle, *Gesammelte Reden und Schriften,* vol. II, p. 215 ff.
120. On this point, see Max Adler, *op. cit.*, p. 176; and Brügel, *Geschichte,* vol. III. p. 374.
121. Mommsen, *op. cit.*, p. 110.
122. Braunthal, *Victor und Friedrich Adler,* p. 54.
123. See the letter from Kautsky to Engels dated 7/31/1888 in Benedikt Kautsky, *Friedrich Engels' Briefwechsel,* pp. 219-220.
124. Braunthal, *Victor und Friedrich Adler,* p. 55.

125. See Kautsky's preface to part XI in Benedikt Kautsky, *Friedrich Engels' Briefwechsel*, p. 213.
126. Ermers, *op. cit.*, p. 174.
127. Krcal, *op. cit.*, pp. 53-54; and Brügel, *Geschichte* vol. III, pp. 380, 386.
128. Victor Adler, "Der Weg nach Hainfeld," p. 151.
129. Brügel, *Geschichte*, vol. III, p. 383.
130. *Ibid.*, p. 385.
131. Otto Bauer, "Die Gesamtpartei," *Der Kampf*, VI (1912), 7.
132. Brügel, *Geschichte*, vol. III, pp. 387-388; the actual program appears, in full, in Berchtold, *op. cit.*, pp. 135-137.
133. Steiner, *op. cit.*, pp. 270-271.
134. Mommsen, *op. cit.*, p. 134.
135. *Ibid.*, p. 139.
136. Victor Adler, "Der Weg nach Hainfeld," p. 153; and "Vor zehn Jahren," p. 3.
137. Mommsen, *op. cit.*, pp. 150 ff.
138. *Verhandlungen des Parteitages der österreichischen Sozialdemokratie in Hainfeld (30./31. Dezember 1888 und 1. Januar 1889)*, p. 3.
139. Brügel, *Geschichte*, vol. IV, p. 5.
140. *Verhandlungen des Parteitages (1888, 1889)*, p.3.
141. Brügel, *Geschichte*, vol. IV, p. 74.
142. Mommsen, *op. cit.*, p. 138.
143. *Verhandlungen des Parteitages (1888, 1889)*, p.3.
144. Bauer's *Introduction*, p. vii.
145. *Verhandlungen des Parteitages (1888, 1889)*, p.8.
146. *Ibid.*, pp. 3-4. For a summation of the program, see William A. Jenks, *Vienna and the Young Hitler* (New York, 1960), pp. 168-169; and Hugo Hantsch, *Die Geschichte Österreichs*, 2 vols. (2nd ed., Graz, 1953), vol. II, pp. 455-457.
147. Carl E. Schorske, *German Social Democracy 1905-1917* (Cambridge, Massachusetts, 1955), pp. 4-5.
148. *Verhandlungen des Parteitages (1888, 1889)*, p. 3.
149. Ermers, *op. cit.*, pp. 174-175; for a penetrating analysis of the function of ideology in the Austrian movement down to 1889, see Franz Strobl, "Zur Ideologie der jungen

österreichischen Arbeiterbewegung," *Weg und Ziel* (1955), pp. 31-45. For more background here, see also volume two of Ferdinand Lassalle's *Reden und Schriften,* 3 vols. (Berlin, 1892).

150. Victor Adler, *Aufsätze, Reden und Briefe,* 11 parts (1st ed., Vienna 1922-25), part 4, p. 88; and *Verhandlungen des Parteitages (1888, 1889),* pp. 32-39, 49-51.
151. *Verhandlungen des Parteitages (1888, 1889),* pp. 37-38.
152. *Ibid.,* pp. 49-51.
153. *Ibid.,* pp. 1-16.
154. *Ibid.,* p. 26; Benedikt Kautsky, *Friedrich Engels' Briefwechsel,* p. 214; and Ermers, *op. cit.,* p. 206.
155. *Gleichheit* ceased publication after Adler and its chief editor Ludwig Bretschneider were accused of printing anarchist diatribes by a provincial court. Its successor, the *Arbeiter-Zeitung,* appeared for the first time on July 12, 1889; Brügel, *Geschichte,* vol. IV, pp. 21-31.
156. See Adler's speech to the congress in *Protokoll des Internationalen Arbeiter-Congresses zu Paris (1889),* pp. 43-45; and Cole, *op. cit.,* vol. III, part I, p. 21.
157. Brügel, *Geschichte,* vol. IV, p. 14.

Chapter II. *The Growth of Organization*

1. Fritz Klenner, *Die österreichischen Gewerkschaften,* 2 vols. (Vienna, 1951-53), vol. I, pp. 242-244. All future references will be to volume I.
2. Heinrich Beer, "Der fünfte Gewerkschaftskongress," *Der Kampf,* I (1907), 49; and Klenner, *ibid.*
3. Brügel, *Geschichte,* vol. IV, pp. 10-11.
4. *Protokoll des Internationalen Arbeiter-Congresses (1889),* pp. 43-44; and Edward Crankshaw, *The Fall of the House of Habsburg* (New York, 1963), p. 297.
5. Julius Deutsch, *Geschichte der österreichischen Gewerkschaftsbewegung* (Vienna, 1908),

p. 179.
6. The Budweis congress of 1893 was actually the third congress of the unified Czech party founded originally in 1887; Otto Bauer, "Die Gesamtpartei," p. 8.
7. Mommsen, *op. cit.*, p. 183.
8. Andrew G. Whiteside, "Industrial Transformation, Population Movement and German Nationalism in Bohemia," *Zeitschrift für Ostforschung*, X (1961, 264; and Mommsen, *op. cit.*, pp. 38 ff.
9. Brügel, *Geschichte*, vol. IV, pp. 81 ff.
10. Anton Schrammel, "Aus der nordwestböhmischen Arbeiterbewegung," *Der Kampf*, VI (1912), 116-117; and Gustav Kränkel,"Aus der Parteigeschichte Westböhmens," *Der Kampf*, III (1910), 428-431.
11. Quoted in Ermers, *op. cit.*, p. 275.
12. Cole, *op. cit.*, vol. III, part 1, pp. 7 ff; Braunthal, *Victor und Friedrich Adler*, p. 77; and Anton Hueber, "Partei und Gewerkschaften in Oesterreich," *Der Kampf*, I (1907), 12.
13. Joll, *op. cit.*, pp. 50-51.
14. *Protokoll des Internationalen Sozialistischen Arbeiterkongresses zu Zürich (1893)*, p. 33; and Brügel, *Geschichte*, vol. IV, p. 221. The original resolution on the May Day celebration may be found in *Protokoll des Internationalen Arbeiter-Congresses (1889)*, p. 123.
15. Schäfer, *op. cit.*, p. 87; Braunthal, *Victor und Friedrich Adler*, p. 80; and *Verhandlungen des zweiten österreichischen sozialdemokratischen Parteitages abgehalten zu Wien am 28., 29. und 30. Juni 1891*, p. 32.
16. Brügel, *Geschichte*, vol. IV, pp. 153-156; and Hannak, *op. cit.*, pp. 77-78.
17. Brügel, *Geschichte*, vol. IV, p. 181.
18. Hannak, *op. cit.*, pp. 78-80.
19. *Verhandlungen des...Parteitages (1891)*, pp. 25-27.
20. The proposals put forward by Pokorny were worked out by a committee composed of twenty-four leading Social Democrats, and were later accepted almost unanimously; *ibid.*, pp. 142-144.

21. *Ibid.*, p. 144.
22. *Ibid.*, pp. 144, 147.
23. The official party newspapers at this time and their unofficial areas of jurisdiction were Vienna and Lower Austria, *Arbeiter-Zeitung* (Vienna); German Moravia and Silesia, *Volksfreund* (Brünn); Slavic Moravia, *Rovnost* (Brünn); German Bohemia, *Freigeist* (Reichenberg); Slavic Bohemia, *Sozialni demokrat* (Prague); Alpinelands, *Arbeiterwille* (Graz); Italian areas *Avanti* (Trieste); Polish areas, *Praca* (Lemberg); and the Slavic element in Vienna, *Dělnicke Listý*; *ibid.*, p. 145.
24. *Ibid.*, pp. 31-33.
25. Bauer, "Die Gesamtpartei," p. 10. Hybeš' attitude toward unification can only be described as an ambiguous one. Ever since the late 1880's he had stood with Adler and the party hierarchy in favor of unification, working energetically to bring it about. But in his own mind unification was something to be differentiated from integration, a distinction that later Czech leaders would also make to the dismay of their German counterparts.
26. *Verhandlungen des dritten österreichischen sozialdemokratischen Parteitages abgehalten zu Wien am 5., 6., 8., und 9. Juni 1892*, pp. 140-145.
27. *Ibid.*, pp. 130-131.
28. *Ibid.*, p. 20.
29. *Ibid.*, pp. 118-119.
30. *Ibid.*, pp. 169-171. The original nine members of the central executive in Vienna were Adler, Reumann, Popp, Ellenbogen, Pokorny, Höger, Presl. Schrammel and Newole, a situation weighing heavily in favor of the Germans; *ibid.*, p. 147.
31. *Ibid.*, pp. 117-118.
32. Krcal, *op. cit.*, pp. 71, 77.
33. Braunthal, *Victor und Friedrich Adler*, pp. 77-78.
34. *Verhandlungen des...Parteitages (1892)*, p. 85. Adler's views directly contradicted the teachings of Marx, especially Marx's law of increasing misery which argues that

the proletariat within capitalism must and
will suffer ever-increasing pauperization.
In the long run, capitalist oppression in
the form of wide-spread unemployment and
depressed wages would drive the working
class to violent revolution. Marx's own
position here might best be summarized as,
"Whoever is the poorest is the most
revolutionary." On this matter, see R.N.
Carew Hunt, *The Theory and Practice of
Communism* (New York, 1951), pp. 58-60.
35. *Verhandlungen des...Parteitages (1892)*, pp.
74-75. For a penetrating analysis of Adler's
defense of moderation and rejection of
extremism, see Axelrod, *op. cit.*, p. 439.
36. Schorske, *op. cit.*, p. 120.
37. Kurt Shell, *The Transformation of Austrian
Socialism* (New York, 1962), pp. 9-10.
38. A discussion of the general background to
this development may be found in Mommsen,
op. cit., p. 247.
39. *Verhandlungen des vierten österreichischen
sozialdemokratischen Parteitages abgehalten
zu Wien vom 25. bis einschliesslich 31.
März 1894*, pp. 3-4.
40. *Ibid.*, p. 15.
41. *Ibid.*, pp. 15-25.
42. *Ibid.*, p. 45.
43. *Ibid.*, p. 194.
44. Bauer, "Die Gesamtpartei," p. 10.
45. *Verhandlungen des fünften österreichischen
sozialdemokratischen Parteitages abgehalten
zu Prag vom 5. bis einschliesslich 11.
April 1896*, pp. 103-104.
46. Mommsen, *op. cit.*, p. 247.
47. *Ibid.*, p. 260; and *Verhandlungen des...
Parteitages (1896)*, p. 126.
48. Mommsen, *op. cit.*, p. 261.
49. As a stop-gap measure the party executive
was expanded in 1896 to include some sixteen members who were to direct and control
the activities of the party. Membership
on the executive committee was roughly
determined by a system of proportional
representation for the various national
groups in the party; *Verhandlungen des...
Parteitages (1896)*, pp. 103, 179-180.

50. *Verhandlungen des sechsten österreichischen sozialdemokratischen Parteitages zu Wien vom 6. bis einschliesslich 12. Juni 1897*, pp. 113-114.
51. The official reasoning behind this decision ran: "The decision first laid down at the Prague party congress and made specific by the sixth party congress to organize Austrian Social Democracy according to independent national groups has had as its goal finding the most practical means possible of organizing the efforts of the multi-lingual proletariat in Austria, aiming as it does at overcoming the difficulties posed by differences of language. In so doing, we recognize the utility of granting full independence to the Social-Democratic organization of every tongue, and thereby believe...that we are creating in the general party and in the general executive those institutions which will better serve ...the common good. *National independence and international unanimity are the fundamental principles of our organization;*" *ibid.*, p. 220. The resolution, from which the above excerpt was taken, was also published in the *A-Z*, June 12, 1897, p. 2.
52. *Verhandlungen des...Parteitages (1897)*, pp. 7, 114.
53. *Ibid.*, pp. 118-119.
54. *Ibid.*, pp. 124-125.
55. *Ibid.*, pp. 130-131.
56. *A-Z*, June 13, 1897, p. 1.
57. *Verhandlungen des...Parteitages (1897)*, p. 113, and *A-Z*, June 10, 1897, p. 2.
58. Ignaz Daszyński, "Die Lage in Oesterreich," *Die Neue Zeit*, XVI (1898), 721-722.
59. Pernerstorfer, "Kleine Erinnerungen," p. 379.
60. Engelbert Pernerstorfer, "Ein kurzes Wort zur Frage des Sozialismus und Nationalismus," *Der Kampf*, V (1911), 57.
61. Hannak, *op. cit.*, p. 105.
62. For an example of the party's response, see *A-Z*, February 16, 1896, p. 2.
63. *Verhandlungen des...Parteitages (1897)*, pp. 22-23.
64. *Ibid.*, p. 8.

65. Franz Soukup, "Die czechische Sozialdemokratie," *Die Zeit,* XXIV (1900), 19; Ferdinand Skaret, "Unsere politische Parteiorganisation," *Der Kampf,* II (1909), 554; and Karl Schwechler, *Die österreichische Sozialdemokratie* (3rd ed., Vienna, 1908), p. 30.
66. For a discussion of the relevance of the press to party activity, see Karl Kautsky, "Das Monopol auf die Presse," *A-Z,* January 1, 1895, p. 2; and Soukup, *op. cit.,* p. 19.
67. Further information on the founding of the *Arbeiter-Zeitung* may be found in Braunthal, *In Search of the Millenium,* p. 247; and Brügel, *Geschichte,* vol. IV, p. 280.
68. Soukup, *op. cit.,* p. 19; and Braunthal, *Victor und Friedrich Adler,* p. 98.
69. Hueber, *op. cit.,* p. 12.
70. Heinrich Beer, "Eine Geschichte der österreichischen Gewerkschaften," p. 414; Fehlinger and Klenner, *op. cit.,* pp. 32-36; Hannak, *op. cit.,* p. 75; Johann C. Allmeyer-Beck, *Minister-präsident Baron Beck* (Munich, 1956), p. 83; and Klenner, *op. cit.,* pp. 161-163.
71. Klenner, *op. cit.,* pp. 163-168.
72. *Ibid.,* p. 167.
73. Deutsch, *op. cit.,* p. 179.
74. Heinrich Beer, "Der fünfte Gewerkschaftskongress," p. 50; and Hueber, *op. cit.,* p. 13.
75. Heinrich Beer, "Der fünfte Gewerkschaftskongress," p. 50.
76. Klenner, *op. cit.,* pp. 172-174.
77. *Ibid.,* p. 174.
78. *Protokoll über die Verhandlungen des 1. Gewerkschaftskongresses abgehalten vom 24. bis 27. Dezember 1893 in Wien,* pp. 5, 31-32.
79. Deutsch, *op. cit.,* pp. 197 ff; and Edouard Beneš, "Le Syndicalisme en Bohême," *Le Mouvement Socialiste,* XXII (1908), 378-379.
80. *Protokoll...des...Gewerkschaftskongresses (1893),* pp. 21-24. The members of the original trade-union commission elected in 1893 were Ludwig Exner, Johann Smitka, Anna Boschek, Anton Hueber, Ludwig Handel, Franz Nader, Robert Preussler, Karl Borgula,

Johann Kahay, Michael Hackel, Ludwig Unger, Josef Mornik, Karl Kořinek and Willibard Pekař. In 1896, Handel and Unger were dropped from the commission (Unger being shifted to the control commission) and were replaced by Josef Tomschik and Wilhelm Kofler. In the same year, the following industrial groups were represented on the commission: clothing, wood-working, bookbinding, building trades, chemicals, metallurgy, textiles, glass and ceramics, food handling, transport and commerce; *Protokoll des II. Österreichischen Gewerkschaftskongresses abgehalten vom 25. bis 29. Dezember 1896*, p. vii.

81. *Protokoll...des...Gewerkschaftskongresses (1893)*, pp. 23-24, 26-29; and *Die Gewerkschaft*, August 1, 1894, pp. 1-2.
82. Braunthal, *Victor und Friedrich Adler*, p. 79.
83. *Protokoll...des...Gewerkschaftskongresses (1893)*, p. 67. Eventually those ties were established with members of the trade-union commission serving on the party's executive committee as well; as an illustration, see here *Exekutivprotokolle der sozialdemokratischen Partei Österreichs*, II (October 8, 1903).
84. *Protokoll...des...Gewerkschaftskongresses (1893)*, pp. 61-69.
85. Jenks, *The Austrian Electoral Reform of 1907*, p. 21.
86. *Ibid.*
87. Victor Adler, *Aufsätze*, 2nd ed., part 10, p. 120.
88. *Ibid.*, pp. 120-121.
89. Bauer's *Introduction*, p. xxi; and *A-Z*, May 8, 1896, p. 2.
90. *Protokoll...des...Gewerkschaftskongresses (1893)*, p. 101.
91. Julius Deutsch, "Anton Hueber," *Neue Österreichische Biographie ab 1815*, 14 vols. (Vienna and Zurich, 1923-1960), vol. XIV, pp. 123-124.
92. *Verhandlungen des...Parteitages (1894)*, pp. 55-59, 75-82, 85-86, 105; and Brügel, *Geschichte*, vol. IV, p. 273.

93. Brügel, *Geschichte,* vol. IV, p. 233; and Hannak, *op. cit.,* pp. 91-92.
94. Klenner, *op. cit.,* pp. 202-204; Heinrich Beer, "Der fünfte Gewerkschaftskongress," p. 50; and *Thätigkeitsbericht der Gewerkschafts-Kommission Oesterreichs für 1894 bis 1896,* pp. 47-48.
95. Mommsen, *op. cit.,* p. 215. For another side to the controversy, see the letter from Konrad Kubala to Victor Adler dated 9/10/1896 in *Der Nachlass Victor Adlers.*
96. *A-Z,* September 17, 1896, p. 2.
97. Deutsch, *Geschichte der österreichischen Gewerkschaften,* pp. 225-226.
98. *Protokoll des...Gewerkschaftskongresses (1896),* pp. 24-27.
99. *Ibid.,* pp. 18-24.
100. *Ibid.,* pp. 29-30.
101. *Ibid.,* pp. 39-40.
102. *Ibid.,* pp. 42-43.
103. *Ibid.,* p. 52.
104. In no mood for compromise, the congress even rejected a modest proposal to increase by one the number of Czech representatives sitting on the existing trade-union commission; *ibid.,* pp. 65-66, 70; Fehlinger and Klenner, *op. cit.,* p. 38; and Wilhelm Kulemann, *Die Gewerkschaftsbewegung* (Jena, 1900), p. 95.
105. Franz Domes, "Wohin steuert der tschechische Separatismus in der Gewerkschaft?"*Der Kampf,* III (1910), 555; and Mommsen, *op. cit.,* p. 228.
106. Fehlinger and Klenner, *op. cit.,* p. 38. The total number of organized Czech workers in Bohemia in 1896 was 31,658, in Moravia 8,674, in Silesia 1,473; Beneš, "Le Syndicalisme en Bohême," p. 379.
107. Mommsen, *op. cit.,* p. 229. Detailed information on the financial resources available to the Viennese commission may be found in Kulemann, *op. cit.,* p. 100.
108. Acceptance of the mandates of three representatives from the Czech trade-union commission by the congress's credentials commission amounted to formal recognition; *Protokoll über die Verhandlungen des III.*

österreichischen Gewerkschafts-Congresses abgehalten zu Wien vom 11. bis 15. Juni 1900, pp. 127, 184; Fehlinger and Klenner op. cit., p. 38; and Deutsch, Geschichte der österreichischen Gewerkschaftsbewegung, p. 257.

109. The labor picture at this time was highlighted by two spectacular walkouts, the general strike of 20,000 miners at Karwin-Ostrau (Ostrava-Karviná) in Silesia in 1896 for higher wages and the strike of 12,000 textile workers in Brünn in 1899 for shorter hours. Strike statistics for the general period 1895-1900 reveal a rising crescendo of labor unrest that peaked at the end of the century. In 1895 only 28,000 workers struck; in 1896, the figure increased to 66,000. The total number of workdays lost in 1895, as a result of strikes, was 300,000 whereas in 1896 it rose to 900,000. In 1900 some 105,000 workers went out on strike, and the number of workdays lost jumped to 3,484,000 indicating that the duration of the average strike was now much longer, A-Z, May 24, 1899, p. 1; A-Z, June 25, 1899, p. 1; A-Z, January 5, 1902, p. 1; Rechenschaftsbericht der Gewerkschafts-Commission Oesterreichs über die Thätigkeit vom 1. Jänner 1897 bis zum 31. Dezember 1899. pp. 108-117; and Beneš, "Le Syndicalisme en Bohême," p. 458.

110. Protokoll...des...Gewerkschafts-Congresses (1900), pp. 128, 163, 166, 192.

111. Heinrich Beer, "Der fünfte Gewerkschaftskongress," p. 50.

112. "Der Aufstieg einer Klasse," Wissenschaft und Weltbild, IV (1951), 312; and Gulick, op. cit., vol. I, p. 28.

113. Whiteside, op. cit., p. 262; and Andrew G. Whiteside, Austrian National Socialism before 1918 (The Hague, 1962), pp. 72-73.

114. See, for example, A-Z, May 23, 1897, p. 3.

115. Verhandlungen des...Parteitages (1897), pp. 198, 201-202; Victor Adler, Aufsätze, 2nd ed., part 7, pp. 178-179; and Karl Cermak, "Partei, Gewerkschaft und Genossenschaft," Der Kampf, VI (1913), 371-372.

116. *Verhandlungen des...Parteitages (1897)*, pp. 194-198; and *A-Z*, June 13, 1897, p. 3.
117. *Verhandlungen des...Parteitages (1897)*, p. 207; Victor Adler, *Aufsätze*, 2nd ed., part 7, p. 179; and Adelheid Popp, "Die erzieherische Bedeutung der Konsumvereine," *Der Kampf*, I (1907), 16.
118. *Verhandlungen des Gesammtparteitages der Sozialdemokratie in Oesterreich abgehalten zu Brünn vom 24. bis 29. September 1899*, pp. 108-119; Benno Karpeles, "Partei und Konsumvereine," *Der Kampf*, III (1910), 554; and *Exekutivprotokolle der sozialdemokratischen Partei Österreichs*, I (November 30, 1899).
119. *Verhandlungen des Gesammtparteitages (1899)*, p. 109.
120. *Ibid.*, pp. 109-113.
121. *A-Z*, April 8, 1909, p. 2.
122. Hannak, *op. cit.*, pp. 82-83.
123. *Ibid.*, pp. 83-84; and *Verhandlungen des Gesammtparteitages (1899)*, pp. 126-133.
124. Two years later the figure was up to 12,000; Adelheid Popp, "Wie stärken wir die Partei," *A-Z*, September 19, 1909, p. 13; and *A-Z*, January 4, 1911, p. 1.
125. Robert Danneberg, "Die österreichische Jugendorganisation," *Der Kampf*, I (1908), 511.
126. *Protokoll über die Verhandlungen des Parteitages der deutschen sozialdemokratischen Arbeiterpartei in Oesterreich abgehalten in Wien vom 30. September bis 4. Oktober 1907*, p. 21.
127. *A-Z*, July 13, 1913, pp. 9-10.
128. Robert Danneberg, "Sozialdemokratische Erziehungsarbeit," *Der Kampf*, II (1909), 453.
129. Ludwig Brügel, *Soziale Gesetzgebung in Österreich von 1848 bis 1918* (Vienna, 1919), p. 147.
130. *A-Z*, May 7, 1897, p. 8.
131. Brügel, *Soziale Gesetzgebung*, p. 145.
132. *Bericht des Verbandes der Genossenschafts-Krankenkassen Wiens sammt der Statistik der Verbandskassen für das Jahr 1895* (Vienna, 1896), p. 5.

133. *A-Z*, May 7, 1897, p. 8.
134. Jakob Brod, "Die Belastung der Industrie durch die Arbeiterversicherung," *Der Kampf*, III (1908), 81.
135. *Die Krankenkasse als sozialpolitische Einrichtung* (Vienna, 1925), p. 4.
136. Klenner, *op. cit.*, p. 28; and *Bericht des Verbandes der Genossenschafts-Krankenkassen Wiens sammt der Statistik der Verbandskassen für das Jahr 1900* (Vienna, 1901), p. 74.
137. *A-Z*, June 30, 1896, p. 1.
138. *A-Z*, October 20, 1895, p. 6; *A-Z*, November 10, 1895, p. 2; *A-Z*, January 24, 1896, p. 2; and *A-Z*, December 6, 1899, p. 7.
139. *A-Z*, July 4, 1896, p. 8; *A-Z*, December 6, 1899, p. 7; Richard Charmatz, *Lebensbilder aus der Geschichte Österreichs* (Vienna, 1947), p. 180; and Helga Schmidt and Felix Czeike, *Franz Schuhmeier* (Vienna, 1964), p. 19.
140. For some examples of the party's organizational efforts, see *Exekutivprotokolle der sozialdemokratischen Partei Österreichs*, I (June 6, 1898-December 29, 1898).

Chapter III. *The Politics of Reform*

1. *Verhandlungen des Parteitages (1888, 1889)*, p. 3; and Strobl, *op. cit.*, p. 45.
2. Francis Coker, *Recent Political Thought* (New York, 1934), p. 66.
3. Adler's remarks were contained in an essay that he wrote in 1890 which appeared under the revealing title of "Lassalle und die Arbeiterbewegung von heute," Victor Adler, *Aufsätze*, 2nd ed., part 4, pp. 83-87.
4. Ermers, *op. cit.*, pp. 215-216; and Max Adler, *op. cit.*, pp. 177-178.
5. Brügel, *Geschichte*, vol. IV, p. 100.
6. Strobl, *op. cit.*, pp. 31-45. Strobl's article is extremely valuable in that it pinpoints the fact that the assimilation of Marxist ideas by the Austrian party was indeed a prolonged process but he erroneous-

ly assumes that the process had gone deeper in 1889 than it actually had. Jacques Droz, "Die Sozialdemokratie in Österreich-Ungarn 1867-1914," in Jacques Droz (ed.), *Geschichte der Sozialismus von 1875 bis 1918* (Frankfurt, 1975), pp. 123-126.

7. Braunthal, *Victor und Friedrich Adler*, p. 109; and Ermers, *op. cit.*, pp. 251-252.
8. *Verhandlungen des...Parteitages (1894)*, p. 78.
9. *Verhandlungen des Parteitages (1888, 1889)*, p. 3; and Schwechler, *op. cit.*, p. 64.
10. Richard Charmatz, *Deutsch-österreichische Politik* (Leipzig, 1907), pp. 300-301.
11. *Ibid.*, p. 301.
12. August Krcal, *Zur Geschichte Arbeiter-Bewegung Oesterreichs 1867-1894* (Berlin, 1894), pp. 46-47; and Karl F. Kocmata, *Dr. Victor Adler und die österreichische Arbeiterbewegung* (2nd ed., Vienna, 1920), p. 7. The final blow for the anarchists came in 1893 when they were excluded from the Second International and the ranks of most of the socialist parties of Europe; *Protokoll des Internationalen...Arbeiter-kongresses (1893)*, pp. 1-10; and Joll, *op. cit.*, p. 71.
13. Braunthal, *Victor und Friedrich Adler*, pp. 77-78.
14. Kocmata, *op. cit.*, p. 10; and Ermers, *op. cit.*, pp. 253-255. Robert Scheu, the son of the early party leader, once referred to Adler as a "conservative politician who closed his eyes to revolution."
15. Ermers, *op. cit.*, pp. 211-212; and Charles F. Elliott, "Quis Custodiet Sacra? Problems of Marxist Revisionism," *Journal of the History of Ideas*, XXVII (1967), 73. On the occasion of the conversion of the *Arbeiter-Zeitung* into a daily on January 1, 1895, Engels sent the paper a congratulatory note which sanctioned the party's policy of moderation and urged restraint upon the Austrian socialist movement. His note ran, in part, as follows: "The first daily newspaper is everywhere characterized as an epoch-making advance in the life of a party,

especially a workers' party. It is the first position from which the party - in the area of the press at least - can combat its opponents with their own weapons. This position you have now conquered; now there is a second one: the franchise and parliament, and this likewise will be assured to you, if you act prudently,...doing what is opportune and, when necessary, waiting, which is in itself to understand when to act;" quoted in Brügel, *Geschichte,* vol. IV, p. 279.

16. Among other things, the Austrian trade-union commission was specifically charged with responsibility for limiting the impact of capitalist exploitation upon the working class; *Protokoll...des...Gewerkschaftskongresses (1893),* pp. 22-23; *Protokoll des...Gewerkschaftskongresses (1896),* pp. 112, 119-120; Hueber, *op. cit.,* p. 12; and Otto Bauer, "Gewerkschaften und Sozialismus," *Der Kampf,* VII (1914), 241.
17. *Verhandlungen des...Parteitages (1892),* p. 75.
18. *Ibid.*
19. The tensions existing between and among these parties are described in Jenks, *Austria Under the Iron Ring,* pp. 275-276.
20. *Verhandlungen des Parteitages (1888, 1889),* p. 4; and Adolf Braun, "Hainfeld," *Der Kampf,* VII (1914), 155.
21. Otto Bauer, "Die Grundfrage unserer Taktik," *Der Kampf,* VII (1913), 53; Schwechler, *op. cit.,* pp. 64-68; and Charmatz, *Deutschösterreichische Politik,* p. 303.
22. See Walther Federn's Introduction in Gulick, *op. cit.,* vol. I, p. vii. The party, with Adler in the lead, insisted, for example, that the social problem could only be settled in parliament, a view which according to two party stalwarts, Dolejši and Neumann, ran counter to the teachings of Marx. The mere suggestion by them of such a "heretical" view caused a veritable storm of protest at the Viennese party congress of 1892; *Verhandlungen des...Parteitages (1892),* pp. 95-96.

23. Bauer, "Gewerkschaften und Sozialdemokratie," p. 241; and Walter F. Hahn, "The Socialist Party of Austria: Retreat from Marx," *Journal of Central European Affairs*, XV (1955), 119.
24. Kocmata, *op. cit.*, p. 9; Mommsen, *op. cit.*, p. 303; and Hahn, *op. cit.*, p. 119.
25. Ermers, *op. cit.*, p. 260.
26. Gustav Strakosch-Grassmann, *Das allgemeine Wahlrecht in Österreich seit 1848* (Leipzig, 1906), p. 54.
27. Victor Adler, *Das allgemeine, gleiche und direkte Wahlrecht und das Wahlunrecht in Österreich* (Vienna, 1893), p. 5.
28. This view, hardly credible to those who know the political history of Austria prior to 1914, was held by other political parties, but for diverse reasons, Jenks, *The Austrian Electoral Reform of 1907*, pp. 106-107.
29. Victor Adler, *Das...Wahlrecht*, p. 6.
30. *Ibid.*, p. 7.
31. Joseph Redlich, *Emperor Francis Joseph of Austria* (New York, 1929), p. 441.
32. Jenks, *Austria Under the Iron Ring*, p. 293.
33. *Verhandlungen des Parteitages (1888, 1889)*, p. 9.
34. *Ibid.*, p. 24.
35. See Bebel's speech to the congress, in *Protokoll des Internationalen...Arbeiterkongresses (1893)*, pp. 7-8.
36. Richard Charmatz, *Österreichs innere Geschichte von 1848 bis 1907*, 2 vols. (2nd ed., Leipzig, 1911-12), vol. II, p. 79; Jenks, *Austria Under the Iron Ring*, p. 293; and Schwechler, *op. cit.*, p. 25.
37. See the letter from Engels to Kautsky dated 3/11/93 in Benedikt Kautsky, *Friedrich Engels' Briefwechsel*, p. 391.
38. *Ibid.*, pp. 391-392.
39. Bauer's *Introduction*, p. viii; and Benedikt Kautsky, *Geistige Strömungen*, p. 7.
40. Brügel, *Geschichte*, vol. IV, pp. 188-189.
41. Victor Adler, "Die Lage in Oesterreich und der sozialdemokratische Parteitag," *Die Neue Zeit*, XII (1893-1894), 234.
42. Charmatz, *Österreichs innere Geschichte*, vol. II, p. 80.

43. Hannak, *op. cit.*, pp. 91-93.
44. Bauer's *Introduction*, p. x. On at least one occasion, Adler expressed the fear that Social-Democratic involvement in the political process might have the effect of making the party seem opportunistic; see his remarks to Engels quoted in Max Adler, *op. cit.*, p. 177.
45. Hannak, *op. cit.*, p. 91.
46. May, *op. cit.*, p. 323.
47. Strauss, *Geschichte*, vol. II, pp. 48-49.
48. The support that Hueber received at the congress came principally from two sources, the miners, primarily of Karwin-Ostrau, and certain radical working-class circles in Vienna; *ibid.*, p. 48; and Victor Adler, "Die Lage in Oesterreich und der sozialdemokratische Parteitag," pp. 236-238.
49. See the letter from Kautsky to Engels dated 2/11/1893 in Benedikt Kautsky, *Friedrich Engels' Briefwechsel*, p. 394.
50. *Verhandlungen des...Parteitages (1894)*, pp. 50-55.
51. *Ibid.*, pp. 98-99; and Viktor Adler, "Bebel und die Sozialdemokratie in Oesterreich," *Der Kampf*, III (1910), pp. 193-194.
52. *Verhandlungen des...Parteitages (1894)*, pp. 50-105.
53. *Ibid.*, p. 105.
54. *Ibid.*
55. Victor Adler, "Die Lage in Oesterreich und der sozialdemokratische Parteitag," pp. 202-204, 234-235. Interestingly, the Social Democrats saw an obvious historical parallel between Bismarck's introduction of universal manhood suffrage and Taaffe's attempt to do so.
56. May, *op. cit.*, p. 323; Strauss, *Geschichte*, vol. II, p. 49; and Strakosch-Grassmann, *op. cit.*, p. 60. If the bill passed, some 1,299,845 voters would have selected the thirteen workers' representatives, some 1,167,357 small taxpayers would have elected the other 34 deputies in the fifth curia, while 1,984,628 "privileged" voters would have continued to select the 353 deputies assigned to the first four curiae.

57. See, for example, Ellenbogen's speech to the party in *Verhandlungen des...Parteitages (1894)*, pp. 52-53; and Adler's comments two years later in *A-Z*, May 8, 1896, p. 2.
58. May, *op. cit.*, p. 323; and Robert Kann, *The Multinational Empire*, 2 vols. (New York, 1950), vol. I, p. 301.
59. *A-Z*, June 19, 1895, p. 1. On the validity of Social-Democratic claims here, see Karl Hugelmann, "Das österreichische Parlament bis zur Staatskatastrophe und Österreichs Zukunft," *Archiv für Politik und Geschichte*, IV (1925), 250-251.
60. *A-Z*, June 21, 1895, p. 2.
61. Gustav Kolmer (ed.), *Parlament und Verfassung in Oesterreich*, 8 vols. (Vienna, 1902-1914), vol. VI, p. v.
62. Strauss, *Geschichte*, vol. II, pp. 49-50.
63. *A-Z*, November 6, 1895, p. 1.
64. Strakosch-Grassmann, *op. cit.*, p. 61.
65. *Ibid.*; May, *op. cit.*, p. 324; and Heinrich Rauchberg, *Die statistische Unterlagen der österreichischen Wahlreform* (Brünn, 1907), p. 13. The old curial system which allotted 85 mandates to the great landowners, 21 to the chambers of commerce and 117 and 136 to the privileged urban and rural voters was left untouched; Kolmer, *op. cit.*, vol. VI, p. 157.
66. Charmatz, *Österreichs innere Geschichte*, vol. II, pp. 102-103.
67. Brügel, *Geschichte*, vol. IV, p. 299.
68. Schwechler, *op. cit.*, p. 27. The mid-Moravian proposals actually took the form of two resolutions, each of which was decisively defeated; *Verhandlungen des... Parteitages (1896)*, pp. 58, 91.
69. *Ibid.*, pp. 50, 81-82.
70. *Ibid.*, pp. 61, 84-85.
71. *Ibid.*, pp. 52-61.
72. *Ibid.*, p. 92. The resolution ran in part: "Badeni's electoral reform does not in any way speak to either the will or the needs of the working people; it has been prompted by the needs of the moment but is only a miserable patch job....Therefore, the struggle to achieve universal suffrage must

be carried forth with all the energy possible."
73. Charmatz, Österreichs innere Geschichte, vol. II, p. 105.
74. Brügel, Geschichte, vol. IV, p. 305.
75. Strauss, Geschichte, vol. II, p. 53.
76. Julius Deutsch, Geschichte der österreichischen Gewerkschaftsbewegung, 2 vols. (Vienna, 1929-1932), vol. I, p. 360. Deutsch's two-volume study of the Austrian Labor movement, which he did later in his life, was an elaboration of his earlier work of the same title and carried the story, of course, up past 1907. Here and after cited as Deutsch, Geschichte, with appropriate volume number.
77. Kurt Skalnik, Dr. Karl Lueger (Vienna, 1954), pp. 86-113.
78. Strauss, Geschichte, vol. II, p. 54; and Schwechler, op. cit., p. 28.
79. Jenks, The Austrian Electoral Reform of 1907, p. 25. For a breakdown of the various parties and clubs, see the table in Kolmer, op. cit., vol. VI, p. 218.
80. Verhandlungen des Parteitages (1888, 1889), p. 4; and Allmeyer-Beck, op. cit., p. 133.
81. Verhandlungen des...Parteitages (1897), pp. 70-73.
82. Ibid., pp. 75-76.
83. Rauchberg, op. cit., p. 17; and Hannak, op. cit., p. 105.
84. Arthur C. Kogan, "The Social Democrats and the Conflict of Nationalities in the Habsburg Monarch," The Journal of Modern History, XXI (1949), 205.
85. Compare Hugelmann, op. cit., p. 254, with Charmatz, Österreichs innere Geschichte, vol. II, pp. 106-108.
86. A-Z, December 20, 1902, p. 1.
87. Suzanne G. Konirsh, "Constitutional Aspects of the Struggle between Germans and Czechs in the Austro-Hungarian Monarchy," The Journal of Modern History, XXVII (1955), 232.
88. Richard Charmatz, Österreichs äussere und innere Politik von 1895 bis 1914 (Leipzig, 1918), p. 51.

89. *Verhandlungen des...Parteitages (1899)*, p. 47; Hannak, *op. cit.*, pp. 116-117; and *Protokoll über die Verhandlungen des Gesammtparteitages der sozialdemokratischen Arbeiterpartei in Oesterreich abgehalten zu Wien vom 2. bis 6. November 1901*, p. 79.
90. *Verhandlungen des Parteitages der deutschen Sozialdemokratie Oesterreichs abgehalten zu Linz vom 29. Mai bis einschliesslich 1. Juni 1898*, p. 48; and *Verhandlungen des... Gesammtparteitages (1899)*, p. 47.
91. Alfred Ableitinger, "The Movement toward Parliamentary Government in Austria since 1900: Rudolf Sieghart's Memoir of June 28, 1903," *Austrian History Yearbook*, II (1966), 128.
92. Charmatz, *Österreichs äussere und innere Politik*, p. 51.
93. *Stenographische Protokolle über die Sitzungen des Hauses der Abgeordneten des österreichischen Reichsrathes* (November 6, 1899), pp. 461-468.
94. Strauss, *Geschichte*, vol. II, p. 103.
95. Charmatz, *Österreichs äussere und innere Politik*, p. 32.
96. *St. P....des Hauses der Abgeordneten* (November 25, 1897), pp. 1813-1814.
97. *A-Z*, November 26, 1897, p. 1.
98. Charmatz, *Österreichs innere Geschichte*, vol. II, p. 115. The leader of the Pan-German movement at this time was Adler's one-time political ally von Schönerer; on his later political career, see Oscar Karbach, "The Founder of Modern Political Antisemitism: Georg von Schönerer," *Jewish Social Studies*, VII (1945), 3-30.
99. Brügel, *Geschichte*, vol. IV, pp. 321-323; May, *op. cit.*, p. 327; and Alfred Fischel, "Minister Immunität," *Die Zeit*, XV (1898), 33. A total of nine deputies were excluded from the House for the next three sittings as an outgrowth of this incident; of that number eight were Social-Democratic deputies; *St. P.... des Hauses der Abgeordneten* (November 26, 1897), pp. 1819-1824; and Strauss, *Geschichte*, vol. II, p. 104.
100. *A-Z*, November 27, 1897, p. 1.

101. *Protokoll...des Gesammtparteitages (1901)*, p. 82.
102. *A-Z*, October 17, 1901, p. 8. The original Social-Democratic contingent of 14 deputies was increased by one when Pernerstorfer, already elected to parliament, joined the party.
103. The principal threat was posed by the Pan-Germans and the German People's Party, although the Young Czechs and the German Progressive Party, a wing of the former German Liberal Party, offered the socialists stiff competition at times; on this point, see Kolmer, *op. cit.*, vol. VI, pp. 217-218; Schwechler, *op. cit.*, p. 29; and *Verhandlungen des Parteitages der deutschen Sozialdemokratie (1898)*, p. 49.
104. Hannak, *op. cit.*, p. 126.
105. Strauss, *Geschichte*, vol. II, pp. 109-110; and Strakosch-Grassmann, *op. cit.*, p. 65.
106. *Full Report of the Proceedings of the International Workers' Congress (London, 1896)*, p. 32.
107. Deutsch, *Geschichte*, vol. II, pp. 365-366.
108. See Adler's comments in *Verhandlungen des Parteitages der deutschen Sozialdemokratie (1898)*, pp. 44-46.
109. Alois Czedik, *Zur Geschichte der k. k. österreichischen Ministerien 1861-1916*, 4 vols. (Vienna, 1917-1920), vol. II, pp. 132-133.
110. See, for example, Bauer's *Introduction*, p. xi.
111. See, as an illustration here, the remarks of Daszyński in *A-Z*, January 28, 1899, pp. 2-3.
112. Franz M. Mayer, Raimund F. Kaindl, Hans Pirchegger and Anton Klein, *Geschichte und Kulturleben Österreichs*, 3 vols. (5th ed., Vienna, 1965), vol. III, p. 248. For a report of Pernerstorfer's comments, see *A-Z*, October 18, 1899, p. 6.
113. May, *op. cit.*, p. 333; and Mayer, et. al., *op. cit.*, vol. III, pp. 248-249.
114. Bauer's *Introduction*, p. xv.
115. *A-Z*, December 22, 1899, p. 1; Julius Braunthal (ed.) *Austerlitz Spricht* (Vienna,

1931), pp. 255-257; and Friedrich Adler (ed.), *Victor Adler Briefwechsel mit August Bebel und Karl Kautsky* (Vienna, 1954), p. 338.
116. May, *op. cit.*, p. 333; and Bauer's *Introduction*, p. xv.
117. Taylor, *op. cit.*, p. 199; Redlich, *op. cit.*, p. 451; and *Protokollbuch des sozialdemokratischen Verbandes*, II (April 8, 1902).
118. *A-Z*, March 13, 1901, p. 1; *A-Z*, January 27, 1903, pp. 2-3; and *A-Z*, September 25, 1903, p. 1. Throughout these years close and intimate ties were maintained between the party executive and its parliamentary faction; on this point, see *Exekutivprotokolle der sozialdemokratischen Partei Österreichs*, II (April 29, 1903, June 25, 1903 and November 24, 1904).
119. *St. P....des Hauses der Abgeordneten* (December 9, 1904), p. 26215; and *A-Z*, December 11, 1904, p. 1.
120. For an interesting assessment of Danneberg's contribution to the party, see Julius Deutsch, *Ein Weiter Weg* (Zurich, 1960), p. 84.
121. Quoted in Braunthal, *In Search of the Millenium*, p. 44.
122. Wilhelm Ellenbogen, *Was will die Sozialdemokratie?* (Vienna, 1899), p. 30.
123. See the comments in Erich Zöllner, *Geschichte Österreichs* (3rd ed., Munich, 1966), p. 429; and Gulick, *op. cit.*, vol. II, pp. 1365-1366. Austro-Marxism was not necessarily a radical creed; more than anything its tenets may best be described as novel.
124. Karl Renner (pseud. Rudolf Springer), "Mösche Säulen," *A-Z*, August 17, 1903, p. 1.
125. *Protokoll über die Verhandlungen des Gesamtparteitages der sozialdemokratischen Arbeiterpartei abgehalten zu Wien vom 9. bis zum 13. November 1903*, pp. 112-114.
126. *Protokoll über die Verhandlungen des Parteitages der deutschen sozialdemokratischen Arbeiterpartei abgehalten zu Aussig vom 15. bis 18. August 1902*, pp. 89-91.
127. At times, Pernerstorfer's overly cautious

policies were subject to ridicule and attack, as they were in 1903 by Anton Hueber and Leopold Winarsky; for Pernerstorfer's own defense at the time, see *Protokoll... des Gesamtparteitages (1903)*, pp. 115-116.

128. As an example, see the content of the speech delivered by Karl Vaněk in 1903 and the resolution which he put forward to the congress, which was readily accepted, on the question of universal suffrage, in *ibid.*, pp. 122-126, 133.

129. Karl Renner (pseud. Rudolf Springer), *Der Kampf der oesterreichischen Nationen um den Staat* (Leipzig, 1902), pp. 215-216.

Chapter IV: *The Widening Nationalities Question*

1. Otto Bauer, *Krieg oder Friede in den Gewerkschaften?* (Vienna, 1910), p. 6. On the same point, see Richard Charmatz, *Das politische Denken in Österreich* (2nd ed., Vienna, 1917), pp. 68 ff.
2. These tendencies, not difficult to discern were chronicled in 1898 by Daszyński in his article, "Die Lage in Oesterreich," pp. 718 ff. Erika Behm and Jürgen Kuczynski, "Die Reflexion der Arbeiterbewegung in der Regierungspresse vor dem Ersten Weltkrieg. Eine vornehmlich quantitative Analyse (Österreich)," *Jahrbuch für Wirtschaftgeschichte* No. 3 (1974), pp. 131-134.
3. Paul Samassa, *Der Völkerstreit im Habsburgerstaat* (Leipzig, 1910), p. 38.
4. The Social Democrats learned this when they lost nearly all of their mandates in western and northern Bohemia in 1901 to Pan-German candidates who played upon the *Grossdeutsch* sympathies of the workers in the area; on this point, see Strauss, *Geschichte*, vol. II, pp. 109-110.
5. Bauer, *Krieg oder Friede in den Gewerkschaften?* p. 6.
6. Berchtold, *op. cit.*, p. 137.
7. *Verhandlungen des Parteitages (1888, 1889)*, p. 3.

8. For an "official" view of the Czech national socialists, see Brügel, *Geschichte*, vol. IV, p. 167.
9. *Verhandlungen des...Parteitages (1891)*, p.43.
10. *Ibid.*
11. *Ibid.*, p. 162.
12. *Ibid.*
13. *Ibid.*, p. 163.
14. *Ibid.*, pp. 164-65, 168-169.
15. *Ibid.*, p. 169. A very brief explanation of these events is contained in the introduction to *Dokumente des Separatismus* (Vienna, 1911), pp. 6-8; a more deliberate examination of the Vávra affair in the history of the movement may be found in Mommsen, *op. cit.*, pp. 139-140, 185-188.
16. Schwechler, *op. cit.*, p. 208.
17. Austrian socialists before 1914 could find little to support their stand on the nationalities question in either Lassalle or Marx; Lassalle's belief in German cultural nationalism seemed to be both misplaced and inappropriate as did Marx's rejection of nationalism, to say nothing about Engels' embarrassing *Grossdeutsch* sentiments; for further information on these points, see Ramm, *Ferdinand Lassalle: Ausgewählte Texte*, pp. 116-129; Heinrich Cunow, "Marx und das Selbstbestimmungsrecht der Nationen," *Die Neue Zeit*, XXXVI (1918), 577-584; and Kann, *op. cit.*, vol. I, pp. 105-106, and vol. II, pp. 154, 170 and 345.
18. *Verhandlungen des...Parteitages (1897)*, pp. 78-79.
19. Mommsen, *op. cit.*, pp. 116-117; Kann, *op. cit.*, vol. II, p. 154; *Verhandlungen des...Parteitages (1896)*, pp. 103-104; *Verhandlungen des...Parteitages (1897)*, pp. 124-125; and Franz Strobl, "Das Brünner Nationalitätenprogramm der österreichischen Sozialdemokratie," *Weg und Ziel* (1949), 287. Pernerstorfer's commitment to nationalism was probably greater than that of Adler's, but not nearly as great as Strobl maintains.
20. *Verhandlungen des...Parteitages (1897)*, p. 7.
21. *Ibid.*, pp. 79-80.
22. In addition to the Germans, Czechs, Poles,

South Slavs and Italians, a Ruthenian group was also formed.
23. *Ibid.*, pp. 117-119, 124-125.
24. See as an illustration here, the report of the Social-Democratic deputy Eduard Rieger in *Verhandlungen des Gesammtparteitages (1899)*, pp. 42-44.
25. Pernerstorfer, "Ein Kurzes Wort zur Frage des Sozialismus und Nationalismus," p. 57.
26. For an informed discussion of the steps that led up to the creation of a separate Czech trade-union commission in January of 1897, see Deutsch, *Geschichte,* vol. I, pp. 341-354.
27. Rudolf Tayerle, "Die gewerkschaftlichen Selbständigkeitsbestrebungen der tschechischen Arbeiter in Österreich," *Die Neue Zeit,* XXIX (1909), 728; Mommsen, *op. cit.*, p. 231; and *Protokoll des...Gewerkschafts-Congresses (1900)*, pp. 207-208. As late as 1903, Roušar, the secretary of the Czech trade-union commission, was still pressing home the theme that coordinated effort was absolutely imperative for the success of the Austrian trade-union movement; on this point, see *Protokoll über die Verhandlungen des vierten österreichischen Gewerkschaftskongresses abgehalten vom 8. bis inklusive 12. Juni 1903 zu Wien*, p. 89.
28. *Bericht der Gewerkschaftskommission Oesterreichs an den Fünften ordentlichen Kongress der Gewerkschaften Oesterreichs in Wien 1907*, p. 114; Czech claims were always higher; see, for example, Tayerle, *op. cit.*, p. 730.
29. Soukup, *op. cit.*, p. 20; Mommsen, *op. cit.*, p. 42; Konirsch, *op. cit.*, p. 247; and Heinrich Rauchberg, *Der nationale Besitzstand in Böhmen,* 3 vols. (Leipzig, 1905), vol. I, pp. 42-44.
30. See Vaněk's report in *Dokumente des Separatismus,* p. 11.
31. Friedrich A. Rager, "National Autonomy in the Austro-Hungarian Monarchy," *Journal of Central European Affairs,* I (1942), 422.
32. Berthold Sutter, *Die Badenischen Sprachenverordnungen von 1897,* (Graz, 1960), vol. I,

pp. 156-157; and William A. Jenks, "The Later Habsburg Concept of Statecraft," *Austrian History Yearbook*, II (1966), 102.
33. The text of the decrees as they applied to Bohemia may be found in Sutter, *op. cit.*, pp. 274-278.
34. May, *op. cit.*, p. 325; and Charmatz, *Österreichs äussere und innere Politik*, p. 25.
35. *A-Z*, April 3, 1897, p. 1.
36. Hannak, *op. cit.*, p. 112.
37. Czedik, *op. cit.*, vol. II, pp. 78-79.
38. Karl G. Hugelmann, *Das Nationalitätenrecht des alten Österreich*, (Vienna, 1934), pp. 179-185.
39. Brügel, *Geschichte*, vol. IV, p. 320.
40. Bauer's *Introduction*, p. x.
41. Mommsen, *op. cit.*, pp. 273-274.
42. *Ibid.*, p. 274.
43. The most obvious incident, of course, was Social-Democratic involvement in the November fiasco, but the party also made use of Article 42 at this time to the disadvantage of parliament; for some of the background here, see Hugelmann, *Das Nationalitätenrecht*, p. 186.
44. *Verhandlungen des...Parteitages (1897)*, pp. 71-72; and *Verhandlungen des Parteitages ...des deutschen Sozialdemokratie (1898)*, p. 55.
45. Karl Kautsky, "Der Kampf der Nationalitäten und das Staatsrecht in Oesterreich," *Die Neue Zeit*, XVI (1897-98), 516-518.
46. *Protokoll...des Gesammtparteitages (1901)*, p. 75.
47. Article 19 of the Austrian constitution of 1867 provided for the equality of all languages in the empire.
48. *Protokoll...des Gesammtparteitages (1901)*, pp. 76-77.
49. *Ibid.*, p. 78.
50. Badeni's attempt at linguistic parity and Gautsch's plan for linguistic accommodation both ended in failure. The Badeni ordinances were superceded by those issued by Gautsch on February 24, 1898; Gautsch's ordinances were in turn rescinded by the government of

Count Manfred Clary on October 14, 1899; the various documents involved here are all contained in Sutter, *op. cit.*, pp. 274-285.
51. Karl Kautsky, "Der Kampf den Nationalitäten und das Staatsrecht in Oesterreich," p. 562.
52. Pernerstorfer, "Ein kurzes Wort zur Frage des Sozialismus und Nationalismus," p. 57.
53. Quoted in *A-Z*, June 9, 1897, p. 2.
54. Oscar Jászi, *The Dissolution of the Habsburg Monarchy* (Chicago, 1929), p. 178.
55. Kann, *op. cit.*, vol. II, p. 154.
56. Friedrich Austerlitz, "Der nationale Kampf und die Sozialdemokratie," *A-Z*, July 20, 1898, p. 2.
57. *Ibid.*
58. Specifically what the Czechs wanted was an autonomous national organizations so as to be able to appeal to the growing number of Czech workers in the city of Vienna; on this score, see *A-Z*, November 5, 1897, p.8.
59. *A-Z*, September 8, 1897, p. 2.
60. Victor Adler, "Die Nationalitätenfrage und der Brünner Parteitag," *A-Z*, September 19, 1899, p. 2.
61. Engelbert Pernerstorfer, "Zur österreichischen Nationalitätenfrage," *A-Z*, September 24, 1899, p. 2.
62. Victor Adler, "Die Nationalitätenfrage und der Brünner Parteitag," p. 2.
63. Friedrich Austerlitz, "Die Sozialdemokratie und die Nationalitätenfrage," *A-Z*, September 3, 1899, p. 2.
64. Victor Adler, "Die Nationalitätenfrage und der Brünner Parteitag," pp. 2-3.
65. Friedrich Austerlitz, "Der Nationalitätenstaat," *A-Z*, September 8, 1899, pp. 2-3.
66. Ignaz Daszyński, "Nationale Selbstverwaltung," *A-Z*, September 23, 1899, p. 2.
67. Rudolf Schlesinger, *Federalism in Central and Eastern Europe* (New York, 1945), p. 210.
68. The most obvious cases were Silesia, with its mixed population of Poles, Czechs and Germans, and Bohemia and Moravia, where the Germans and Czechs faced one another in an atmosphere of increasing crisis.
69. *Verhandlungen des Gesammtparteitages (1899)*, p. xiv. An English translation of the

original resolution placed before the congress by the general executive may be found in Kogan, *op. cit.*, p. 208.
70. *Verhandlungen des Gesammtparteitages (1899)*, p. 86.
71. *Ibid.*, p. 92.
72. *Ibid.*, pp. 86-88.
73. *Ibid.*, p. 77.
74. *Ibid.*, p. 78.
75. *Ibid.*, pp. 78-80.
76. *Ibid.*, pp. 87-88.' Synopses of the events described here may be found in Kogan, *op. cit.*, pp. 207-209; and Brügel, *Geschichte*, vol. IV, pp. 337-343.
77. *Verhandlungen des Gesammtparteitages (1889)*, p. 104.
78. *Ibid.* Compare and contrast here, Kogan, *op. cit.*, p. 208, and Kann, *op. cit.*, vol. II, p. 155. For a comparison between the Brünn program and the last-minute efforts of the Emperor Karl in 1918 to save his empire, see Rolf Woldan, "Der Österreichische Staatsgedanke und seine Wandlungen im Zeitalter Franz Josephs," *Mitteilungen des osterreichischen Instituts für Geschichtsforschung*, XI (1929), 852-853.
79. Alfred Werner, "Austria has a Mission," *Journal of Central European Affairs*, VII (1948), 408-409.
80. Kann, *op. cit.*, vol. II, p. 148.
81. Even as late as 1917, the idea of the empire dissolving into its component parts was still regarded as fantastic and inconceivable by Austrian socialism; on this point, see Julius Braunthal, *The Tragedy of Austria* (London, 1948), p. 31. By contrast, for Lenin's support of the idea of self-determination, see the essay "Theses on the National Question," in Lenin, *Collected Works*, 38 vols. (Moscow, 1960-1967), vol. 19, pp. 243-251.
82. Alfred Fischel (ed.), *Materialien zur Sprachenfrage in Österreich* (Brünn, 1902), pp. 33 ff; Allmeyer-Beck, *op. cit.*, pp. 67-68; and Kann, *op. cit.*, vol. I, pp. 374-375.
83. For brief biographical sketches, see the article on Karl Renner by Adolf Schärf

and the one on Otto Bauer by Julius Deutsch in *Neue Österreichische Biographie ab 1815*, vol. IX, pp. 9-30, and vol. X, pp. 209-218.
84. Deutsch, *Ein Weiter Weg*, p. 87.
85. Schlesinger, *op. cit.*, p. 218.
86. *Verhandlungen des Gesammtparteitages (1899)*, p. 85; and Kogan, *op. cit.*, p. 209.
87. Renner used two pseudonyms, Synopticus and the better known Rudolf Springer. Renner used these pseudonyms because of his politically sensitive position as a librarian in the Austrian parliament.
88. Kann, *op. cit.*, vol. II, p. 159. Examples that seemed to support Renner's case were the British Empire and Switzerland; it is clear that Renner badly misread the temper of the times. Nonetheless, he continued to assume the existence of the Austrian state; on this point, see Arthur Kogan, *Socialism in the Multi-National State* (unpubl. Ph.D. dissertation, Harvard, 1946), p. 208. All references hereafter will be to Kogan's published, rather than his unpublished, work.
89. Karl Renner (pseud. Synopticus), *Staat und Nation* (Vienna, 1899), p. 13.
90. Renner also published another study of nationalism under the pseudonym of Synopticus entitled *Staat und Parlament* (Vienna, 1901).
91. Once again he used a pseudonym, this time Rudolf Springer.
92. Renner, *Der Kampf der oesterreichischen Nationen*, pp. 12-13.
93. *Ibid.*, p. 42; and Jászi, *op. cit.*, p. 179.
94. Renner, *Der Kampf der öesterreichischen Nationen*, pp. 60-62.
95. Hugo Hantsch, *Die Nationalitätenfrage im alten Österreich* (Vienna, 1953), p. 71.
96. Karl Renner (pseud. Rudolf Springer), *Grundlagen und Entwicklungsziele der österreichisch-ungarischen Monarchie* (Vienna, 1906, p. 208; and Kann, *op. cit.*, vol. II, p. 159. The translation is Professor Kann's.
97. Evidence of Renner's attempt to make use of the personality principle may be found in

his work, *Der Kampf der öesterreichischen Nationen,* pp. 35 ff.
98. *Ibid.,* pp. 40-44.
99. *Ibid.,* pp. 182-188; and Jaszi, *op. cit.,* p. 179.
100. Kann, *op. cit.,* vol. II, p. 159.
101. Kogan, *op. cit.,* p. 213.
102. Renner, *Der Kampf der oesterreichischen Nationen,* pp. 199-200.
103. *Ibid.,* p. 190.
104. *Ibid.,* pp. 190-191.
105. May, *op. cit.,* p. 48.
106. Specifically they were: Moravia, Silesia, Galicia, Bukovina, the German Alpine lands, Bohemia, Carniola and the Littoral (Trieste and its hinterland).
107. Kann, *op. cit.,* vol. II, pp. 159-160.
108. *Ibid.,* p. 160.
109. The party never did reject the monarchical principle; what it wanted specifically was a constitutional monarchy buttressed by democratic institutions.
110. Kann, *op. cit.,* vol. II, p.160. Renner maintained throughout his writings a belief in a strong central government; this point is stated succinctly in Schlesinger, *op. cit.,* p. 215.
111. See for example Renner's *Der nationale Streit um die Aemter und die Sozialdemokratie* (Vienna, 1908); again published under his pseudonym Rudolf Springer.
112. For example, the ideas of Synopticus were certainly known at this time to Pernerstorfer, see *Verhandlungen des Gesammtparteitages (1899),* p. 87.
113. On this score, see Carl Brockhausen, "Grundlagen und Entwicklungsziele der österreichisch-ungarischen Monarchie," *Österreichische Rundschau,* X (1907), 1-11; and Aurel von Onciul, "Das österreichische Problem," *Österreichische Rundschau,* II (1905), 205-216.
114. See for example, Alfred Meissner, "Löst die nationale Autonomie das nationale Problem?" *Der Kampf,* I (1908), 271-276; and Karl Mann, "Das Selbstbestimmungsrecht der österreichischen Nationen," *Der Kampf,* XI

(1918), 201-205.
115. For additional evidence here, see Karl Reinold, *Die österreichische Sozialdemokratie und der Nationalismus* (Vienna, 1910), pp. 19-45.
116. Renner, *Grundlage und Entwicklungsziele*, p. 246; and Kann, *op. cit.*, vol. II, p. 160.
117. The *Ausgleich* of 1867 was more than anything a settlement that accorded exclusively with the dynastic interests of the Hapsburgs; for more evidence on this conclusion, see Josef Redlich, *Das österreichische Staats- und Reichsproblem*, 2 vols. (Leipzig, 1920-26), vol. II, pp. 672-680.
118. May, *op. cit.*, pp. 348-349.
119. *Ibid.*, p. 349; and Charmatz, *Österreichs innere Geschichte*, vol. II, pp. 128 ff.
120. *A-Z*, August 30, 1903, p. 1.
121. Friedrich Austerlitz, "Die Krise des Dualismus in Österreich," *Die Neue Zeit*, XXI (1902-1903), 548-552.
122. Renner, *Grundlagen und Entwicklungsziele*, pp. 165 ff.
123. *Protokoll...des Gesammtparteitages (1903)*, pp. 133-151.
124. *Ibid.*, pp. 152-153.
125. *Ibid.*, p. 153.
126. *Ibid.*, pp. 155-156.
127. *Ibid.*, pp. 165-166.
128. For a discussion of this consideration, see Mommsen, *op. cit.*, p. 6.
129. Meissner makes this point in his article, "Löst die nationale Autonomie das nationale Problem?", already cited.
130. Schlesinger, *op. cit.*, p. 223.
131. See, for example, Otto Bauer, *Die österreichische Revolution* (Vienna, 1923), p. 1 and *passim*; and Braunthal, *The Tragedy of Austria*, p. 31.
132. Hantsch, *Die Nationalitätenfrage im alten Österreich*, pp. 73-74.
133. Kann, *op. cit.*, vol. II, p. 168.
134. Otto Bauer, *Die Nationalitätenfrage und die Sozialdemokratie* (2nd ed., Vienna, 1924), pp. 1-8, 19-22. The second edition of this book is identical in every way with the original edition which was published

in 1907; the only exception being that the second edition contains a new preface; all future references will be therefore to that second edition.
135. *Ibid.*, p. 24.
136. *Ibid.*, p. 531.
137. *Ibid.*, p. 135.
138. *Ibid.*, p. 101.
139. *Ibid.*, p. 532.
140. *Ibid.*, and Schlesinger, *op. cit.*, p. 224. For a summation of Bauer's ideas, see Ludo M. Hartmann, "Die Nationalitäten und die Sozialdemokratie," *Neue Gesellschaft,* VII (1907), 263-272.
141. Otto Bauer, "Bemerkungen zur Nationalitätenfrage," *Die Neue Zeit,* XXVI (1908), 795-798. Bauer was replying to a long critique contained in the article by Karl Kautsky entitled "Nationalität und Internationalität," *Die Neue Zeit,* XXVI (1908), 1-36.
142. As an illustration here, see Ignaz Daszyński, "Die Nationalitätenfrage in der osteuropäischen Sozialdemokratie," *Sozialistische Monatshefte,* XIV (1910), 1068-1072.

Chapter V: *The Search for a Social Policy*

1. *Verhandlungen...des Gesammtparteitages (1899),* p. 99.
2. Karl Kautsky, *The Road to Power,* tr. by A. M. Simons (Chicago, 1909), p. 50.
3. *Verhandlungen des Parteitages (1888, 1889),* p. 4.
4. *Congrès International Ouvrier Socialiste tenu à Bruxelles du 16 au 23 août 1891 (Rapport),* p. 35.
5. Far and away, the best discussion of these reforms can be found in Jenks, *Austria Under the Iron Ring,* pp. 179-195, 196-220.
6. Wilhelm Weber, "Sozialpolitik und Sozialrecht von 1848 bis 1945," in Hans Mayer (ed.), *Hundert Jahre Österreichischer Wirtschaftsentwicklung 1848-1948* (Vienna, 1949), p. 581.
7. Karl Kautsky, *Das Erfurter Programm*

(Stuttgart, 1892), p. 196.
8. *Ibid.*, pp. 229-231.
9. *Verhandlungen des Parteitages (1888, 1889)*, p. 56.
10. *Ibid.*, pp. 49-51.
11. *Ibid.*, p. 51.
12. On this point, see Ermers, *op. cit.*, p. 149; and the resolution presented to the 1889 congress of the Second International by Bebel and Jules Guesde, which was modified by William Morris and Kier Hardie in *Protokoll des Internationalen Arbeiter-Congresses (1889)*, pp. 121-122.
13. Adolf Braun, *Die Gewerkschaften, ihre Entwicklung und Kämpfe* (Nuremberg, 1914), p. 147.
14. Brügel, *Soziale Gesetzgebung*, pp. 133-134.
15. Karl Pŕibram, *Der Normalarbeitstag in den gewerblichen Betrieben und im Bergbaue Österreichs* (Vienna, 1906), p. 16.
16. *Ibid.*, p. 15.
17. *Protokoll des Internationalen Arbeiter-Congresses (1889)*, p. 123.
18. Friedrich Hertz, *Die Produktionsgrundlagen der österreichischen Industrie vor und nach dem Kriege* (Vienna, 1917), p. 173.
19. Robert Danneberg, *Das sozialdemokratische Programm* (6th ed., Vienna, 1919), p. 39.
20. Brügel, *Soziale Gesetzgebung*, p. 134; and *Verhandlungen des...Parteitages (1891)*, p. 112.
21. Danneberg, *Das sozialdemokratische Programm*, p. 61.
22. Deutsch, *Geschichte*, vol. I, p. 368.
23. Klenner, *op. cit.*, p. 287.
24. Kulemann, *op. cit.*, p. 99.
25. Klenner, *op. cit.*, p. 285.
26. *Ibid.*, p. 288; and Pŕibram, *op. cit.*, p. 26.
27. Quoted in Jenks, *Vienna and the Young Hitler*, p. 37.
28. *Ibid.*
29. Matthias Eldersch, "Die Reform der Krankenversicherung," *Der Kampf*, II (1908), 120.
30. Hertz, *op. cit.*, p. 5.
31. For the party's attitude toward the *Krankenkassen*, see the speech by Jakob Reumann in

Verhandlungen des...Parteitages (1891), pp. 113-114.
32. Victor Adler was most likely correct when he made this assertion in 1901; see his comments in *Protokoll...des Gesammtparteitages (1901)*, p. 102.
33. Brügel, *Soziale Gesetzgebung*, p. 171; and Weber, *op. cit.*, p. 581.
34. Weber, *op. cit.*, pp. 582-583.
35. For a case in point, see Kolmer, *op. cit.*, vol. VI, pp. 94-95.
36. *Protokoll des...Gewerkschaftskongresses (1896)*, pp. 107-112.
37. *Ibid.*, pp. 112-113.
38. *Ibid.*, p. 114.
39. *Verhandlungen des...Parteitages (1897)*, pp. 136-150.
40. *Ibid.*, pp. 161-162.
41. *Verhandlungen des...Gesammtparteitages (1899)*, pp. 99-101.
42. *Protokoll...des Gewerkschafts-Congresses (1900)*, p. 221.
43. On the intensity of this development, see Pulzer, *op. cit.*, p. 119; and Jenks, *Vienna and the Young Hitler*, pp. 189-190; for an illustration of the party's response, see *A-Z*, May 29, 1895, p. 3.
44. Czeike, *op. cit.*, pp. 64, 77, 79.
45. The essential core of Bernstein's thought is contained in his classic study *Die Voraussetzungen des Sozialismus und die Aufgabe der Sozialdemokratie* (Stuttgart, 1899).
46. *Ibid.*, pp. v-viii, 7; and Eduard Bernstein, "Der Kampf der Sozialdemokratie und die Revolution der Gesellschaft," *Die Neue Zeit*, XVI (1897-98), 555.
47. Bernstein, *Die Voraussetzungen*, pp. v-viii.
48. Schorske, *op. cit.*, p. 19.
49. See, for example, Karl Kautsky, *Bernstein und das sozialdemokratische Programm* (Stuttgart, 1899); and Rosa Luxemburg, *Reform and Revolution* (English edition, Bombay, 1951).
50. Victor Adler, *Aufsätze*, 2nd ed., part 6, p. 227.
51. Bernstein, *Die Voraussetzungen*, p. viii.

52. Victor Adler, "Revisionismus und Reformismus," *A-Z*, October 16, 1898, p. 3.
53. Victor Adler, Bernstein's Theorie und Taktik," *A-Z*, April 2, 1899, p. 3.
54. Victor Adler, "Zur Revision des Parteiprogramms," *A-Z*, September 22, 1901, pp. 2-3. The decision to undertake the revision was made by the party at its Brünn congress in 1899; *Verhandlungen des...Gesammtparteitages (1899)*, pp. 94-95.
55. Bernstein had argued that from a sociological point of view there was no such thing as a process of absolute pauperization at work in capitalism; here, see Eduard Bernstein, *Der Revisionismus in der Sozialdemocratie* (Amsterdam, 1909), p. 41.
56. For a summary of his earlier position, see Victor Adler, *Aufsätze*, 1st ed., part 4, pp. 92-94.
57. Victor Adler, "Zur Revision des Parteiprogramm," pp. 2-3.
58. Adler was exposed to the ideas of Bernstein in two ways, personally and ideationally. In the middle of 1898 he and the German leader August Bebel met with Bernstein in Zurich to discuss the consequences of Bernstein's modification of Marxism. Adler also became acquainted with Bernstein's thought when he was called upon to review Bernstein's major work for the *Arbeiter-Zeitung*. Whether these exposures were equivalent to assimilation is still subject to dispute, although the weight of the evidence indicates that he was significantly influenced by Bernstein. On the various facets of the story here, see Friedrich Adler, *Victor Adler Briefwechsel*, p. 251; Victor Adler, "Bernstein's Theorie und Taktik," p. 3; Ermers, *op. cit.*, pp. 251-252; and Bauer's *Introduction*, p. xvii.
59. In the main, what Kautsky objected to in Bernstein's case, and later in the case of Adler, was that they had attacked basic Marxian suppositions; he seems to have been oblivious to the discrepancy between theory and practice at times, and yet, curiously sensitive about maintaining the purity and

integrity of Marxist ideas; on this point, see Schorske, *op. cit.*, pp. 16-24; for a brief glimpse of Kautsky's own feelings at the time of the revisionist controversy, see Benedikt Kautsky (ed.), *Ein Leben für den Sozialismus: Erinnergungen an Karl Kautsky* (Hannover, 1954), pp. 21-25. For a summation of Bernstein's position here, see Peter Gay, *op. cit.*, p. 138.

60. Hunt, *op. cit.*, pp. 58-60. On the continuing influence of Lassalle at this time, see Norbert Leser, *Begegnung und Auftrag: Beiträge zur Orientierung im zeitgenossischen Sozialismus* (Vienna, 1963), pp. 199-213.
61. Leopold Winarsky, "Zur Revision des Parteiprogramm," *A-Z*, October 8, 1901, p. 7.
62. Karl Kautsky, "Die Revision des Programms der Sozialdemokratie in Oesterreich," *Die Neue Zeit*, XX (1901-02), 70.
63. *Ibid*.
64. *Ibid*., pp. 73-74. Kautsky himself believed at the turn of the century that a sharpening of class antagonisms was occurring due to the declining economic position of the working class; for his views, see Karl Kautsky, *The Road to Power*, p. 94; and Karl Kautsky, *Bernstein und das Sozialdemokratie: Eine Antikritik* (Stuttgart, 1899), pp. 114-117. It should be noted here that Kautsky did not take the exact same line in dealing with Bernstein as he did with Adler.
65. Kautsky, "Die Revision des Programms der Sozialdemokratie in Oesterreich," p. 74. Kautsky's criticism did force a change in the wording of the final draft of the Viennese program; the first two paragraphs of the program which were ultimately accepted in 1901, and which formed the crux of the dispute between Adler and Kautsky, ran as follows:

The Social-Democratic Labor Party in Austria strives on behalf of all the people, without regard to nationality, race or sex, for their emancipation from the chains of economic dependence, for the elimination of political oppression and for their elevation from intellectual confinement. The cause of these unsatisfactory conditions is not to be found in particular political institutions, but rather in the fact that essentially the whole society is conditioned and dominated by those individual owners who monopolize the means of production. The possessors of the capacity to work, the working class, fall therefore into the most oppressive dependence upon the possessors of the means of working, which include land--that is, upon the great landowning and capitalistic classes, whose political and economic domination is expressed in the class state of today.

Technical progress, the growing concentration of production and property, the union of every economic force in the hand of capitalists and capitalistic groups, have the effect of depriving ever-widening circles of small industrial employers and peasants, formerly independent, of their means of production, and brings them as wage-workers, employees, or debtors, into direct or indirect dependence on the capitalists. The mass of proletarians grows; the degree of their exploitation also rises; and, in consequence, the standard of living of ever-deepening strata of the working people contrasts more and more with the rapidly rising productivity of their own work and the expansion of the wealth they themselves create.

Protokoll...des Gesammtparteitages (1901), pp. 3, 123. The full text may be found in the 1901 protocol; and English translation of the document may be found in R.C.K. Ensor (ed.), *Modern Socialism* (London, 1907), pp. 334-338.

66. Criticism of Adler was also heard in Polish circles; see, as an illustration, Max Zetterbaum, "Zur Revision des Parteiprogramms," *A-Z*, October 10, 1901, pp. 6-7.
67. Up until the last, he shied away from an

all-out confrontation with his critics; for more on this particular point, see Victor Adler, *Aufsätze*, 2nd ed., part 6, p. 301.
68. Unwilling to heat up the situation any more than it was already, Adler adamantly refused to answer Kautsky in *Neue Zeit* even though Kautsky offered to supply the space needed; for Adler's reasoning see his letter to Kautsky in Friedrich Adler, *Victor Adler Briefwechsel*, p. 373.
69. Victor Adler, *Aufsätze*, 2nd ed., part 6, p. 315.
70. *Ibid.*, p. 238; the public character of the dispute between Adler and Kautsky was paralleled in their private correspondence, which was more frank and open than their public debate; for example, at one juncture, speaking about the Hainfeld program, Kautsky curtly advised Adler "to leave it as it is;" for the salient feature of their interchange, see Friedrich Adler, *Victor Adler Briefwechsel*, pp. 353, 357-358, 375.
71. Karl Kautsky, "Die Revision des Parteiprogramms der Sozialdemokratie in Oesterreich," p. 68.
72. *Protokoll...des Gesammtparteitages (1901)*, pp. 96-97.
73. *Ibid.*, p. 101.
74. *Ibid.*
75. *Ibid.*
76. *Ibid.*, pp. 102, 103, 110.
77. *Ibid.*, pp. 112-113.
78. *Ibid.*, pp. 3, 123; for the text here, see footnote 65. During the congress, Kautsky repeatedly expressed the fear that certain portions of the new program would be misunderstood. That unhoped-for result occurred shortly after the congress when an official governmental memorandum circulated to the effect that, led by Adler, Austrian socialism had shed its radicalism in the process of making concessions to Bernstein's thinking; on this point, see the long explanatory footnote in Brügel, *Geschichte*, vol. IV, p. 347.
79. *Protokoll...des Gesammtparteitages (1901)*, pp. 123-124. The original text of the

Hainfeld program, which Kautsky favored, ran:

> The Social-Democratic Labor Party in Austria strives on behalf of all the people, without regard to nationality, race, or sex, for their emancipation from the chains of economic dependence, for the elimination of political oppression and for their elevation from intellectual confinement. The cause of these unsatisfactory conditions is not to be found in particular political institutions, but rather in the fact that essentially the whole society is conditioned and dominated by those individual owners who monopolize the means of production. The possessors of the capacity to work, the working class, are thereby cast into the role of slaves vis-à-vis the owners of the means of production, the capitalistic class, whose political and economic domination finds expression in the existing state. This unique possession of the means of production, which expresses itself politically in the class state, also means economically increasing poverty and a growing pauperization for ever-widening levels of the population.

Verhandlungen des Parteitages (1888, 1889), p. 3.

80. Protokoll...des Gesammtparteitages (1901), p. 124.
81. Ibid., pp. 124-126, 129-133.
82. Ibid., p. 137.
83. Ibid., p. 124.
84. In the period after the congress, the war of words between Kautsky and Adler, never personal but always pointed, continued unabated; in this regard, see Karl Kautsky, "Steigt die Ausbeutung der Arbeiter?" A-Z, December 15, 1901, p. 9; and Victor Adler, "Eine Programmanderung," in Anton Tesarek (ed.), Grosse Gestalten des Sozialismus (Vienna, 1947), vol. I, p. 62.
85. Braunthal, The International, pp. 274-284; and Joll, op. cit., p. 102.
86. J. Lenz, The Rise and Fall of the Second

International (New York, 1932), p. 58.
87. See here, *Internationaler Sozialisten-Kongress zu Amsterdam 14. bis 20. August 1904*, pp. 67, 69, 70; and the explanatory footnote in Friedrich Adler, *Victor Adler Briefwechsel*, p. 432.
88. *Internationaler Sozialisten-Kongress (1904)*, p. 70.
89. See Kautsky's letter in Friedrich Adler, *Victor Adler Briefwechsel*, pp. 431-432. Further background on Kautsky's position may be gleaned from Erich Matthias, "Kautsky und der Kautskyanismus," *Marxismus-Studien*, II (1957), 151-197.
90. Compare *Protokoll...des Gesammtparteitages (1901)*, pp. 4-5, and Ensor, *op. cit.*, pp. 337-338, with *Verhandlungen des Parteitages (1888, 1889)*, pp. 3-4.
91. *Protokoll...des Gesammtparteitages (1901)*, p. 182.
92. Brügel, *Soziale Gesetzgebung*, p. 232.
93. *A-Z*, March 14, 1901, p. 1.
94. *St. P....des Hauses der Abgeordneten* (February 18, 1902), pp. 8982-8993.
95. *Ibid.* (June 2, 1902), pp. 13629-13631, 13634-13636.
96. *A-Z*, October 22, 1901, p. 1; details concerning the petition drive may be found in Karl Renner's pamphlet *Was haben die Sozialdemokraten geleistet?* (Vienna, 1907).
97. Brügel, *Soziale Gesetzgebung*, p. 232.
98. Hertz, *op. cit.*, pp. 5-6.
99. Deutsch, *Geschichte*, vol. I, pp. 390 ff.
100. *Protokoll...des Gesammtparteitages (1903)*, pp. 168-169.
101. *Ibid.*, p. 169.
102. *Die Gewerkschaft*, June 10, 1904, pp. 118-123.
103. *Protokoll...des Gesammtparteitages (1903)*, pp. 169-171, 176.

Chapter VI: *The Achievement of Electoral Reform*

1. W. Beaumont, "Le Suffrage Universel en Autriche," *Annales des Sciences Politiques*,

XXII (1907), 618.
2. For a brief estimate of the party's capabilities at this time, see Victor Heller, "The Economic and Political Background of Austria's Reconstruction," *Journal of Central European Affairs*, VI, (1946), 286.
3. Schiller Marmorek, *L'Obstruction au Parlement Autrichien* (Paris, 1908), p. 94; and Joseph Redlich, *Austrian War Government* (New Haven, 1929), p. 41.
4. Otto Bauer, "Geschäftsordnungsreform oder Absolutismus?" *Der Kampf*, VIII (1913), 97.
5. Redlich, *Austrian War Government*, p. 43.
6. The Austrian party shared with Kautsky an ingrained assumption that Social-Democratic parties were revolutionary parties but not revolution-making parties; for further information on this point, see Karl Kautsky, *Das Erfurter Programm*, p. 217; and Karl Kautsky, *The Road to Power*, p. 50.
7. *A-Z*, October 17, 1901, p. 8.
8. Charles Brocard, *La Démocratie Socialiste Allemande et Autrichienne et les Élections de 1907* (Paris, 1909), pp. 147-148.
9. Kolmer, *op. cit.*, vol. VIII, pp. 615-616; and Marmorek, *op. cit.*, p. 110.
10. Charmatz, *Österreichs innere Geschichte*, vol. II, pp. 159-161.
11. Marmorek, *op. cit.*, p. 111.
12. Brügel, *Geschichte*, vol. IV, pp. 349-350.
13. Jenks, *The Austrian Electoral Reform of 1907*, pp. 27-30.
14. Strakosch-Grassmann, *op. cit.*, p. 78; and Charmatz, *Österreichs innere Geschichte*, vol. II, p. 162.
15. Strauss, *Geschichte*, vol. II, p. 127.
16. Brügel, *Geschichte*, vol. IV, pp. 351-353.
17. *St. P....des Hauses der Abgeordneten* (September 27, 1905), pp. 31577-31582.
18. *Ibid.* (September 26, 1905), pp. 31421-31423.
19. Jenks, *The Austrian Electoral Reform of 1907*, pp. 38-39; and Strauss, *Geschichte*, vol. II, p. 134.
20. *St. P....des Hauses der Abgeordneten* (October 6, 1905), pp. 32228-32231, 32258-32272.
21. Rudolf Sieghart, *Die letzten Jahrzehnte*

einer Grossmacht (Berlin, 1932), p. 86.
22. Jenks, The Austrian Electoral Reform of 1907, p. 39.
23. Allmeyer-Beck, op. cit., p. 141; and Ottakar Czernin, Oesterreichs Wahlrecht und Parlament (Prague, 1905), pp. 58-65.
24. A-Z, October 19, 1905, p. 1.
25. Strakosch-Grassmann, op. cit., p. 73.
26. Protokoll über die Verhandlungen des Gesammtparteitages der sozialdemokratischen Arbeiterpartei in Oesterreich abgehalten zu Wien vom 30. Oktober bis zum 2. November 1905, p. 75.
27. Ibid., pp. 87, 95-98.
28. Ibid., p. 120; Stanley W. Page, "The Russian Proletariat and the World Revolution: Lenin's View to 1914," The American Slavic and East European Review, X (1951), 6; see also, the letter from the St. Petersburg soviet to the Austrian central executive dated 12/31/1905 in Der Nachlass Victor Adlers.
29. Protokoll...des Gesammtparteitages (1905), pp. 120-122.
30. Ibid., pp. 123-124.
31. Quoted in Strauss, Geschichte, vol. II, p. 130.
32. Braunthal, In Search of the Millenium, p. 59.
33. Protokoll...des Gesammtparteitages (1905), pp. 125-132.
34. Ibid., pp. 68-69, 125-126.
35. Schorske, op. cit., p. 33; and Eduard Bernstein, "Die Potenz politischer Massenstreik," Sozialistische Monatshefte, XIV (1910), 482-486.
36. Internationaler Sozialisten-Kongress (1904), pp. 24-25, 30.
37. For almost a year prior to the 1905 congress of the Austrian party, Adler had been throwing cold water upon the idea of a general strike. As early as September, 1904, Adler had warned that the general strike was a dangerous and doubled-edged sword. On the one hand, he contended, it could bring practical success, but, on the other, he inferred, it might easily develop

into a struggle that could come perilously close to rebellion or insurrection; on this point, see the comments contained in Victor Adler, *Aufsätze*, 2nd ed., part 7, pp. 114-126.
38. *Protokoll...des Gesammtparteitages (1905)*, pp. 133-136.
39. *Sitzungsprotokolle der Gewerkschaftskommission Oesterreichs (September-December, 1905)*, pp. 147-150.
40. Strakosch-Grassmann, *op. cit.*, p. 83.
41. Strauss, *Geschichte*, vol. II, p. 134.
42. Sieghart, *op. cit.*, p. 83; and Beaumont, *op. cit.*, p. 620.
43. Jenks, *The Austrian Electoral Reform of 1907*, p. 41.
44. *Ibid.*, pp. 42-43.
45. Julius Deutsch, *Geschichte der deutschösterreichischen Arbeiterbewegung* (2nd ed., Vienna, 1922), p. 30.
46. Strakosch-Grassmann, *op. cit.*, p. 83.
47. Jenks, *The Austrian Electoral Reform of 1907*, p. 44; *A-Z*, November 28, 1905, p. 1; and Braunthal, *Austerlitz Spricht*, pp. 66-70.
48. Jenks, *The Austrian Electoral Reform of 1907*, p. 44.
49. *St. P....des Hauses der Abgeordneten* (November 30, 1905), p. 32454.
50. *Ibid.*, pp. 32446-32459.
51. *Ibid.* (December 1, 1905), pp. 32511-32514.
52. *Ibid.* (December 5, 1905), pp. 32601-32613.
53. Fehlinger and Klenner, *op. cit.*, pp. 38-39. The results here were not unexpected since the various trade-union secretaries meeting in Stuttgart in 1902 had already decided this question in favor of the principle of international organization; on this point, see "Auszug aus dem Protokoll über die Verhandlungen der internationalen Konferenz der Landessekretäre in Stuttgart im Jahre 1902," in *Protokoll des ausserordentlichen österreichischen Gewerkschaftskongresses abgehalten vom 8. bis inklusive 10. Dezember 1905 zu Wien*, p. 17.
54. Deutsch, *Geschichte*, vol. I, pp. 414-420.
55. *Sitzungsprotokolle der Gewerkschaftskommis-*

sion Oesterreichs (November-December, 1905), pp. 149-150.
56. *Protokoll der...Gewerkschaftskongresses (1905)*, pp. 9-10, 24-25, 53.
57. *Ibid.*, pp. 29-30, 33-34.
58. *Ibid.*, p. 53.
59. Fehlinger and Klenner, *op. cit.*, p. 39.
60. Rauchberg, *Die statistische Unterlagen*, p.1.
61. Sieghart, *op. cit.*, p. 86.
62. Rauchberg, *Die statistische Unterlagen*, p.1.
63. Beaumont, *op. cit.*, pp. 623-624; and Brügel, *Geschichte*, vol. IV, pp. 370-371.
64. Beaumont, *op. cit.*, p. 624. Of the 455 mandates that Gautsch proposed to create, 205 would have gone to the Germans, 20 to the Rumanians and Italians and 230 to the Slavs; Charmatz, *Österreichs innere Geschichte*, vol. II, pp. 165-166.
65. Beaumont, *op. cit.*, p. 625.
66. *A-Z*, February 24, 1906, pp. 1-2.
67. Brügel, *Geschichte*, vol. IV, p. 371.
68. Bauer's *Introduction*, p. xxi; and Gay, *op. cit.*, p. 78.
69. *St. P....des Hauses der Abgeordneten* (March 7, 1906), pp. 34825-34828.
70. *Ibid.* (March 9, 1906), pp. 34985-34986.
71. Sieghart, *op. cit.*, p. 87.
72. *St. P....des Hauses der Abgeordneten* (March 9, 1906), p. 34987.
73. *Ibid.*, p. 34988.
74. *Ibid.*, pp. 34992-34997.
75. For Grabmayr's speech, see *ibid.* (March 7, 1906), pp. 34834-34839.
76. Charmatz, *Österreichs innere Geschichte*, vol. II, p. 166.
77. Czedik, *op. cit.*, vol. III, p. 286.
78. Jenks, *The Austrian Electoral Reform of 1907*, p. 57.
79. Brocard, *op. cit.*, pp. 139-140. For the party's response to these events, see *Parteivertretungsprotokolle der sozialdemokratischen Partei Österreichs*, I (May 2, 1906).
80. Beaumont, *op. cit.*, p. 627.
81. *St. P....des Hauses der Abgeordneten* (May 15, 1906), pp. 36147-36149.
82. Charmatz, *Österreichs innere Geschichte*,

vol. II, p. 169.
83. May, *op. cit.*, p. 338. Hungarian claims for a separate customs area all but incensed Renner, who considered the Hungarian demands to be another parasitical attempt on the part of the Magyars to do economic harm to Austria; on this point, see Jászi, *op. cit.*, p. 181.
84. *A-Z*, May 29, 1906, p. 1; and Sieghart, *op. cit.*, pp. 94-95.
85. Sieghart, *op. cit.*, p. 92.
86. Ableitinger, *op. cit.*, p. 131; and Brügel, *Geschichte*, vol. IV, pp. 372-373.
87. Max Beck, "Der Kaiser und die Wahlreform," in Eduard von Steinitz (ed.), *Erinnerungen an Franz Joseph I* (Berlin, 1931), p. 209.
88. Hannak, *op. cit.*, p. 144; and Beck, *op. cit.*, p. 203.
89. Victor Adler, *Aufsätze*, 2nd ed., part 10, p. 344.
90. *A-Z*, June 7, 1906, p. 2.
91. *A-Z*, June 13, 1906, p. 2; see also, *Parteivertretungsprotokolle der sozialdemokratischen Partei Österreichs*, I (June 13, 1906).
92. *A-Z*, June 18, 1906, p. 1.
93. Again, as before, the trade-union commission failed to give serious consideration to the idea; on this point see *Sitzungsprotokolle der Gewerkschaftskommission Oesterreichs (June-July, 1906)*, pp. 157-159.
94. Beck, *op. cit.*, pp. 210-211.
95. Victor Adler, *Aufsätze*, 2nd ed., part 10, pp. 350-351.
96. *Ibid.*, pp. 350, 352-353.
97. *Ibid.*, p. 354.
98. *Ibid.*, p. 367.
99. *St. P....des Hauses der Abgeordneten* (September 13, 1906), p. 436. Article 7 of the new law constituted the key provision of the act guaranteeing universal manhood suffrage; Edmund Bernatzik (ed.), *Die österreichischen Verfassungsgesetze* (Vienna, 1911), pp. 757-758.
100. Beaumont, *op. cit.*, p. 629.
101. *A-Z*, September 18, 1906, p. 3.
102. *St. P....des Hauses der Abgeordneten*

(November 8, 1906), pp. 39598-39599.
103. *Ibid.*, p. 39602.
104. Beck, *op. cit.*, p. 215. The final distribution of seats gave the Slavs 259 (107 for the Czechs; 82 for the Poles; 33 for the Ruthenians; 24 for the Slovenes; and 13 for the Serbo-Croats), the Germans 233, the Italians 19 and the Rumanians 5, Brocard, *op. cit.*, p. 140.
105. Jenks, *The Austrian Electoral Reform Bill of 1907*, pp. 88-89.
106. Strauss, *Geschichte*, vol. II, p. 140.
107. For further evidence here, see *Sitzungsprotokolle der Gewerkschaftskommission Oesterreichs (December, 1906)*, pp. 164-165.
108. Jenks, *The Austrian Electoral Reform of 1907*, pp. 89-90.
109. *Ibid.*, pp. 132-133; and Hannak, *op. cit.*, p. 145.
110. Beaumont, *op. cit.*, p. 631. The history of the long road leading up to electoral reform in Austria is recorded in outline in Hans Kelsen, *Kommentar zur österreichischen Reichsratswahlordnung* (Vienna, 1907), pp. 1-20; a copy of the 1907 law may be found, in full, in Bernatizik, *op. cit.*, pp. 756-781.
111. *St. P....des Hauses der Abgeordneten* (January 11, 1907), pp. 41441-41453.
112. Victor Adler, *Aufsätze*, 2nd ed., part 10, p. 457; see also, Fritz Austerlitz, *Das neue Wahlrecht* (Vienna, 1907).
113. V. Hussey Walsh, "Through the Austrian General Election," *Fortnightly Review*, LXXXI (1907), p. 981; and Brocard, *op. cit.*, p.163.
114. Walsh, *op. cit.*, p. 982.
115. Schwechler, *op. cit.*, pp. 37-38.
116. Hannak, *op. cit.*, p. 149.
117. Ermers, *op. cit.*, p. 298; and Brügel, *Geschichte*, vol. V, p. 41.
118. Brügel, *Geschichte*, vol. V, p. 40. The relative figures appear as 4,505, 552 and 1,033,565 in Brocard, *op. cit.*, p. 156.
119. Brocard, *op. cit.*, pp. 156-157, 160-162.
120. Marmorek, *op. cit.*, p. 119.
121. Allmeyer-Beck, *op. cit.*, p. 158.
122. Jenks, *The Austrian Electoral Reform of 1907*,

pp. 199-200.
123. Bauer's *Introduction*, p. xxiv.
124. Brügel, *Geschichte*, vol. V, p. 44.
125. *A-Z*, June 27, 1907, p. 1.
126. *A-Z*, September 26, 1907, p. 9.
127. *St. P....des Hauses der Abgeordneten* (June 27, 1907), pp. 95-97.
128. Taylor, *op. cit.*, pp. 212-213.
129. *St. P....des Hauses der Abgeordneten* (November 26, 1908), p. 7627. The bill was actually submitted early in November.
130. Ermers, *op. cit.*, p. 299.
131. Taylor, *op. cit.*, p. 165; and Mommsen, *op. cit.*, p. 6.

Chapter VII: *The Disintegration of Austrian Socialism*

1. Otto Bauer, "Gesammtparteitag und Gewerkschaftsfrage," *Der Kampf*, V (1911), 560.
2. The more complete story is contained in Domes, *op. cit.*, pp. 555-556.
3. Deutsch, *Geschichte*, vol. I, pp. 413-414.
4. Weber, *op. cit.*, p. 582.
5. Deutsch, *Geschichte*, vol. I, p. 414.
6. *Ibid.*
7. See Škatula's letter in *Protokoll des ausserordentlichen Gewerkschaftskongresses (1905)*, pp. 9-10.
8. Reinold, *op. cit.*, pp. 47-48.
9. See the report issued by the Prague commission on June 16, 1905 in *Protokoll des ausserordentlichen Gewerkschaftskongresses (1905)*, pp. 10-11.
10. "Auszug aus dem Protokoll über die Verhandlungen der internationalen Konferenz der Landessekretäre in Amsterdam im Jahre 1905," in *ibid.*, p. 12.
11. *Ibid.*
12. *Ibid.*, p. 13.
13. *Ibid.*
14. *Ibid.*, pp. 13-14. The vote, which was 10 to 0, reaffirmed the 1902 decision of the Stuttgart Conference of Trade-Union Secretaries which provided that there was

to be only one trade-union central in each country.
15. See the report of Němec's article in *ibid.*, p. 14. The minutes of the Amsterdam conference (June 23-24, 1905) dealing with the Czech dispute may be found, in full, in *Bericht der Gewerkschaftskommission Oesterreichs an den Fünften ordentlichen Kongress der Gewerkschaften Oesterreichs in Wien 1907*, pp. 22-24.
16. Reinold, *op. cit.*, p. 49.
17. Quoted in *ibid.*
18. *Ibid.*, pp. 49-50.
19. On the subject of Czech autonomy, see Edvard Beneš, *Le Problème Autrichien et la Question Tchèque* (Paris, 1908), p. 294 ff.
20. *Protokoll des ausserordentlichen Gewerkschaftskongresses (1905)*, pp. 21-25-30.
21. *Ibid.*, p. 41.
22. *Ibid.*, pp. 33-34.
23. *Ibid.*, p. 32.
24. *Protokoll...des Gesammtparteitages (1905)*, pp. 85-86.
25. Reinold, *op. cit.*, pp. 50-51.
26. Heinrich Beer, "Der fünfte Gewerkschaftskongress," p. 50.
27. Tayerle, "Die gewerkschaftlichen Selbständigkeitsbestrebungen der tschechischen Arbeiter in Österreich," p. 733.
28. *Bericht der Gewerkschaftskommission (1907)*, p. 114.
29. Beneš, "Le Syndicalisme en Bohême," p. 462.
30. *Protokoll des ausserordentlichen Gewerkschaftskongresses (1905)*, p. 57; and Deutsch, *Geschichte*, vol. I, p. 421.
31. Fehlinger and Klenner, *op. cit.*, pp. 40-41.
32. As in the years before 1907, the Trade-Union Commission did have an overwhelmingly German character; in part this was the result of history since the German unions arose first and their leaders came to dominate unions that the Czechs came to penetrate only later. In 1907, the commission members were Heinrich Beer (Metalworkers), Anna Boschek (Women), Alexander Da Rin (Ceramic workers), Josef Swořaček (Bookbinders), Julius Grünwald (Bookbinders),

Ferdinand Hanusch (Textile workers), Anton Hueber (Secretary), Rudolf Müller (Railway workers), Heinrich Möller (Shoemakers), Thomas Mrkwička (Carpenters), Franz Nader (Construction workers), Anton Schrammel (Chemical workers), Franz Silberer (Backers), and Johann Suchanek (Turners); *Verhandlungsprotokolle des Fünften ordentlichen Gewerkschaftskongresses Oesterreichs abgehalten vom 21. bis inklusive 25. Oktober 1907 zu Wien*, pp. 219, 221-222, 224.

33. Deutsch, *Geschichte*, vol. I, p. 424.
34. Anton Nĕmec, "Proletariat, Demokratie und die tschechische Nation," *Der Kampf*, I (1907), 19.
35. *Revolte des Separatismus* (Vienna, 1911), p.3.
36. *A-Z*, November 15, 1911, pp. 11-12.
37. *Bericht der Gewerkschafts-Kommission Oesterreichs an den VI. ordentlichen Kongress der Gewerkschaften Oesterreichs in Wien 1910*, p. 6; and Strauss, *Geschichte*, vol. II, p. 221.
38. Victor Adler, *Aufsätze*, 2nd ed., part 7, p. 163.
39. Strauss, *Geschichte*, vol. II, pp. 220-221.
40. Domes, *op. cit.*, p. 554.
41. Reinold, *op. cit.*, p. 93.
42. *Ibid.*, p. 95.
43. *Verhandlungen des...Parteitages (1897)*, p. 8.
44. Bauer, "Gesamtparteitag und Gewerkschaftsfrage," 556-564; on this point, see also *Parteivertretungsprotokolle der sozialdemokratischen Partei Österreichs*, I and II, especially the period after 1906.
45. *Protokoll...des Parteitages der deutschen ...Arbeiterpartei (1907)*, pp. 83-94; and *Protokollbuch des sozialdemokratischen Abgeordnetenverbandes* (Plenum), I (November 7, 1907).
46. Friedrich Adler, "Minderwertig im Internationalismus," *Der Kampf*, IV (1911), 497.
47. Ermers, *op. cit.*, pp. 302-303.
48. *Dokumente des Separatismus*, p. 15.
49. *Ibid.*, pp. 14-15; and *Parteivertretungsprotokolle der sozialdemokratischen Partei Österreichs*, I (March 3 and 7, 1910).

50. See Vaněk's brochure "Wollen wir unter Kuratel sein oder frei?" in *Dokumente des Separatismus,* pp. 23, 26-27, 29, 31-33.
51. *Ibid.*
52. *Ibid.,* pp. 37 ff.
53. Franz Soukup, "Der Parteitag der tschechischen Sozialdemokratie," *Der Kampf,* III (1909), 4.
54. For a summary of Czech contentions here, see Otto Bauer, "Krieg oder Friede?" *Der Kampf,* IV (1910), 11.
55. Strauss, *Geschichte,* vol. II, p. 222.
56. Bauer, *Krieg oder Friede in den Gewerkschaften?* p. 5.
57. *Ibid.,* pp. 9-12.
58. Strauss, *Geschichte,* vol. II, p. 222.
59. Klenner, *op. cit.,* p. 319.
60. *Ibid.*
61. By 1912, the number had swelled to 104,000 in the Czech unions, *A-Z,* July 23, 1913, p. 8. The defections took place for the most part in the territories with overwhelming Czech population majorities. The Czech unions located in heterogeneous population areas tended to remain faithful to the international organization in Vienna; Braunthal, *In Search of the Millenium,* p. 117.
62. Ernst Lieben, "Der Separatismus in der Genossenschaftsbewegung," *Der Kampf,* III (1910), 418-420.
63. *Dokumente des Separatismus,* p. 54; Reinold, *op. cit.,* pp. 105-107; *Protokolle des deutschen Clubs,* I (June 6, 1910); and *St. P....des Hauses der Abgeordneten* (June 23, 1910, pp. 3729-3730, 3736-3737.
64. Konirsh, *op. cit.,* p. 247.
65. Karl Renner, "Die nationaler Minderheitsschulen," *Der Kampf,* III (1910), 250-257.
66. Otto Bauer, "Ein nationaler Gegensatz," *A-Z,* July 1, 1910, pp. 1-2.
67. *Dokumente des Separatismus,* pp. 55-58.
68. *Internationaler Sozialisten-Kongress zu Kopenhagen 28. August bis 3. September 1910,* p. 128.
69. *Ibid.*
70. Mommsen, *op. cit.,* pp. 435-436.

71. Victor Adler, *Aufsätze*, 2nd ed., part 8, pp. 11-12.
72. *Internationaler Sozialisten-Kongress (1910)*, pp. 43-44.
73. *Ibid.*, p. 45.
74. *Ibid.*, pp. 46-47, 50-51, 82-84, 93-94.
75. *Ibid.*, pp. 49-50, 88-89.
76. *Ibid.*, pp. 47-48.
77. *Ibid.*, p. 95; and *Dokumente des Separatismus*, p. 76.
78. Otto Bauer, "Kopenhagen," *Der Kampf*, III (1910), 536.
79. *Internationaler Sozialisten-Kongress (1910)*, pp. 44, 95.
80. *Dokumente des Separatismus*, p. 86.
81. *Ibid.*, pp. 89-113.
82. *Verhandlungs-Protokoll des Sechsten ordentlichen Gewerkschafts-Kongresses abgehalten vom 17. bis 22. Oktober 1910 zu Wien*, p. 250.
83. The Czech message was to a large degree written between the lines and would most likely have been lost to those who responded to the Czechs viscerally rather than carefully as the Germans did quite obviously.
84. See for example, Victor Adler, *Aufsätze*, 2nd ed., part 8, pp. 11-17.
85. *Ibid.*, p. 18.
86. *Verhandlungs-Protokoll des Sechsten... Gewerkschafts-Kongresses (1910)*, pp. 252-255. Some evidence exists that Adler was of two minds during the separatist crisis; that there was a private Adler, who was willing to pursue one course, and a public Adler, who followed another. If Adler was ever in favor of an accommodation with Němec, he kept the fact fairly well hidden during the later stages of the controversy; for some revealing points on this question, see Anto Hueber, "Im Kampf um die Einheit der Gewerkschaften," in *Victor Adler im Spiegel seiner Zeitgenossen* (Vienna, 1968), pp. 99-100.
87. Otto Bauer, "Zu neuen Form," *Der Kampf*, X (1911), 446-447.
88. *Revolte des Separatismus*, p. 32; and Deutsch, *Geschichte*, vol. I, p. 426.

89. *Revolte des Separatismus,* pp. 32-33.
90. *Ibid.,* pp. 34-37.
91. Ermers, *op. cit.,* p. 304.
92. Strauss, *Geschichte,* vol. II, pp. 227-228. The new party should be distinguished from the older one which had clung nostalgically and hopefully to the title of the Czechoslovakian Social-Democratic Labor Party. For more background material on the fears which separatism occasioned both inside and outside of Austria, see Paul Umbreit, "Zur Entwicklungsgeschichte des Separatismus in Österreich," *Die Neue Zeit,* XXX (1911), 470-474.
93. *Protokoll über die Verhandlungen des Parteitages der deutschen sozialdemokratischen Arbeiterpartei in Oesterreich abgehalten in Innsbruck vom 29. Oktober bis 2. November 1911,* p. 92.
94. Edmund Burian, "Tschechische Literatur über Sozialismus und Separatismus," *Der Kampf,* V (1912), 295-301.
95. Bauer, "Zu neuen Formen," p. 446.
96. *Dokumente des Separatismus,* p. 124.
97. *A-Z,* June 15, 1911, p. 6; Kelsen, *op. cit.,* pp. 189-191; and Bernatzik, *op. cit.,* p. 784.
98. Ermers, *op. cit.,* p. 305.
99. Brügel, *Geschichte,* vol. V, p. 108.
100. *Protokoll...des deutschen sozialdemokratischen Arbeiterpartei (1911),* pp. 213, 216.
101. *Ibid.,* pp. 215-216, 282.
102. Deutsch, *Geschichte der deutschösterreichischen Arbeiterbewegung,* p. 34; Otto Bauer, "Galizische Parteitage," *Der Kampf,* V (1912), 157-158. On this point, see also *Parteivertretungsprotokolle der sozialdemokratischen Partei Österreichs,* II (June 20, 1912).
103. *A-Z,* November 6, 1912, p. 2.
104. *A-Z,* June 24, 1912, p. 1. The article by Němec was reprinted as "Die Pfiffigkeit der deutschen Sozialdemokraten," *Der Kampf,* IV (1911), 104.
105. Friedrich Adler, "Minderwertig im Internationalismus," 496; and Karl Renner, "Nach Innsbruck," *Der Kampf,* V (1911), 104.

106. Otto Bauer, "Zum Innsbrucker Parteitag," *Der Kampf*, V (1911), 49-56.
107. Victor Adler, "Die separatistische Krise," *Der Kampf*, IV (1911), 531.

Chapter VIII: *The Coming of World War I*

1. Otto Bauer, "Der zweite Balkankrieg," *Der Kampf*, VI (1913), 481.
2. Otto Bauer, "Der Weg zur Macht," *Der Kampf*, II (1909), 337; Benedikt, *op. cit.*, p. 176; Ermers, *op. cit.*, pp. 311-312; and Sieghart, *op. cit.*, p. 132.
3. Bienerth's close political connections with the heir to the Austrian throne Franz Ferdinand and the architect of Austria's forward policy in the Balkans, the foreign minister Count Alois Aehrenthal, were in themselves, considered ominous; May, *op. cit.*, p. 425.
4. Sieghart, *op. cit.*, pp. 128-129.
5. Hugelmann, *Das Nationalitätenrecht*, p. 243.
6. In the early part of November, weeks before his resignation, Beck submitted a new Old Age and Invalid Insurance Act to parliament, an event which the socialists deemed as one of the most significant in the history of Austria's social development; *A-Z*, November 4, 1908, p. 1.
7. Czedik, *op. cit.*, vol. IV, p. 9.
8. *A-Z*, November 17, 1908, p. 1.
9. *St. P....des Hauses der Abgeordneten* (December 10, 1908), pp. 7864-7865.
10. Georges Blondel, "Les Dernières Élections en Autriche-Hongrie," *La Réforme Sociale*, LXII (1911), 221.
11. Brügel, *Geschichte*, vol. V, p. 61.
12. Czedik, *op. cit.*, vol. IV, pp. 17-19.
13. Sieghart, *op. cit.*, p. 147.
14. Adler, *Aufsätze*, 2nd ed., part 8, p. 307.
15. *Ibid.*
16. *Ibid.*, pp. 315-318; and *A-Z*, October 8, 1909, pp. 1-2.
17. *St. P....des Hauses der Abgeordneten* (December, 15-19, 1909) pp. 1013-1144.

18. *Ibid.*, pp. 1059-1060, 1065-1066, 1135-1139.
19. Karl Renner, "Die Entwaffnung der Obstruktion," *Der Kampf*, III (1910), 145.
20. Strauss, *Geschichte*, vol. II, pp. 200-201.
21. *Verhandlungs-Protokoll...Gewerkschafts-Kongresses (1910)*, p. 308.
22. Friedrich Adler, "Der Wert des Parlamentarismus," *Der Kampf*, IV (1911), 415.
23. *Ibid.*, pp. 413-415.
24. Jenks, *The Austrian Electoral Reform of 1907*, p. 204; May, *op. cit.*, p. 428, Zöllner, *op. cit.*, p. 439; Blondel, *op. cit*, pp. 218-219; and Hantsch, *Die Geschichte Österreichs*, vol. II, p. 538. The Christian Socialist total was only 77 but that party operated as a more effective unit than the Social Democrats after 1911.
25. Friedrich Austerlitz, "Sieg und Niederlage in Österreich," *Die Neue Zeit*, XXIX (1911), 466-468.
26. Czedik, *op. cit.*, vol. IV, pp. 331-337.
27. Sieghart, *op. cit.*, pp. 148-149.
28. Czedik, *op. cit.*, vol. IV, pp. 391-399.
29. Charmatz, *Österreichs äussere und innere Politik*, p. 114.
30. Bauer, "Geschäftsordnungsreform oder Absolutismus," pp. 97-99.
31. Compare here, Charmatz, *Österreichs innere Geschichte*, vol. II, p. 175; and Czedik, *op. cit.*, vol. IV, pp. 432-433.
32. One observer insists that they never did, as a practical matter, exercise any influence upon the parliamentary majority; on this point, see Sieghart, *op. cit.*, pp. 353-354.
33. *Protokoll des Verhandlungen des Parteitages der deutschen sozialdemokratischen Arbeiterpartei in Oesterreich in Wien vom 31. Oktober zum 4. November 1912*, p. 225.
34. *Ibid.* In mid-July of 1914, the house committee working on the bill that would have brought Austria abreast of Germany and England in the field of social legislation finally completed its work. The *Arbeiter-Zeitung* spoke to the great significance of the bill saying that in the design resided the central interest of the masses in the

work of parliament. The lower house, the paper happily predicted, would vote the Old Age and Invalid Insurance Act into law within two or three sittings, once the then prorogued parliament reconvened for its fall session. Ironically, the war intervened and there was never to be a fall session; see *A-Z*, July 10, 1914, p. 1.
35. Brügel, *Soziale Gesetzgebung*, pp. 232-233.
36. *Bericht der Reichskommission der Gewerkschaften Oesterreichs an den Siebenten ordentlichen Kongress der Gewerkschaften Oesterreichs (1913)*, pp. 13-26.
37. *Protokoll des Siebenten ordentlichen Kongresses der Gewerkschaften Oesterreichs abgehalten vom 6. bis zum 10. Oktober 1913 in Wien*, p. 230.
38. As an illustration here, see Siegfried Schab, "[Artikel] 14, Obstruktion und Sozialdemokratie," *Der Kampf*, VII (1913), 22-25.
39. Strauss, *Geschichte*, vol. II, pp. 207-209.
40. *Protokolle der Verhandlungen des Parteitages der deutschensozialdemokratischen Arbeiterpartei in Oesterreich abgehalten in Wien vom 31. Oktober bis zum 4. November 1913*, pp. 179-184.
41. *Ibid.*, pp. 174-176, 187, 195. On this point, see also *Protokolle des deutschen Clubs*, III (March 4, 1914).
42. Fehlinger and Klenner, *op. cit.*, pp. 41-42.
43. See for example, Heinrich Beer's speech in *Verhandlungsprotokoll des...Gewerkschaftskongresses (1907)*, pp. 180-181.
44. *Bericht der Gewerkschafts-Kommission (1910)*, p. 71.
45. The sum involved here jumped from some 4,641,726 *Kronen* in 1904 to some 8,120,763 *Kronen* in 1907; *ibid.*, p. 73. Roughly translated the comparable figures would have been $1,160,000 and $2,030,000; the *Krone* was worth approximately 20 cents before World War I.
46. *Ibid.*, p. 74.
47. Klenner, *op. cit.*, p. 340.
48. Hertz, *Die Produktionsgrundlage*, pp. 173-174.
49. Frederick Hertz, *The Economic Problem of the*

Danubian States (London, 1947), pp. 33-34.
50. Klenner, op. cit., pp. 310-311, 336-337; and Strauss, Geschichte, vol. II, pp. 187-188.
51. Otto Bauer, "Krise und Teuerung," Der Kampf, I (1907), 116.
52. Bericht der Gewerkschafts-Kommission (1910), p. 71.
53. Bericht der Reichskommission der Gewerkschaften (1913), p. 29.
54. Protokoll...des Parteitages der deutschen sozialdemokratischen Arbeiterpartei (1912), pp. 42-43.
55. Friedrich Hertz, Die Schwierigkeiten der industriellen Produktion in Oesterreich (Vienna, 1910), p. 43.
56. Danneberg, Das sozialdemokratische Programm, p. 79.
57. See for example, Matthias Eldersch, "Die neue Sozialversicherungsvorlage," Der Kampf, V (1911), 127-132.
58. For more background material on this point, see Hans Fehlinger, "Internationale Uebereinkommen betreffend die Sozialversicherung," Archiv für Sozialwissenschaft und Sozialpolitik, LX (1928), 180-186.
59. Karl Renner, "Fünf Kampfjahre," Der Kampf, VI (1912), 1-5.
60. Benedikt, op. cit., p. 178.
61. Hannak, op. cit., pp. 164-165.
62. Verhandlungs-Protokoll des...Gewerkschafts-Kongresses (1910), p. 365.
63. Brügel, Geschichte, vol. V, p. 109.
64. Strauss, Geschichte, vol. II, p. 180; and Charmatz, Österreichs äussere und innere Politik, p. 111.
65. Victor Adler, Aufsätze, 2nd ed., part 8, pp. 447-451.
66. St. P....des Hauses der Abgeordneten (October 5, 1911), pp. 606-617.
67. For more on Austro-Marxism, see the studies by Norbert Lesser, Zwischen Reformismus und Bolshewismus: Der Austromarxismus als Theorie und Praxis (Vienna, 1968); and Paul M. Zulehener, Kirche und Austromarxismus (Vienna, 1967).
68. This theme is, of course, the implication of Renner's principal work, Der Kampf der

69. oesterreichischen Nationen um den Staat. See here, Adler's article, "Der Nachlass von Marx, Engels und Lassalle," in Tesarek, op. cit., p. 109.
70. Adolf Braun, "Marx und die Gewerkschaften," Der Kampf, I (1908), 249-251.
71. Benedikt Kautsky, Geistige Strömungen, pp. 10-11.
72. This question is raised in Wolkan, op. cit., pp. 857-858.
73. Carlton J.H. Hayes, The Historical Evolution of Modern Nationalism (New York, 1931), pp. 27-33.
74. For a wider discussion of these points, see Cole, op. cit., vol. III, part 2, pp. 552-555, 557.
75. Otto Bauer, "Der Arbeiter und die Nation," Der Kampf, V (1912), 401-406.
76. Otto Bauer, "Der Weg zur Macht," pp. 337-344.
77. Otto Bauer, "Der Grundfrage unserer Taktik," p. 53.
78. Ibid., pp. 53-54.
79. Ibid., p. 53.
80. Ibid., p. 62. For Bauer's views on the growth of the capitalist economy, see "Die Teuerung," Der Kampf, VII (1912), 443-461.
81. Bauer, "Gewerkschaften und Sozialismus," pp. 241-242.
82. On these points, see Otto Bauer, Der Übergang vom Kapitalismus zum Sozialismus (Wiener Neustadt, 1958), pp. 1-31; and his earlier piece on the same subject, Der Weg zum Sozialismus (Vienna, 1919).
83. Max Adler, "Marxismus und Materialismus," Der Kampf, III (1910), 564-571.
84. Max Adler, "Der soziale Sinn der Lehre von Karl Marx," Archiv für die Geschichte des Sozialismus und der Arbeiterbewegung, IV (1914), 1-29; and Max Adler, Marxistische Probleme (Stuttgart, 1913), pp. 35-39.
85. Max Adler, Marx als Denker (3rd rev. ed., Berlin, 1925), pp. 68-78, 156-165; and part II (Kausalität und Teleologie im Streite um die Wissenschaft) in Max Adler, "Marx' Verhältnis zur Erkenntniskritik," Marx-Studien, I (1904), 314-322.

86. See here, as an illustration, Friedrich Adler, "Wozu brauchen wir Theorien?" *Der Kampf*, II (1909), 256-263.
87. May, *op. cit.*, p. 414.
88. *Die Sozialdemokratie und der Frieden: Reden der sozialdemokratischen Abgeordneten über die bosnische Frage und die Kriegsgefahr* (Vienna, 1909), pp. 5-6.
89. *St. P....des Hauses der Abgeordneten* (December 18, 1908), pp. 8199-8207.
90. *Ibid.* (December 3, 16-18, 1908), pp. 7709, 8062-8102, 8112-8221.
91. Otto Bauer, "Oesterreich und der Imperialismus," *Der Kampf*, II (1908), 19-20; and Heinrich Weber, "Das südslawische Problem," *Der Kampf*, II (1909), 289-294.
92. Bauer's *Introduction*, p. xxviii.
93. Schwechler, *op. cit.*, pp. 215-218.
94. *VIIe Congrès Socialiste International tenu à Stuttgart du 16 au 24 août 1907 (Compte Rendu Analytique)*, p. 148.
95. *Ibid.*, p. 152.
96. *Ibid.*, p. 421.
97. *Internationaler Sozialisten-Kongress (1910)*, pp. 34-35, 38.
98. May, *op. cit.*, pp. 460-461.
99. Joll, *op. cit.*, pp. 152-153.
100. Ermers, *op. cit.*, p. 312.
101. *St. P....des Hauses der Abgeordneten* (October 22, 1912), p. 5297 (Anhang III-2509).
102. *Protokoll...des Parteitages der deutschen... Arbeiterpartei (1912)*, p. 116.
103. *Ausserordentlicher Internationaler Sozialisten-Kongress zu Basel am 24. und 25. November 1912*, p. 23.
104. *Ibid.*, pp. 24-25.
105. *Ibid.*, pp. 13-14.
106. *Ibid.*, pp. 17-18.
107. Ermers, *op. cit.*, p. 313.
108. Brügel, *Geschichte*, vol. V, p. 119.
109. May, *op. cit.*, pp. 464-467.
110. Otto Bauer, *Der Balkankrieg und die deutsche Weltpolitik* (Berlin, 1912), pp. 3-4, 48-49.
111. Friedrich Austerlitz, "Oesterreich nach dem Balkankrieg," *Der Kampf*, VI (1913), 385.
112. Z.A.B. Zeman, *The Break-Up of the Habsburg*

113. *Monarchy 1914-1918* (London, 1961), p. 36.
113. Fritz Fellner (ed.), *Das politische Tagebuch Josef Redlichs,* 2 vols. (Graz, 1953-54), vol. I, pp. 235-239.
114. *A-Z,* June 29, 1914, p. 1; and Braunthal, *Austerlitz Spricht,* pp. 77-79.
115. *A-Z,* July 23, 1914, p. 1.
116. Zeman, *op. cit.,* pp. 37-38.
117. Czedik, *op. cit.,* vol. IV, p. 427.
118. Arthur J. May, *The Passing of the Hapsburg Monarchy,* 2 vols. (Philadelphia, 1966), vol. I, pp. 62-63.
119. *Ibid.,* p. 64; and *A-Z,* July 24, 1914, p.1.
120. Czedik, *op. cit.,* vol. IV, p. 42.
121. Joll, *op. cit.,* p. 163.
122. Braunthal, *The International,* p. 352.
123. Ermers, *op. cit.,* p. 317.
124. Brügel, *Geschichte,* vol. V, p. 177; Joll, *op. cit.,* pp. 178-179; Engelbert Pernerstorfer, *Zeitfragen* (2nd ed., Vienna, 1918), pp. 55-57; and *Sitzungsprotokolle des Vorstandes der deutschen sozialdemokratischen Partei* (July 23, 26, 28 and 30, 1914).
125. Quoted in Charmatz, *Lebensbilder,* p. 201.
126. Shell, *op. cit.,* p. 12.
127. Eduard Beneš (pseud. É. Bělský), *Le Socialisme Autrichien et la Guerre* (Paris, 1915), pp. 5-10.
128. *A-Z,* July 28, 1914, p. 1.

BIBLIOGRAPHY

I. Victor Adlers Nachlass

II. Party Archives

A. Vorstands-und Exekutivprotokolle der sozialdemokratischen Partei Österreichs

Exekutivprotokolle I (1897-1900)
Exekutivprotokolle II (1900-1904)
Parteivertretungsprotokolle I (1906-1910)
Parteivertretungsprotokolle II (1910-1913)
*Sitzungsprotokolle des Parteivorstandes der
   deutschen sozialdemokratischen Partei
   (1913-1914)*

B. Fraktionsprotokolle des sozialdemokratischen Verbandes

*Protokollbuch des sozialdemokratischen Verbandes
   II (1898-1903)*
*Verband der sozialdemokratischen Abgeordneten
   (Vorstand) (1907-1909)*
Abgeordnetenverband (Plenum) I (1907-1908)
Abgeordnetenverband (Plenum) II (1907-1908)
Protokolle des deutschen Clubs I (1907-1911)
Protokolle des deutschen Clubs II (1911-1912)
Protokolle des deutschen Clubs III (1912-1914)
Vorstand des deutschen Clubs (1911-1913)

III. Protocols

A. Party Protocols

*Verhandlungen des Parteitages der österreichischen
   Sozialdemokratie in Hainfeld (30./31.
   Dezember 1888 und 1. Januar 1889).*
*Verhandlungen des zweiten österreichischen sozialdemokratischen Parteitages abgehalten zu Wien
   am 28., 29. und 30. Juni 1891.*
*Verhandlungen des dritten österreichischen sozialdemokratischen Parteitages abgehalten zu Wien
   am 5., 6., 7., 8. und 9. Juni 1892.*
Verhandlungen des vierten österreichischen sozialdemokratischen Parteitages abgehalten zu Wien

vom 25. bis einschliesslich 31. März 1894.
Verhandlungen des fünften österreichischen sozialdemokratischen Parteitages abgehalten zu Prag vom 5. bis einschliesslich 11. April 1896.
Verhandlungen des sechsten österreichischen sozialdemokratischen Parteitages zu Wien vom 6. bis einschliesslich 12. Juni 1897.
Verhandlungen des Gesammtparteitages der Sozialdemokratie in Oesterreich abgehalten zu Brünn vom 24. bis·29. September 1899.
Protokoll über die Verhandlungen des Gesammtparteitages der sozialdemokratischen Arbeiterpartei in Oesterreich abgehalten zu Wien vom 2. bis 6. November 1901.
Protokoll über die Verhandlungen des Gesamtparteitages der sozialdemokratischen Arbeiterpartei abgehalten zu Wien vom 9. bis zum 13. November 1903.
Protokoll über die Verhandlungen des Gesamtparteitages der sozialdemokratischen Arbeiterpartei in Oesterreich abgehalten zu Wien vom 30. Oktober bis zum 2. November 1905.
Verhandlungen des Parteitages der deutschen Sozialdemokratie abgehalten zu Linz vom 29. Mai bis einschliesslich 1. Juni 1898.
Protokoll über die Verhandlungen des Parteitages der deutschen sozialdemokratischen Arbeiterpartei abgehalten zu Aussig vom 15. bis 18. August 1902.
Protokoll über die Verhandlungen des Parteitages der deutschen sozialdemokratischen Arbeiterpartei in Oesterreich abgehalten in Wien vom 30. September bis 4. Oktober 1907.
Protokoll des Parteitages der deutschen sozialdemokratischen Arbeiterpartei in Oesterreich abgehalten in Reichenberg vom 19. bis 24. September 1909.
Protokoll über die Verhandlungen des Parteitages der deutschen sozialdemokratischen Arbeiterpartei in Oesterreich abgehalten in Innsbruck vom 29. Oktober bis 2. November 1911.
Die Verhandlungen der deutschen sozialdemokratischen Arbeiterpartei in Oesterreich abgehalten vom 31. bis zum 4. November 1912 in Wien.
Protokolle der Verhandlungen des Parteitages der deutschensozialdemokratischen Arbeiter-

*partei in Oesterreich abgehalten in Wien vom
31. Oktober bis zum 4. November 1913.*

B. Trade-Union Protocols

Protokoll über die Verhandlungen des 1. Gewerkschaftskongresses abgehalten vom 24. bis 27. Dezember 1893 in Wien.
Protokoll des II. österreichischen Gewerkschaftskongresses abgehalten vom 25. bis 29. Dezember 1896.
Protokoll über die Verhandlungen des III. österreichischen Gewerkschafts-Congresses abgehalten zu Wien vom 11. bis 15. Juni 1900.
Protokoll über die Verhandlungen des vierten österreichischen Gewerkschaftskongresses abgehalten vom 8. bis inklusive 12. Juni 1903 zu Wien.
Protokoll des ausserordentlichen österreichischen Gewerkschaftskongresses abgehalten vom 8. bis inklusive 10. Dezember 1905 zu Wien.
Verhandlungsprotokolle des Fünften ordentlichen Gewerkschaftskongresses Oesterreichs abgehalten vom 21. bis inklusive 25. Oktober 1907 zu Wien.
Verhandlungs-Protokoll des Sechsten ordentlichen Gewerkschafts-Kongresses abgehalten vom 17. bis 22. Oktober 1910 zu Wien.
Protokoll des Siebenten ordentlichen Kongresses der Gewerkschaften Oesterreichs abgehalten vom 6. bis zum 10. Oktober 1913 in Wien.
Sitzungsprotokolle der Gewerkschaftskommission Oesterreichs vom 7. Mai 1895 bis 31. Dezember 1906.

C. Protocols of the Second International

Protokoll des Internationalen Arbeiter-Congresses zu Paris (1889).
Congrès International Ouvrier Socialiste tenu à Bruxelles du 16 au 23 août 1891 (Rapport).
Protokoll des Internationalen Sozialistischen Arbeiterkongresses zu Zürich (1893).
Full Report of the Proceedings of the International Workers' Congress 1896.
Compte Rendu Sténographique Non Officiel de la Version Française du cinquième Congrès

Socialiste International tenu à Paris du 23
au 27 September 1900.
Internationaler Sozialisten-Kongress zu Amsterdam
14. bis 20. August 1904.
VIIe Congrès Socialiste International tenu à
Stuttgart du 16 au 24 août 1907 (Compte Rendu
Analytique).
Internationaler Sozialisten-Kongress zu Kopenhagen
28. August bis 3. September 1910.
Aussenordentlicher Internationaler Sozialisten-
Kongress zu Basel am 24. und 25. November
1912.

IV. Trade-Union Reports

Thätigkeitsbericht der Gewerkschafts-Kommission
Oesterreichs für 1894 bis 1896.
Rechenschaftsbericht der Gewerkschafts-Commission
Oesterreichs über die Thätigkeit vom 1.
Jänner 1897 bis zum 31. Dezember 1899.
Rechenschaftsbericht der Gewerkschaftskommission
Oesterreichs uber ihre Thätigkeit vom 1.
Jänner 1900 bis 31. Dezember 1902.
Bericht der Gewerkschaftskommission Oesterreichs
an den Fünften ordentlichen Kongress der
Gewerkschaften Oesterreichs in Wien 1907.
Bericht der Gewerkschafts-Kommission Oesterreichs
an den VI. ordentlichen Kongress der Gewerk-
schaften Oesterreichs in Wien 1910.
Bericht der Reichskommission der Gewerkschaften
Oesterreichs an der Siebenten ordenlichen
Kongress der Gewerkschaften Oesterreichs
(1913).

V. Parliamentary Debates

Stenographische Protokolle über die Sitzungen des
Hauses der Abgeordneten des österreichischen
Reichsrathes, 1897-1914.

VI. General Literature

Ableitinger, Alfred, "The Movement toward Parlia-
    mentary Government in Austria since 1900:
    Rudolf Sieghart's Memoir of June 28, 1903,"
    Austrian History Yearbook, II (1966), 111-135.

Adler, Friedrich, "Wozu brauchen wir Theorien?" *Der Kampf*, II (1909), 256-263.
———. "Der Wert des Parlamentarismus," *Der Kampf*, IV (1911), 413-415.
———. "Minderwertig im Internationalismus," *Der Kampf*, IV (1911), 495-499.
——— (ed.), *Victor Adler Briefwechsel mit August Bebel und Karl Kautsky* (Vienna, 1954).
Adler, Max, "Marx' Verhältnis zur Erkenntniskritik," *Marx-Studien*, I (1904), 290-324.
———. "Marxismus und Materialismus," *Der Kampf*, III (1910), 564-571.
———. "Der soziale Sinn der Lehre von Karl Marx," *Archiv für die Geschichte des Sozialismus und der Arbeiterbewegung*, IV (1914), 1-29.
———. "Ferdinand Lassalles fünfzigster Todestag," *Der Kampf*, VII (1914), 482-486.
———. "Zur Würdigung Victor Adlers," *Archiv für die Geschichte des Sozialismus und die Arbeiterbewegung*, XI (1925), 174-183.
———. *Marx als Denker* (3rd rev. ed., Berlin, 1925).
Adler, Victor, *Das allgemeine, gleiche und direkte Wahlrecht und das Wahlunrecht in Oesterreich* (Vienna, 1893).
———. "Die Lage in Oesterreich und der sozialdemokratische Parteitag," *Die Neue Zeit*, XII (1893-94), 197-205, 232-241.
———. "Der Weg nach Hainfeld," *Der Kampf*, II (1909), 145-154.
———. "Bebel und die Sozialdemokratie in Oesterreich," *Der Kampf*, III (1910), 193-194.
———. "Die separatistische Krise," *Der Kampf*, IV (1911), 529-534.
———. "Peukerts Erinnerungen," *Der Kampf*, VII (1914), 302-307.
———. *Aufsätze, Reden und Briefe*, 11 parts (1st ed., Vienna, 1922-25; 2nd ed., Vienna, 1929).
Allmeyer-Beck, Johann C., *Minister-präsident Baron Beck* (Munich, 1956).
"Der Aufstieg einer Klasse," *Wissenschaft und Weltbild*, IV (1951), 309-313.
Austerlitz, Friedrich, "Die Krise des Dualismus in Österreich," *Die Neue Zeit*, XXI (1902-1903), 545-558.

_____ *Das neue Wahlrecht* (Vienna, 1907).
_____ "Sieg und Niederlage in Österreich," *Die Neue Zeit*, XXIX (1911), 466-473.
_____ "Oesterreich nach dem Balkankrieg," *Der Kampf*, VI (1913), 385-392.
Axelrod, Paul, "Adler und die russische Sozialdemokratie," *Der Kampf*, V (1912), 437-440.
Baron, Salo W., *Die politische Theorie Ferdinand Lassalles* (Leipzig, 1923).
Bauer, Otto, "Krise und Teuerung," *Der Kampf*, I (1907), 116-123.
_____ "Oesterreich und der Imperialismus," *Der Kampf*, II (1908), 17-22.
_____ "Bemerkungen zur Nationalitätenfrage," *Die Neue Zeit*, XXVI (1908), 792-802.
_____ "Der Weg zur Macht," *Der Kampf*, II (1909), 337-344.
_____ *Krieg oder Friede in den Gewerkschaften?* (Vienna, 1910).
_____ "Kopenhagen," *Der Kampf*, III (1910), 529-536.
_____ "Krieg oder Friede?" *Der Kampf*, IV (1910), 7-14.
_____ "Zu neuen Formen," *Der Kampf*, IV (1911), 445-451.
_____ "Zum Innsbrucker Parteitag," *Der Kampf*, V (1911), 49-56.
_____ "Gesamtparteitag und Gewerkschaftsfrage," *Der Kampf*, V (1911), 556-564.
_____ "Galizische Parteitage," *Der Kampf*, V (1912), 154-162.
_____ "Die Gesamtpartei," *Der Kampf*, VI (1912), 5-17.
_____ "Der Arbeiter und die Nation," *Der Kampf*, V (1912), 401-406.
_____ *Der Balkankrieg und die deutsche Weltpolitik* (Berlin, 1912).
_____ "Der zweite Balkankrieg," *Der Kampf*, VI (1913), 481-489.
_____ "Der Grundfrage unserer Taktik," *Der Kampf*, VII (1913), 49-63.
_____ "Geschäftsordnungsreform oder Absolutismus?" *Der Kampf*, VIII (1913), 97-105.
_____ "Gewerkschaften und Sozialismus," *Der Kampf*, VII (1914), 241-248.
_____ "Die Teuerung," *Der Kampf*, VII (1914), 443-461.

———————— *Der Weg zum Sozialismus* (Vienna, 1919).
———————— *Die österreichische Revolution* (Vienna, 1923).
———————— *Die Nationalitätenfrage und die Sozialdemokratie* (2nd ed., Vienna, 1924).
———————— *Der Übergang vom Kapitalismus zum Sozialismus* (Wiener Neustadt, 1958).
Beaumont, W., "Le Suffrage Universel en Autriche," *Annales des Sciences Politiques*, XXII (1907), 618-640.
Beer, Heinrich, "Der fünfte Gewerkschaftskongress," *Der Kampf*, I (1907), 49-52.
———————— "Eine Geschichte der österreichischen Gewerkschaften," *Der Kampf*, I (1908), 410-415.
Beer, Max, *The General History of Socialism and Social Struggles*, 2 vols. (New York, 1952).
Benedikt, Heinrich, *Die wirtschaftliche Entwicklung in der Franz-Joseph Zeit* (Vienna, 1958).
Beneš, Edouard, "Le Syndicalisme en Bohême," *Le Mouvement Socialiste*, XXIII (1908), 372-384, 457-467.
———————— *La Problème Autrichien et la Question Tchèque* (Paris, 1908).
———————— (pseud. É. Bělský), *Le Socialisme Autrichien et la Guerre* (Paris, 1915).
———————— "Le mouvement ouvrier tschéchoslovaque," *Le Monde Slave*, II (1918), 236-245.
Berchtold, Klaus (ed.), *Österreichische Parteiprogramme 1868-1966* (Vienna, 1967).
Bernatzik, Edmund (ed.), *Die österreichischen Verfassungsgesetze* (Vienna, 1911).
Bernstein, Eduard, "Der Kampf der Sozialdemokratie und die Revolution der Gesellschaft," *Die Neue Zeit*, XVI (1897-98), 484-497, 548-557.
———————— *Die Voraussetzungen des Sozialismus und die Aufgabe der Sozialdemokratie* (Stuttgart, 1899).
———————— *Der Revisionismus in der Sozialdemocratie* (Amsterdam, 1909).
———————— "Die Potenz politischer Massenstreik," *Sozialistische Monatshefte*, XIV (1910), 482-488.
Blondel, Georges, "Les Dernières Élections en Autriche-Hongrie," *La Réforme Sociale*, LXII (1911), 218-221.
Braun, Adolf, "Marx und die Gewerkschaften,"

_____ *Der Kampf,* I (1908), 249-256.
_____ *Die Gewerkschaften, ihre Entwicklung und Kämpfe* (Nuremberg, 1914).
_____ "Hainfeld," *Der Kampf,* VII (1914), 151-158.
Braunthal, Julius (ed.), *Austerlitz Spricht* (Vienna, 1931).
_____ *In Search of the Millenium* (London, (1945).
_____ *The Tragedy of Austria* (London, 1948).
_____ *Victor und Friedrich Adler* (Vienna, (1965).
_____ *History of the International 1864-1914* (New York, 1967).
Braun-Vogelstein, Julie, *Ein Menschenleben: Heinrich Braun und sein Schicksal* (Tübingen, 1932).
Brocard, Charles, *La Démocratie Socialiste Allemande et Autrichienne et les Élections de 1907* (Paris, 1909).
Brockhausen, Carl, "Grundlagen und Entwicklungsziele der österreichisch-ungarischen Monarchie," *Österreichische Rundschau,* X (1907), 1-11.
Brod, Jakob, "Die Belastung der Industrie durch die Arbeiterversicherung," *Der Kampf,* III (1908), 80-82.
Brügel, Ludwig, *Soziale Gesetzgebung in Österreich von 1848 bis 1918* (Vienna, 1919).
_____ *Geschichte der österreichischen Sozialdemokratie,* 5 vols. (Vienna, 1922-1925).
Bunzel, Julius, *Die Anfänge der modernen Arbeiterbewegung in der Steiermark* (Leipzig, 1913).
_____ (ed.), "Eine amtliche Darstellung der Anfänge der österreichischen Arbeiterbewegung," *Vierteljahrsschrift für Sozial-und Wirtschaftsgeschichte,* XII (1914), 284-299.
_____ *Die erste Lassallebewegung in Oesterreich* (Leipzig, 1914).
Burian, Edmund, "Tschechische Literatur über Sozialismus und Separatismus," *Der Kampf,* V (1912), 295-303.
Buttinger, Joseph, *In the Twilight of Socialism* (New York, 1953).
Cermak, Karl, "Partei, Gewerkschaft und Genossenschaft," *Der Kampf,* VI (1913), 371-376.

Charmatz, Richard, *Deutsch-österreichische Politik* (Leipzig, 1907).
_____ *Österreichs innere Geschichte von 1848 bis 1907*, 2 vols. (2nd ed., Leipzig, 1911-12).
_____ *Das politische Denken in Österreich* (2nd ed., Vienna, 1917).
_____ *Österreichs äussere und innere Politik von 1895 bis 1914* (Leipzig, 1918).
_____ *Lebensbilder aus der Geschichte Österreichs* (Vienna, 1947).
Coker, Francis, *Recent Political Thought* (New York, 1934).
Cole, G.D.H., *A History of Socialist Thought*, 5 vols. (London, 1954-60).
Crankshaw, Edward, *The Fall of the House of Habsburg* (New York, 1963).
Cunow, Heinrich, "Marx und das Selbstbestimmungsrecht der Nationen," *Die Neue Zeit*, XXXVI (1918), 577-584.
Czedik, Alois, *Zur Geschichte der k. k. österreichischen Ministerien 1861-1916*, 4 vols. (Vienna, 1917-20).
Czeike, Felix, *Liberale, Christlichsoziale und Sozialdemokratische Kommunalpolitik (1861-1934)* (Vienna, 1962).
Czernin, Ottakar, *Oesterreichs Wahlrecht und Parlament* (Prague, 1905).
Danneberg, Robert, "Die österreichische Jugendorganisation," *Der Kampf*, I (1908), 511-516.
_____ "Sozialdemokratische Erziehungsarbeit," *Der Kampf*, II (1909), 453-462.
_____ *Das sozialdemokratische Programm* (6th ed., Vienna, 1919).
Daszyński, Ignaz, "Die Lage in Oesterreich," *Die Neue Zeit*, XVI (1898), 718-723.
_____ "Die Nationalitätenfrage in der osteuropäischen Sozialdemokratie," *Sozialistische Monatshefte*, XIV (1910), 1068-1072.
Deutsch, Julius, *Geschichte der österreichischen Gewerkschaftsbewegung* (Vienna, 1908).
_____ *Geschichte der deutschösterreichischen Arbeiterbewegung* (2nd ed., Vienna, 1922).
_____ *Geschichte der österreichischen Gewerkschaftsbewegung*, 2 vols. (Vienna, 1929-32).
_____ *Ein Weiter Weg* (Zurich, 1960).
Dokumente des Separatismus (Vienna, 1911).
Domes, Franz, "Wohin steuert der tschechische

Separatismus in der Gewerkschaft?" *Der Kampf,* III (1910), 554-558.

Eldersch, Matthias, "Die Reform der Krankenversicherung," *Der Kampf,* II (1908), 120-128.

―――――― "Die neue Sozialversicherungsvorlage," *Der Kampf,* V (1911), 127-132.

Ellenbogen, Wilhelm, *Was will die Sozialdemokratie?* (Vienna, 1899).

Elliott, Charles F., "Quis Custodiet Sacra? Problems of Marxist Revisionism," *Journal of the History of Ideas,* XXVIII (1967), 71-86.

Ensor, R.C.K. (ed.), *Modern Socialism* (London, 1907).

Ermers, Max, *Victor Adler* (Vienna, 1932).

Fehlinger, Hans, "Internationale Uebereinkommen betreffend die Sozialversicherung," *Archiv für Sozialwissenschaft und Sozialpolitik,* LX (1928), 180-186.

―――――― and Fritz Klenner, *Die österreichische Gewerkschaftsbewegung* (Vienna, 1948).

Fellner, Fritz (ed.), *Das politische Tagebuch Josef Redlichs,* 2 vols. (Graz, 1953-54).

Fischel, Alfred, "Minister Immunität," *Die Zeit,* XV (1898), 33.

―――――― (ed.), *Materialien zur Sprachenfrage in Österreich* (Brünn, 1902).

Fischer, Eric, "The Negotiations for the National Ausgleich in Austria in 1871," *Journal of Central European Affairs,* III (1942), 134-145.

Gay, Peter, *The Dilemma of Democratic Socialism: Eduard Bernstein's Challenge to Marx* (New York, 1952).

Gulick, Charles A., *Austria from Habsburg to Hitler,* 2 vols. (Berkeley, 1948).

Hahn, Walter F., "The Socialist Party of Austria: Retreat from Marx," *Journal of Central European Affairs,* XV (1955), 115-133.

Hannak, Jacques, *Im Sturm eines Jahrhunderts* (Vienna, 1952).

Hannich, Josef, *Erinnerungen* (Warnsdorf, 1910).

Hantsch, Hugo, *Die Geschichte Österreichs,* 2 vols. (2nd ed., Graz, 1953).

―――――― *Die Nationalitätenfrage im alten Österreich* (Vienna, 1953).

Hartmann, Ludo M., "Die Nationalitäten und die Sozialdemokratie," *Neue Gesellschaft,* V

(1907), 263-272.
Hayes, Carlton J.H., *The Historical Evolution of Modern Nationalism* (New York, 1931).
Heller, Victor, "The Economic and Political Background of Austria's Reconstruction," *Journal of Central European Affairs,* VI (1946), 283-302.
Hertz, Friedrich, *Die Schwierigkeiten der industriellen Produktion in Österreich* (Vienna, 1910).
_____ *Die Produktionsgrundlagen der österreichischen Industrie vor und nach dem Kriege* (Vienna, 1917).
_____ *The Economic Problem of the Danubian States* (London, 1947).
Hillebrand, Oswald, "Die erste sozialdemokratische Organisation in Oesterreich," *Der Kampf,* VI (1913), 350-356.
Hofmann, Werner, *Ideengeschichte der sozialen Bewegung des 19. und 20. Jahrhunderts* (Berlin, 1962).
Hueber, Anton, "Partei und Gewerkschaften in Oesterreich," *Der Kampf,* I (1907), 11-14.
Hugelmann, Karl, "Das österreichische Parlament bis zur Staatskatastrophe und Österreichs Zukunft," *Archiv für Politik und Geschichte,* IV (1925), 229-273.
_____ *Das Nationalitätenricht des alten Österreich* (Vienna, 1934).
Hunt, R.N. Carew, *The Theory and Practice of Communism* (New York, 1951).
Jászi, Oscar, *The Dissolution of the Habsburg Monarchy* (Chicago, 1929).
Jenks, William A., *The Austrian Electoral Reform of 1907* (New York, 1950).
_____ *Vienna and the Young Hitler* (New York, 1960).
_____ *Austria Under the Iron Ring* (Charlottesville, Virginia, 1965).
_____ "The Later Habsburg Concept of Statecraft," *Austrian History Yearbook,* II (1966), 92-109.
Joll, James, *The Second International 1889-1914* (London, 1955).
Kann, Robert, *The Multinational Empire,* 2 vols. (New York, 1950).
Karbach, Oscar, "The Founder of Modern Political

Antisemitism: Georg von Schoenerer," *Jewish Social Studies*, VII (1945), 3-30.

Kautsky, Benedikt, *Geistige Strömungen im österreichischen Sozialismus* (Vienna, 1953).

_____ (ed.), *Ein Leben für den Sozialismus: Erinnerungen an Karl Kautsky* (Hannover, 1954).

_____ (ed.), *Friedrich Engels' Briefwechsel mit Karl Kautsky* (Vienna, 1955).

_____ (ed.), *Erinnerungen und Erörterungen von Karl Kautsky* (The Hague, 1960).

Kautsky, Karl, *Das Erfurter Programm* (Stuttgart, 1892).

_____ "Der Kampf der Nationalitäten und das Staatsrecht in Oesterreich," *Die Neue Zeit*, XVI (1897-98), 516-524.

_____ *Bernstein und die Sozialdemokratie: Eine Antikritik* (Stuttgart, 1899).

_____ *Bernstein und das sozialdemokratische Programm* (Stuttgart, 1899).

_____ "Die Revision des Programs der Sozialdemokratie in Oesterreich," *Die Neue Zeit*, XX (1901-02), 68-82.

_____ "Nationalität und Internationalität," *Die Neue Zeit*, XXVI (1908), 1-36.

_____ *The Road to Power*, tr. by A.M. Simons, (Chicago, 1909).

Kelsen, Hans, *Kommentar zur österreichischen Reichsratswahlordnung* (Vienna, 1907).

Klenner, Fritz, *Die österreichischen Gewerkschaften*, 2 vols. (Vienna, 1951-53).

_____ *Die österreichischen Gewerkschaften: Eine Monographie* (Vienna, 1967).

Kocmata, Karl F., Dr. *Victor Adler und die österreichische Arbeiterbewegung* (2nd ed., Vienna, 1920).

Kogan, Arthur, *Socialism in the Multi-National State* (unpubl. Ph.D. dissertation, Harvard, 1946).

_____ "The Social Democrats and the Conflict of Nationalities in the Habsburg Monarchy," *The Journal of Modern History*, XXI (1949), 204-217.

Kolmer, Gustav (ed.), *Parlament und Verfassung in Oesterreich*, 8 vols. (Vienna, 1902-1914).

Konirsh, Suzanne G., "Constitutional Aspects of the Struggle between Germans and Czechs in the Austro-Hungarian Monarchy," *The Journal of Modern History*, XXVII (1955), 231-261.

Koŕalka, Jiŕi, "Über die Anfänge der sozialistischen Arbeiterbewegung in der Tschechoslowakei," *Zeitschrift für Geschichtswissenschaft*, IX (1961), 111-143.

──────── "Die deutsch-österreichische nationale Frage in den Anfängen der sozialdemokratischen Partei," *Historica*, III (1961), 109-158.

Kränkel, Gustav, "Aus der Parteigeschichte Westböhmens," *Der Kampf*, III (1910), 428-432.

Die Krankenkasse als sozialpolitische Einrichtung (Vienna, 1925).

Krcal, August, *Zur Geschichte Arbeiter-Bewegung Oesterreichs 1867-1894*, (Berlin, 1894).

──────── *Blätter aus der Geschichte der Arbeiterbewegung Oesterreichs (1867-1894)*, (Zurich, 1913).

Kulemann, Wilhelm, *Die Gewerkschaftsbewegung* (Jena, 1900).

Lassalle, Ferdinand, *An die Arbeiter Berlins* 3rd ed., Leipzig, 1872).

──────── *Reden und Schriften*, 3 vols. (Berlin, 1892).

──────── *Gesammelte Reden und Schriften*, 12 vols. (Berlin, 1919).

Lenin, Vladimir, *Collected Works*, 38 vols. (Moscow, 1960-67).

Lenz, J., *The Rise and Fall of the Second International* (New York, 1932).

Leser, Norbert, *Begegnung und Auftrag: Beiträge zur Orientierung im zeitgenossischen Sozialismus* (Vienna, 1963).

──────── *Zwischen Reformismus und Bolshewismus: Der Austromarxismus als Theorie und Praxis* (Vienna, 1968).

Lieben, Ernst, "Der Separatismus in der Genossenschaftsbewegung," *Der Kampf*, III (1910), 418-420.

Luxemburg, Rosa, *Reform and Revolution* (English ed., Bombay, 1951).

Mann, Karl, "Das Selbstbestimmungsrecht der österreichischen Nationen," *Der Kampf*, XI (1918), 201-215.

Marmorek, Schiller, *L'Obstruction au Parlement Autrichien* (Paris, 1908).

Matthias, Eric, "Kautsky und der Kautskyanismus,"

Marxismus-Studien, II (1957), 151-197.
May, Arthur J., *The Hapsburg Monarchy 1867-1914* (Cambridge, Massachusetts, 1960).
_____ *The Passing of the Hapsburg Monarchy*, 2 vols. (Philadelphia, 1966).
Mayer, Franz M., et. al., *Geschichte und Kulturleben Österreichs*, 3 vols. (5th ed., Vienna, 1965).
Mayer, Hans (ed.), *Hundert Jahre österreichischer Wirtschaftsentwicklung 1848-1948* (Vienna, 1949).
Meissner, Alfred, "Löst die nationale Autonomie das nationale Problem?" *Der Kampf*, I (1908), 271-276.
Mommsen, Hans, *Die Sozialdemokratie und die Nationalitätenfrage im habsburgerischen Vielvölkerstaat* (Vienna, 1963).
Němec, Anton, "Proletariat, Demokratie und die tschechische Nation," *Der Kampf*, I (1907), 19-23.
_____ "Die Pfiffigkeit der deutschen Sozialdemokraten," *Der Kampf*, IV (1911), 112-113.
Nitti, Francesco S., *Catholic Socialism* (2nd ed., London, 1908).
Obermann, Karl and Josef Polisensky (eds.), *Aus 500 Jahren deutsch-tschechoslowakischer Geschichte* (Berlin, 1958).
Oberwinder, Heinrich, *Die Arbeiterbewegung in Oesterreich* (Vienna, 1875).
_____ *Sozialismus und Sozialpolitik* (Berlin, 1887).
Onciul, Aurel von, "Das österreichische Problem," *Österreichische Rundschau*, II (1905), 205-216.
Page, Stanley W., "The Russian Proletariat and the World Revolution: Lenin's View to 1914," *The American Slavic and East European Review*, X (1951), 1-13.
Pernerstorfer, Engelbert, "Kleine Erinnerungen," *Der Kampf*, III (1910), 376-379.
_____ "Ein kurzes Wort zur Frage des Sozialismus und Nationalismus," *Der Kampf*, V (1911), 56-58.
_____ *Zeitfragen* (2nd ed., Vienna, 1918).
Peukert, Josef, *Erinnerungen eines Proletariers aus der revolutionären Arbeiterbewegung* (Berlin, 1913).

Pinson, Koppel S., *Modern Germany* (New York, 1954).
Popp, Adelheid, "Die erzieherische Bedeutung der Konsumvereine," *Der Kampf*, I (1907), 16-18.
Preussler, Robert, "Erinnerungen aus der Arbeiterbewegung," *Der Kampf*, III (1910), 469-475.
Přibram, Karl, *Der Normalarbeitstag in den gewerblichen Betrieben und im Bergbaue Österreichs* (Vienna, 1906).
Pulzer, P.G.J., *The Rise of Political Anti-Semitism in Germany and Austria* (New York, 1964).
Rager, Friedrich A., "National Autonomy in the Austro-Hungarian Monarchy," *Journal of Central European Affairs*, I (1942) 417-427.
Ramm, Thilo, *Ferdinand Lassalle als Rechts-und Sozialphilosoph* (Meisenheim, 1953).
_____(ed.), *Ferdinand Lassalle: Ausgewählte Texte* (Stuttgart, 1962).
Rath, R. John, *The Viennese Revolution of 1848* (Austin, Texas, 1957).
Rauchberg, Heinrich, *Der nationale Besitzstand in Bohmen*, 3 vols. (Leipzig, 1905).
_____ *Die statistische Unterlagen der österreichischen Wahlreform* (Brünn, 1907).
Redlich, Josef, *Das österreichische Staats-und Reichsproblem*, 2 vols. (Leipzig, 1920-26).
_____ *Emperor Francis Joseph of Austria* (New York, 1929).
_____ *Austrian War Government* (New Haven, 1929).
Reinhold, Karl, *Die österreichische Sozialdemokratie und der Nationalismus* (Vienna, 1910).
Renner, Karl, (pseud. Synopticus), *Staat und Nation* (Vienna, 1899).
_____ (pseud. Synopticus), *Staat und Parlament* (Vienna, 1901).
_____ (pseud. Rudolf Springer), *Der Kampf der oesterreichischen Nationen um den Staat* (Leipzig, 1902).
_____ (pseud. Rudolf Springer), *Grundlagen und Entwicklungsziele der österreich-ungarischen Monarchie* (Vienna, 1906).
_____ *Was haben die Sozialdemokraten geleistet?* (Vienna, 1907).
_____ (pseud. Rudolf Springer), *Der nationale Streit um die Aemter und die Sozialdemokratie*

(Vienna, 1908).
_____ "Die Entwaffnung der Obstruktion," *Der Kampf*, III (1910), 145-148.
_____ "Die nationaler Minderheitsschulen," *Der Kampf*, III (1910), 446-449.
_____ "Nach Innsbruck," *Der Kampf*, V (1911), 103-109.
_____ "Fünf Kampfjahre," *Der Kampf*, VI (1912), 1-5.
_____ *An der Wende zweier Zeiten: Lebenserinnerungen* (Vienna, 1946).
Die Revolte des Separatismus (Vienna, 1911).
Rocker, Rudolf, *Johann Most: Das Leben eines Rebellen* (Berlin, 1924).
Samassa, Paul, *Der Völkerstreit im Habsburgerstaat* (Leipzig, 1910).
Schab, Siegfried, "[Artikel] 14, Obstruktion und Sozialdemokratie," *Der Kampf*, VII (1913), 22-25.
Schäfer, Anton, "Aus der Geschichte der nordböhmischen Arbeiterbewegung," *Der Kampf*, III (1909), 87-84.
Scheu, Heinrich, *Erinnerungen* (Vienna, 1912).
Schlesinger, Rudolf, *Federalism in Central and Eastern Europe* (New York, 1945).
Schmidt, Helga and Felix Czeike, *Franz Schuhmeier* (Vienna, 1964).
Schorske, Carl E., *German Social Democracy 1905-1917* (Cambridge, Massachusetts, 1955).
Schrammel, Anton, "Aus der nordwestböhmischen Arbeiterbewegung," *Der Kampf*, VI (1912), 116-119.
Schwechler, Karl, *Die österreichische Sozialdemokratie* (3rd ed., Vienna, 1908).
Shell, Kurt, *The Transformation of Austrian Socialism* (Albany, New York, 1962).
Sieghart, Rudolf, *Die letzten Jahrzehnte einer Grossmacht* (Berlin, 1932).
Skalnik, Kurt, *Dr. Karl Lueger* (Vienna, 1954).
Skaret, Ferdinand, "Unsere politische Parteiorganisation," *Der Kampf*, II (1909), 553-556.
Soukup, Franz, "Die czechische Sozialdemokratie," *Die Zeit*, XXIV (1900), 18-20.
_____ "Der Parteitag der tschechischen Sozialdemokratie," *Der Kampf*, III (1909), 4-8.
Die Sozialdemokratie und der Frieden: Reden der sozialdemokratischen Abgeordneten über die

bosnische Frage und die Kriegsgefahr
(Vienna, 1909).
Steiner, Herbert, *Die Arbeiterbewegung Österreichs 1867-1889* (Vienna, 1964).
_____ *Bibliographie zur Geschichte der österreichischen Arbeiterbewegung,* 2 vols. (Vienna, 1962-67).
Steinitz, Eduard von (ed.), *Erinnerungen an Franz Joseph I* (Berlin, 1931).
Strakosch-Grassmann, Gustav, *Das allgemeine Wahlrecht in Österreich seit 1848* (Leipzig, 1906).
Strauss, Emil, "Die nationale Frage in der Frühzeit der tschechischen Arbeiterbewegung," *Der Kampf,* XIV (1919), 253-258.
_____ *Geschichte der deutschen Sozialdemokratie Böhmens,* 2 vols. (Prague, 1925-26).
Strobl, Franz, "Das Brünner Nationalitätenprogramm der österreichischen Sozialdemokratie," *Weg und Ziel* (1949), 283-288.
_____ "Zur Idelogie der jungen österreichischen Arbeiterbewegung," *Weg und Ziel* (1955), 31-45.
Sutter, Berthold, *Die Badenischen Sprachenverordnungen von 1897* (Graz, 1960).
Tayerle, Rudolf, "Die gewerkschaftlichen Selbständigkeitsbestrebungen der tschechischen Arbeiter in Österreich," *Die Neue Zeit,* XXIX (1909), 727-738.
Taylor, A.J.P., *The Habsburg Monarchy 1809-1918* (London, 1948).
Tesarek, Anton (ed.), *Grosse Gestalten des Sozialismus* (Vienna, 1947).
Umbreit, Paul, "Zur Entwicklungsgeschichte des Separatismus in Österreich," *Die Neue Zeit,* XXX (1911), 470-474.
Victor Adler im Spiegel seiner Zeitgenossen (Vienna, 1968).
Walsh, V. Hussey, "Through the Austrian General Election," *Fortnightly Review,* LXXXI (1907), 977-990.
Weber, Heinrich, "Das südslawische Problem," *Der Kampf,* II (1909), 289-294.
Werner, Alfred, "Austria has a Mission," *Journal of Central European Affairs,* VII (1948), 406-413.
Whiteside, Andrew G., "Industrial Transformation, Population Movement and German Nationalism

in Bohemia," *Zeitschrift für Ostforschung,* X (1961), 261-271.

──────────── *Austrian National Socialism before 1918* (The Hague, 1962).

Wolfgramm, Eberhard, "Zur Erforschung der tschechoslowakischen Arbeiterbewegung bis 1918 in der tschechoslowakischen Geschichtswissenschaft," *Zeitschrift für Geschichtswissenschaft,* VIII (1960), 1223-1237.

Wolkan, Rolf, "Der österreichische Staatsgedanke und seine Wandlungen im Zeitalter Franz Josephs," *Mitteilungen des österreichischen Instituts für Geschichtsforschung,* XI (1929), 833-864.

Zeman, Z.A.B., *The Break-Up of the Habsburg Monarchy 1914-1918* (London, 1961).

Zöllner, Erich, *Geschichte Österreichs* (3rd ed., Munich, 1966).

Zulehener, Paul M., *Kirche und Austromarxismus* (Vienna, 1967).

VII. Biographical and Statistical Material

Bericht des Verbandes der Genossenschafts-Krankenkassen Wiens sammt der Statistik der Verbandskassen für das Jahr 1895.

Bericht des Verbandes der Genossenschafts-Krankenkassen Wiens sammt der Statistik der Verbandskassen für das Jahr 1900.

Neue Österreichische Biographie ab 1815, 14 vols. (Vienna und Zurich, 1923-60).

INDEX

Adler, Friedrich, 175, 180, 189, 193, 199
Adler, Max, 189, 192-193
Adler, Victor, 17, 31, 32, 38, 47, 65, 67, 78-79, 83, 89; on the origins of Austrian socialism, 18-22, 24-25; on revolution, 34-35; on the trade unions, 45-46; on the co-operative, 51-52; on political reform, 57-63; on parliament, 70-71; on electoral reform, 134-137, 139-150; on separatism, 161, 168-172, 174-175; on the decline of parliament, 183, 184; on the standard of living, 188-189; and on foreign policy, 194-195, 196, 197
Aehrenthal, Count Alois, 194
Anarchism, 14-16, 34, 59, 136
Anti-Semitism, 19, 112-113
Arbeiter-Zeitung, 31, 40, 41, 48, 74, 87, 88-89, 90, 117, 121, 145, 178, 197-198
Article 14, 73, 76, 163, 182
Article 42, 73, 129, 133, 179-180
Auersperg, Count Charles, 5

Ausgleich, 4, 74, 99-100, 101, 178, 193-194
Austerlitz, Friedrich, 87-88, 89, 100, 101, 197-198
Austrian Social Democracy, 1-2, 27; its origins, 3, 7; early divisions, 7-8, 10; on anarchism, 15-16; national divisions, 10, 81-84, 86, 88, 116, 153-176; founding congress, 23-25; organization, 27-42, 83-84; party membership, 29, economic goals, 112; political goals, 130, 181; on electoral reform, 132, 134-137, 148-149; its final collapse

Badeni, Count Casimir, 40, 69, 74, 76, 85, 86
Baernreither, Josef, 154
Bakunin, 15
Bardof, Josef, 21-22
Bauer, Otto, 65, 81, 90, 101-103, 118, 166, 167, 170, 175, 182, 187, 189, 191-192
Bebel, August, 7, 8, 64, 67, 124-125
Beck, Karl, 2
Beck, Max, 144-146, 149-150, 177-178, 182, 187
Bernstein, Eduard, 113; Revisionism, 113-115, 116, 117, 118, 120
Bienerth, Richard von, 178, 179, 181, 194-195

Braun, Adolf, 106, 190
Braun, Heinrich, 20
Bretschneider, Ludwig, 29
Brod, Jakob, 122
Bruha, Anton, 175
Brünn party congress (1887), 23
Brünn party congress (1899), 87, 88, 90-94, 102, 162
Budoucnost, 13
Burian, Adolf, 14, 25, 175
Bylandt, Count Artur, 142

Central Executive Committee, 33, 35, 38, 39, 67, 132, 163
Charmatz, Richard, 177
Christian Socialists, 64, 71, 75, 112, 133, 149-150, 181, 194
Cilli affair, 68
Clary, Count Manfred, 76
Communist Manifesto, 118
Constitutional rights, 4, 6-7, 9, 77, 102-103, 131, 144
Cooperatives, 51-52, 167
Czech Social Democracy, 10-11, 13-14, 23, 32, 35-40, 48-49, 153-154, 158-159, 160, 161-162, 165
Czech Social-Democratic Labor Party, 173, 174-175

Danneberg, Robert, 77-78
Daszyński, Ignaz, 37, 71, 72, 75, 84, 87, 89, 90, 122, 133, 139, 194
Der Kampf, 190
Diamand, Hermann, 171
Die Neue Zeit, 18, 67
Die Zukunft, 15, 16
Domes, Franz, 171

Eldersch, Ferdinand, 126-127
Electoral campaigns, 71, 75
Ellenbogen, Wilhelm, 45, 67, 78, 100-101, 122, 123, 134-135
Engels, Friedrich, 60, 64, 122, 191
Erfurt program, 122

Fejervary, Baron Geza, 131
Fischhof, Adolf, 93
Franz, Ferdinand, 133, 197-198
Franz, Joseph, 4, 131, 137, 143, 144, 147, 151, 202
Freundlich, Emmy, 53
Friedjung, Heinrich, 19, 177
Friedländer, D.S., 34

Gautsch, Baron Paul, 86, 130-131, 132-133, 137-138, 143, 144, 181-182, 202
General Strike, 45-47, 65, 67-68, 70, 135-137, 145, 147
General Workers Educational Union, 5, 10, 18

Gerin, Antonio, 91
German Liberals, 68, 72
German Nationals, 64, 141, 181
Gleichheit, 20-21
Grabmayr, Karl von, 143
Grohs, Konrad, 7

Hainfeld party congress, 23-25, 28, 31, 82, 106-107, 112, 117
Hannich, Josef, 24, 25, 71, 105, 112
Hanusch, Ferdinand, 183
Hartung, Herman, 5, 6, 7
Hitler, Adolf, 109
Höger, Karl, 44, 47, 59
Hohenlohe, Prince Konrad, 143-144
Hohenwart, Count Charles, 9, 10
Hueber, Anton, 15, 45, 47, 48, 59, 66, 78, 140, 156, 161, 171, 172, 203
Hybeš, Josef, 14, 22, 32, 49, 59, 71, 82, 84

Independent Socialist Party, 34, 45, 59-60
Internationalism, 24, 83, 87, 91-92
Italian Social Democracy, 23, 38, 172

Jaros, Rudolf, 171
Juarès, Jean, 196, 199

Jura, Franz, 168, 169, 171

Kaler-Reinthal, Emile, 11-12, 13
Kautsky, Karl, 17-18, 20, 22, 25, 66, 87, 103, 106, 114, 115, 116, 117, 120-121, 123-125, 130, 202
Kielmansegg, Prince Erich, 69
Kiesewetter, Wilhelm, 71
Kleedorfer, E.F., 44, 66
Körber, Ernst von, 75-76, 125, 130
Kořinek, Karl, 48
Kossuth, Francis, 131
Kramař, Karel, 181
Krankenkassen, 53, 54-55, 68, 109-110, 126, 202
Kristan, Etbin, 94-95, 171
Kristoffy, Josef, 131-132

Lassalle, Ferdinand, 3, 6; ideas of, 7, 10-11, 13, 17-18, 20-21, 24-25, 35, 57-58, 61, 78, 134, 183, 189
Legien, Karl, 44, 155
Liebermann, Aron, 91
Liebknecht, Wilhelm, 7, 8
Linz Program, 19
Lueger, Karl, 71, 113
Luxemburg, Rosa, 17, 114, 115, 116

Marx, Karl, 2; marxism, 7-8, 10-11, 13, 18, 21, 24-25, 57-59, 62,

293

78, 113-114, 116, 117-118, 119, 184; and austro-marxism, 189-193
May Day celebration, 29
Meissner, Albert, 2
Modracek, Franz, 163
Most, Johann, 9, 14

Nationalism, 24, 63, 87, 89-93, 95-103; czech nationalism, 28, 76, 82, 84, 85, 98-99, 139-140, 148, 154-156, 162-163, 166, 173; german nationalism, 68, 76, 84, 85, 140, 148, 162-163, 166, 199; polish nationalism, 194-195, 199; slovene nationalism, 68
Němec, Anton, 37, 38, 39, 49, 84, 87, 92, 101, 123, 140, 156, 159, 169, 171, 197, 199
Neudörfl party congress, 13

Oberwinder, Heinrich, 6, 7, 9, 10, 11, 13, 21

Palacky, Francis, 93
Papst, Johann, 9
Paris Commune, 12
Parliament, 30, 40-41, 61, 68-69, 72-77, 110, 125, 127, 132-134, 140-141, 143-147, 163, 178-180, 182, 184, 188

Pecka, Josef B., 11, 13
Pernerstorfer, Engelbert, 17, 18, 19, 40, 76, 79, 83, 87, 89, 91, 92, 134, 196
Pfingstprogramm, 94
Pittoni, Valentino, 38, 194
Plekhanov, George, 124, 169, 192
Pokorny, Rudolf, 31, 33-34, 59
Polish Social Democracy, 23, 36, 172
Popp, Adelheid, 53, 59
Popp, Julius, 15, 22, 25
Prague party congress, 37-38
Pravo lidu, 41, 156, 170

Radimsky, August, 39
Reform, 25, 34, 40-41, 42, 60-61, 106, 114, 140-141
Renner, Karl, 78, 90, 94-98, 101, 102, 175, 184, 189, 190-191
Reumann, Jakob, 33, 36, 111, 125
Revolution, 25, 34-35, 60-61, 66, 78, 106, 114
Revolution of 1848, 2
Rissmann, Johann, 22, 25, 34
Roušar, Josef, 50, 84, 154
Rovnost, 164

Scheu, Andreas, 8, 9, 10, 13, 14
Scheu, Heinrich, 9
Scheu, Josef, 8
Schlesinger, Theresa, 53
Schönerer, Georg von, 19

Schrammel, Anton, 180
Schuhmeier, Franz, 45, 52, 55, 122, 145
Schulze-Delitzch, Herman, 3, 4, 7, 8, 19
Schwarzinger, Johann, 18
Schweitzer, Johann von, 6, 8
Second International, 27, 29, 64, 75-76, 107-108, 124, 168-170, 195-196, 197, 199
Seliger, Josef, 91, 171
Separatism, 32, 36, 38, 49-50, 162-176, 184
Skaret, Ferdinand, 134
Skatula, Emmanuel, 155
Slovene Social Democracy, 23, 37-38, 172
Smitka, Johann, 44
Social-Democratic Youth Organization, 53-54
Social reforms, 10, 17, 60, 102, 105-106, 107, 111, 114, 125, 178, 182, 183, 187
Socialism, 21
Soukup, Franz, 39, 84, 86, 157-158, 171, 197
St. Margareten party congress, 14
Standard of living, 20, 52, 105, 109-110, 117, 119, 186-187, 188
Stanek affair, 167-168
Stein, Victor, 175
Steinbach, Emil, 46

Steiner, Josef, 70, 71, 122, 156, 157
Stürgkh, Count Karl von, 196

Taaffe, Count Edward, 16, 59, 64, 65-66
Taushinsky, Hyppolit, 7
Tayerle, Rudolf, 171
Thun, Count Leo, 76
Tomschek, Josef, 132
Trade-Union movement, 3-4; strike activity, 8-9, 138, 186; disorganization, 13, 27-28, 139-140, 160-161, 162-167, 173; organizational efforts, 42-45, 110; membership, 43, 48, 51, 84, 109, 158, 161, 167, 168, 185; czech desires, 48-49, 50, 84, 153, 157-158, 171-172; political desires, 59, 183-184; and social reforms, 107-108, 111, 185-186
Tusar, Vlastimil, 164, 171, 173

Vandervelde, Émile, 124
Vaněk, Karl, 70, 84, 86, 157, 159-160, 164-165
Vávra, Jan, 82
Verkauf, Leo, 55, 71, 74, 111-112
Volksstimme, 7
Vollmar, Georg von, 15
Vormärz, 1
Vorwärts, 114
Voting procedures, 4, 5; universal manhood suffrage, 40, 46, 61-63, 69, 81, 127, 131, 132, 177-178; electoral

reform, 64, 66, 68,
  69-70, 130, 134-135,
  140-141, 144-148,
  150; 1907 elections,
  148-149
Viennese party congress,
  (1891), 30-31, 82
Viennese party congress,
  (1892), 28, 32
Viennese party congress,
  (1894), 35-36
Viennese (Wimberger)
  party congress (1897),
  38-40, 72
Viennese party congress
  (1901), 118-123

Wahrheit, 22-23
Winarsky, Leopold, 100,
  119, 121
Windischgrätz, Prince
  Alfred, 66, 68-69
Wittek, Count Heinrich
  von, 76
Women's Auxiliary, 53
Workers Education Union,
  29
Working-Class demon-
  strations, 9, 64, 67,
  126, 132, 137-138,
  146, 188
World War I, 193-194,
  196, 197-198

Young Czechs, 64, 72,
  75, 129, 133

Zapotocky, Ladislav,
  11, 13, 14
Zavertnik, Ferdinand,
  37-38
Zeller, Eduard, 71

ABOUT THE AUTHOR:

Dr. Vincent J. Knapp is Associate Professor of History at the State University of New York at Potsdam. Professor Knapp received his undergraduate training in European history at Syracuse University and was later awarded a Ph.D. in the area from the University of Rochester in 1964. In addition to his training in this country, Dr. Knapp was associated with the Historical Institute at the University of Vienna from 1960-1961. More recently, during the 1977-1978 academic year, he was an Associate Member of the Cambridge Group for the History of Population and Social Structure at Cambridge University. Currently, Dr. Knapp is a member of The American Historical Association, The New York State Association of European Historians and The Inter-University Center for European Studies in Montreal.

Professor Knapp's articles and reviews have appeared in numerous journals both in this country and abroad, including The American Historical Review, The Journal of Urban History, The Canadian Historical Review and The Australian Journal of Politics and History. He is also the author of a major study of the European standard of living since 1700, which was published in book form by Prentice-Hall in 1976 under the title, Europe in the Era of Social Transformation, 1700-Present.

LIBRARY OF DAVIDSON COLLEGE

Books on regular loan may be checked out for **two weeks**. Books must be presented at the Circulation Desk in order to be renewed.

A fine is charged after date due.

Special books are subject to special regulations at the discretion of the library staff.